Hands-On Cybersecurity for Architects

Plan and design robust security architectures

Neil Rerup
Milad Aslaner

BIRMINGHAM - MUMBAI

Hands-On Cybersecurity for Architects

Commissioning Editor: Vijin Boricha
Reviewers: Diya Qudaih, Gregory Saxton, and Abhijit Mohanta
Acquisition Editor: Prateek Bharadwaj
Content Development Editor: Nithin George Varghese
Technical Editor: Prashant Chaudhari
Copy Editor: Safis Editing
Project Coordinator: Virginia Dias
Proofreader: Safis Editing
Indexer: Aishwarya Gangawane
Graphics: Tom Scaria
Production Coordinator: Shantanu Zagade

First published: July 2018

Production reference: 1280718

Published by Packt Publishing Ltd.
Livery Place
35 Livery Street
Birmingham
B3 2PB, UK.

ISBN 978-1-78883-026-3

www.packtpub.com

To my wife, Lisa, who supported me in my journey through the IT industry through the years, as frustrating as it must have been. To my oldest son, Nathan, who is a better version of myself and who has a very bright future in front of him. And to my youngest son, Connor, who has greatness within him, if he just reaches out to grab it.

–Neil Rerup

This book is dedicated to my family and friends, who have always supported me in pursuing my dreams.

–Milad Aslaner

`mapt.io`

Mapt is an online digital library that gives you full access to over 5,000 books and videos, as well as industry leading tools to help you plan your personal development and advance your career. For more information, please visit our website.

Why subscribe?

- Spend less time learning and more time coding with practical eBooks and Videos from over 4,000 industry professionals

- Improve your learning with Skill Plans built especially for you

- Get a free eBook or video every month

- Mapt is fully searchable

- Copy and paste, print, and bookmark content

PacktPub.com

Did you know that Packt offers eBook versions of every book published, with PDF and ePub files available? You can upgrade to the eBook version at `www.PacktPub.com` and as a print book customer, you are entitled to a discount on the eBook copy. Get in touch with us at `service@packtpub.com` for more details.

At `www.PacktPub.com`, you can also read a collection of free technical articles, sign up for a range of free newsletters, and receive exclusive discounts and offers on Packt books and eBooks.

Contributors

About the authors

Neil Rerup is the President and Chief Security Architect of an architecture firm that provides architectural services (enterprise and solution) to enterprises across North America. He is an enterprise architect who came out of the world of cybersecurity. He has worked on a number of projects for enterprises around the world and has worked in various architecture domains, including security, networking, and applications. He was responsible for the security architecture for the Vancouver 2010 Winter Olympics, securing the critical infrastructure of numerous utilities, and is also responsible for large enterprise solutions for companies around the world.

> *I'd like to acknowledge Randy Stroud, for teaching me the professionalism for security architecture; John Lilleyman, for expanding my understanding of Enterprise Architecture; and Steve Zalewski, for being a sounding board on my thoughts around enterprise security architecture.*

Milad Aslaner is a mission-focused security professional with more than 11 years of international experience in product engineering; product management; and business evangelism for cybersecurity, data privacy, and enterprise mobility. He has been an award-winning speaker and technical expert at global conferences, such as Microsoft Ignite, Microsoft Tech Summit, and Microsoft Build.

> *I would like to express my appreciation to my mother, who shaped me into the person I am today; my siblings, Aydin and Aylin Aslaner, who motivated me to get into this industry; my soulmate, Salpie Dawood, who continuously pushes me to become a better person; my supporting friends, Dr. Erdal Ozkaya, Karam Masri, Joao Botto, Antonio Vasconcelos, and Yasin Söğütlü; and finally, Packt Publishing, for the great partnership.*

About the reviewer

Abhijit Mohanta works as a malware researcher for Juniper Threat Labs. He worked as malware researcher for Cyphort, MacAfee, and Symantec. He has expertise in reverse engineering and experience working with antivirus and sandbox technologies. He is the author of the book *Preventing Ransomware: Understand, Prevent, and Remediate Ransomware Attacks*, published by Packt Publishing. He has a number of blogs on malware research, and also has a couple of patents related to malware detection.

Packt is searching for authors like you

If you're interested in becoming an author for Packt, please visit `authors.packtpub.com` and apply today. We have worked with thousands of developers and tech professionals, just like you, to help them share their insight with the global tech community. You can make a general application, apply for a specific hot topic that we are recruiting an author for, or submit your own idea.

Table of Contents

Preface

There has been so much written over the years on the subject of security. IT security. Information security. Cybersecurity. All focused on security. But here's the problem: from a more practical point of view, security is more about quality assurance for your architectures rather than being about ensuring that risks are mitigated.

Most people forget that the core business of an enterprise is **business**. It's not security in any form. Security—more specifically, cybersecurity—is meant to provide a clear understanding to the business as to what the security risks are and how to potentially mitigate those cybersecurity risks. And that brings us to cybersecurity and how it integrates into architectures.

There are going to be many different types of people—coming from diverse backgrounds—reading this book, but our intent is to focus on the second word in "security architecture", which is **architecture**. Every architecture should have a focus on security. If you are working on a network architecture, you have to keep in mind things such as security zones and access control lists. If you are putting together an infrastructure architecture, you have to keep in mind what roles the solution will use and how you will harden the various components. And, if you are working on an application architecture, you want to be thinking about how to ensure that the application is designed and coded so that there are as few vulnerabilities in the application as possible.

This book will talk about all the different things that an architect gets involved in and how security is integrated into those activities. There is a heavy slant toward thinking like a security architect, since there isn't much difference between a security architect or any other architect. They all do the same things—they create the same types of artifacts and they support architects in different architecture domains in the same ways. The only difference is the realm of focus.

There are different areas that an architect will focus on, depending on whether they are an enterprise-level architect, a solution-level architect, or a supporting-level architect. And, with each, there are security aspects that have be considered, just as there are aspects that every architect has to think about from other non-security domains. There are governance aspects, strategy and program-level aspects, and solution-level aspects, for instance. Plus, if you are doing your job correctly, you should be interfacing with the biggest stakeholder of them all—the operations teams—since they, too, have to deal with your solution. But they'll have to deal with it long after you are gone.

Enjoy this book and read it for what it's worth. And, hopefully, it will provide you with a view into your own architecture domain and not just into the security architecture domain. Thank you, and we hope this book helps you.

Who this book is for

If you are a security, network, or a system administrator interested in taking up high-level responsibilities, such as designing and implementing complex security structures and modules, then this book is for you. This book is also ideal for non-security architects who want to understand how to integrate security into their solutions.

What this book covers

Chapter 1, *Security Architecture History and Overview*, gives you an overview of what security architecture covers. This will include a summary of the different layers in security architecture and how they are integrated. This chapter will also talk about the different types of security architects and how what they do differs depending on the needs of the organization. It will also describe the origins of architecture in general, IT/cybersecurity in general, and the evolution of security architecture.

Chapter 2, *Security Governance*, grants you an understanding of the importance of governance in security generally, as well as in security architecture specifically. The focus will be on how you can't approach security from a *personal* point of view; rather, an approach that the entire organization agrees to in order to ensure an organization-wide approach to security is required.

Chapter 3, *Reference Security Architecture*, will give you an actual **Reference Security Architecture (RSA)** that you can use, as well as an understanding of how to use it and when to use it. The RSA is meant to ensure that the various areas in security architecture are not missed and are included in activities that the architect performs, regardless of what level of architecture is being worked on (whether it's an enterprise-, solution-, or technical-level architecture, for example).

Chapter 4, *Cybersecurity Architecture Strategy*, talks about the process of creating strategies and roadmaps. This will leverage the information given in the previous chapter and build upon it. It will talk about various inputs into strategies, the development of the SWOT analysis, the requirements of the organization and how they drive strategy, the resulting output of the strategy of specific projects, and a roadmap of delivering those projects.

Chapter 5, *Program- and Strategy-Level Work Artifacts*, looks at how, at the program and strategy layers, the enterprise security architect has to create a number of things to allow for a communication of the strategy elements to associated stakeholders within the organization, whether it's upward to the executive level or downward to the technical staff. This section talks about these artifacts, what they are used for, and what should be included in each artifact.

Chapter 6, *Security Architecture in Waterfall Projects*, goes into how the vast majority of organizations out there use a waterfall methodology for delivering their projects. That being so, it's important to first understand the various stages in a project delivery life cycle before you try to understand how a security architect works with those stages. It's also important to remember that a security architect may play two different roles in these phases: a solution architect role for security-specific projects, or a support role to non-security-based projects.

Chapter 7, *Security Architecture Project Delivery Artifacts*, explains how, since architecture is all about communication, it's important to understand the artifacts that a security architect will work with and deliver in each phase of the project-delivery life cycle. So, to that end, this chapter explores the different phases of that life cycle and some of the artifacts that are associated with them.

Chapter 8, *The Architecture Design Document*, follows on from the previous chapter, which talked about the various artifacts that are delivered by the security architect in each phase of a project, of which the biggest by far is the **Architecture Design Document (ADD)**. This chapter focuses just on the ADD and what should go into it. At the end of the day, this document is the core of what the architect does and is used to describe the solution that is to be implemented.

Chapter 9, *Security Architecture and Operations*, reminds you that security architecture strategies take input from various stakeholders, and so it's important to consider the requirements of the various operations groups. These are stakeholders that not only receive the output of projects but also give input into the creation of new strategies. This chapter discusses this interaction.

Chapter 10, *Practical Security Architecture Designs*, proceeds from the quite true premise that any organization today needs to assume that they have been compromised. This is not only important for the **Security Operations Center (SOC)**, but also for the cybersecurity architects, so that they are able to build a comprehensive security architecture that can protect, detect, and respond to cyber attacks. By reading this chapter, you will understand the key requirements regarding security for mail, networks, identity, endpoints, BYOD, IoT, and infrastructure, as well as get insights on real-world cyber attacks and design practices.

Chapter 11, *Trends in Security Architecture Technology*, looks at the trends in various areas with regards to security and what the security architect should be thinking about down the road.

Chapter 12, *The Future of Security Architecture*, concludes the book by talking about what the future holds for the role of the security architect.

To get the most out of this book

This book is written for those individuals that are designing or architecting IT solutions. The solutions don't necessarily have to be security solutions, but can be for any architecture tower. To get the most out of this book, you should have an understanding of how to architect a solution and the various activities that are involved in the running of an IT organization.

Conventions used

There are a number of text conventions used throughout this book.

CodeInText: Indicates code words in text, database table names, folder names, filenames, file extensions, pathnames, dummy URLs, user input, and Twitter handles. Here is an example: "That's the reason why the factors for both don't start with 0."

A block of code is set as follows:

```
html, body, #map {
 height: 100%;
 margin: 0;
 padding: 0
}
```

When we wish to draw your attention to a particular part of a code block, the relevant lines or items are set in bold:

```
[default]
exten => s,1,Dial(Zap/1|30)
exten => s,2,Voicemail(u100)
exten => s,102,Voicemail(b100)
exten => i,1,Voicemail(s0)
```

Any command-line input or output is written as follows:

```
$ mkdir css
$ cd css
```

Bold: Indicates a new term, an important word, or words that you see onscreen. For example, words in menus or dialog boxes appear in the text like this. Here is an example: "Select **System info** from the **Administration** panel."

 Warnings or important notes appear like this.

 Tips and tricks appear like this.

Get in touch

Feedback from our readers is always welcome.

General feedback: Email `feedback@packtpub.com` and mention the book title in the subject of your message. If you have questions about any aspect of this book, please email us at `questions@packtpub.com`.

Errata: Although we have taken every care to ensure the accuracy of our content, mistakes do happen. If you have found a mistake in this book, we would be grateful if you would report this to us. Please visit `www.packtpub.com/submit-errata`, selecting your book, clicking on the Errata Submission Form link, and entering the details.

Piracy: If you come across any illegal copies of our works in any form on the Internet, we would be grateful if you would provide us with the location address or website name. Please contact us at `copyright@packtpub.com` with a link to the material.

If you are interested in becoming an author: If there is a topic that you have expertise in and you are interested in either writing or contributing to a book, please visit `authors.packtpub.com`.

Reviews

Please leave a review. Once you have read and used this book, why not leave a review on the site that you purchased it from? Potential readers can then see and use your unbiased opinion to make purchase decisions, we at Packt can understand what you think about our products, and our authors can see your feedback on their book. Thank you!

For more information about Packt, please visit `packtpub.com`.

1
Security Architecture History and Overview

Security architecture is a combination of two things that, over the last two decades, have been steadily changing. Security architecture, as written in this book, is architecture focused on security. It's not security with an architecture leaning. Many people will talk about security architecture and focus on the security aspect of that term but, by doing that, they ignore the build capability associated with any architecture tower, even in a security architecture tower.

To understand security architecture, you must first understand architecture in general. At first glance, security and architecture are diametrically opposed. Security, by its nature, is meant to slow things down, to break things, and to understand how things can be broken. Architecture, on the other hand, is meant to build things up to make them more useful. It's the process of understanding security and architecture separately that allows you to understand the importance of security architecture.

The following topics will be covered in this chapter:

- The history of architecture and security architecture
- Security in the different architectures, including:
    - Security in network architecture
    - Security in infrastructure architecture
    - Security in application architecture
    - Security in virtual architectures
    - Security in the cloud
- Architecture layers in an organization
- The different security architecture roles
- The importance of templatization
- Security architecture principles

The history of architecture

In order for you to understand what a security architect and security architecture do it's important to understand where security architecture came from. So, let's start with architecture and its history.

Architecture as a practice is young, only starting in the mid-1980s. One of the very first architecture frameworks was the Zachmann Framework, which came out in 1987. John Zachman, created it when he was working with IBM. It was meant to codify how to look for solutions and ensure that no aspect of a solution was missed. People took the Zachman framework and started to adjust it, based on their organization's needs and personality.

That's the thing about frameworks: very few organizations truly follow a set framework, simply because very few organizations are the same as others. Each organization is unique and has its own characteristics. Different-sized organizations have different stakeholders. They have different internal processes. And, as a result, a fixed framework can never truly be ported from one organization to another.

But an architecture is not a framework. Rather, an architecture, is the end result of a framework. Remember, an architecture is about communication of ideas and whatever form that takes has to be usable by the organization. If you create an architecture and that architecture is never used or followed, what is the point of creating it in the first place? The framework is just a structure used to create the architecture and ensure a consistent level of quality for the architecture itself.

Because of that, different types of architecture frameworks started to be developed over the years. NIST created their own framework, which was originally very heavily influenced by the Zachman framework. But frameworks have been evolving ever since, each trying to improve how to communicate a solution or an idea. It has gotten to the point where people are more focused on creating frameworks and filling out templates, than they are on communicating.

Today, the ISO has documented over 67 different architecture frameworks (`http://www.iso-architecture.org/ieee-1471/afs/frameworks-table.html`). The most well-known one is probably **The Open Group Architecture Forum** (**TOGAF**). TOGAF, as an architecture framework, is quite useful. It starts from a high-level conceptual state and brings the architecture down to a much more physical interpretation. The problem with TOGAF is that it was created before the concept of security architecture was conceived. As a result, it doesn't take into consideration how to deal with security risk.

The closest that TOGAF ever got to integrating security into their architectural framework was when they created a white paper in 2005 (W055: Guide to Security Architecture in TOGAF), expressing an intent to integrate security and risk management into their architecture framework. But that never occurred and, to this day, TOGAF still considers the only architecture towers to be those that cover networks, infrastructure, applications, and information.

One of the things learned over the years is that security cannot be an add-on. Security must be integrated into all aspects of a solution; otherwise, by nature, vulnerabilities and weaknesses are injected into the solution.

That brings us to SABSA. **Sherwood Applied Business Security Architecture (SABSA)** is a framework that took components of TOGAF and Zachman's to create a uniquely security-based architecture framework. SABSA started in 2007 and has been growing ever since. Like TOGAF, it created several different views, going from a very high-level business view, down to a much more physical/technical view. But, unlike TOGAF, SABSA added a third dimension, which talks about specific security activities.

From a security point of view, SABSA works very well. Unfortunately, it is just about security and it isn't something that is widely adopted among an entire IT organization. As a result, we end up with multiple frameworks in a single organization and that just causes more problems. Which one takes priority? When the different frameworks are in conflict, how do you solve a conflict? Security people tend to have a "my way or the highway" approach to doing business and that doesn't work when the core business of an organization is not security.

There are two other security architecture frameworks that you can think about. The first is the iCode security architecture and the second is the open safety and security architecture framework. We were talking about an architecture framework that is focused on security. Very few architectural frameworks have security built into them and, as a result, you have to tack security onto your architecture approach. And when that happens, like I said earlier, vulnerabilities are bound to occur.

The history of security architecture

Architecture, when it comes to the field of information technology space, is all about planning and building. In this day and age, there are typically four separate architecture towers and they are described following the traditional OSI model (from the bottom up). But each architecture tower has led to the continued growth of security architecture.

Security in network architecture

Network architecture is all about designing network-level structures. Everything from LANs to MANs to WANs, network architecture is all about ensuring that the communication of information from one device to another can occur smoothly and without interruption.

It's important to remember that network architecture is probably the very first place that IT started to plan. Most solutions were originally centered around the mainframe, which meant that any connection was typically in a star topology, where the mainframe was in the center and then connections were serialized outward from the mainframe.

When smaller devices such as servers and workstations came about, architected solutions started to have to focus on client/server topologies. But for those solutions to work, you had to ensure that communication from the client (which was typically a thick application that had one dedicated purpose, which was to interface with the server's application) was able to communicate directly to the server. How could that be done? Well, that was where networks came about.

Back in the late 1980s and early 1990s, there were several network protocols that were being used. Today, networks at the physical layer are predominantly Ethernet-based but, back then, you had Ethernet (of the 10 M variety only), Token Ring, FDDI, a number of serial protocols including RS-232 (which was used to connect printers and auxiliary devices to computers), and others. Fiber optics cabling was starting to come into vogue so there was great interest in using it, simply because of the speeds that it could provide. But, because of cost, fiber only ended up being put into place for networks covering large areas.

If you go up the OSI stack, you get to the network communication layers, which include the network layer and the transport layer. Today, we make use of TCP/IP. But IP networks didn't become the standard until the early 1990s and, before that, we had things such as AppleTalk (for any of you Apple geeks, the protocol to network Apple computers), IPX, Banyan VINES, DECNet, and many more.

Security? Well, as with all things in IT, security has always come as an add-on. There are these great breakthroughs with regards to networking and the first thing that people do is figure out how to get around the protocols. Remember, protocols and designs have one intended consequence and, typically, two unintended consequences. The same goes for networking. You had this great ability, but it didn't fully meet people's needs. They would have to figure out a hack for how to get around the problem.

When you look at the history of networking, you see many devices that you don't see today, such as bridges and hubs. Bridges were used because they were meant to bridge from one network protocol to another. When we started to standardize on TCP/IP, bridges started to disappear.

You also saw devices that had secondary purposes that aren't used today, such as switches and routers. Switches, like today, were meant to allow for communication between individual computers but in logical groupings. That was the beginning of virtualization. But you didn't have VLANs at the time, so routers were used to control who could access a network or network segment.

At the outer edge of the company, you would have a router, not a switch like today. You could put **Access Control Lists** (**ACLs**) on routers and then use those router ACLs to control traffic flow. But soon you started to see people find ways to bypass those ACLs. Routers, by their nature, don't track where traffic originated from and, if you pretended you were responding to traffic originating from inside the company, the router would let you bypass the ACL.

And so the firewall was invented. There needed to be a device that could act like a router, because it needed to control access into the enterprise and direct traffic to the appropriate segments, but it needed to be able to discern where traffic hitting it was originating from. Check point came to prominence because it came up with a technology called **Stateful Inspection**, which in simple terms, allowed a router to have a table that was used to track traffic leaving, and traffic returning, and matching the communication.

You could say that the creation of the firewall was the first step down the road of security architecture. When a technology is created, it's announced to great fanfare and is then implemented without thinking fully about the consequences. People like new sparkling toys and like to appear to be doing things, so they act quickly. But quickly isn't necessarily the best way; there will be more on that in later chapters.

Now, firewalls were originally put just at the outer edge of the company. Why would you need firewalls inside when all the problems come from outside, right? Well, network administrators soon came to realize that the view of attacks from outside was wrong. Back around 2000, multiple studies came out showing anywhere from 65% to 90% of all attacks come from inside the organization (which, by the way, hasn't changed). They started to ask, if a firewall worked so well on the outside edge, can it also be used inside the network?

And this led to network zoning or, as it is now called, security zones. The DMZ is the most commonly known security zone and is used to ensure that services are exposed to external customers, but also that those services can't be used as a jumping off point into the internal areas of the network.

And so, security architecture was born. Most security professionals were originally people from the network arena. They understood networking concepts and how to structure them for protection. And, because most security people are frustrated hackers, they understood how to break network protocols for their own benefit.

They started looking at dial-up modems and replacing them with a new technology call VPNs. They started replacing hubs with something called VLANs on switches. **Denial-of-Service (DoS)** attacks started to become less successful because we started to architect multiple ingress/egress points in the network, as well as limiting the amount of bandwidth a specific port or protocol could use. And all these technologies started to be centralized so that they were easier to control and manage.

So, all was good with the world. But an unexpected shift occurred when, because people couldn't bypass simple network barriers, exploitation of the OSI stack at the infrastructure layer began, simply because that was using the network to communicate.

Security in infrastructure architecture

Infrastructure is defined as those things that communicate directly on the network itself. Commonly, they are servers but there are other devices that have very specific functions and that are in the form of appliances. But, at the end of the day, all these devices have a network interface card in them and they where applications will reside.

Back at around the turn of the century, Microsoft was gaining a reputation for having very poor code quality with regards to their operating system. Remember, Microsoft had created an operating system in the mid–1980s called MS-DOS, which allowed for the easy implementation and support of higher-level applications. As applications demanded more and more capabilities and power, operating systems needed to become more and more robust. Plus, because IT was beginning to catch the eye of the more technically inclined, there were more and more people wanting to learn about information technology.

But people, by their very nature, tend to be lazy. That's not necessarily a bad thing but it's something to be kept in mind. If you can find a simple way of doing things, why do something that is harder, even if it is a better way. And that's a lesson to remember when you are doing any security architecture work. The more complex you make something, the higher the likelihood that people won't use it.

People wanted to use all those shiny new tools called computers. But they didn't have the time to learn how to program in BASIC or Fortran. The creation of operating systems made it much easier to use computers. But, as with anything that is programmed, there are going to be issues and errors. Whenever I write a report, I can guarantee that I have made either spelling mistakes or grammatical mistakes. They are unintended but they will exist. The same happened with the creation of operating systems. And it was those issues and errors that were then used to breach company network environments.

Remember, firewalls were being put into place and it became much harder to get into a company's environment. But Microsoft, which was the predominant operating system supplier, and Novell, with its NetWare networking operating system, were more concerned with pumping out solutions to make it easier to use computers and networks than with ensuring the security of their customers. There was money to be made.

So, by the late 1990s, Microsoft was gaining a reputation for having poor coding practices. When you look at the history of Microsoft operating systems, they kept the same core code and then kept adding more and more adaptions to it to make the operating system do what application developers needed or what end customers wanted. And it was this spaghetti code that was causing all these problems.

Patch Tuesday was introduced in 2003 and became a running joke because Microsoft kept having to issue patches to their code. It was getting to the point that they were losing contracts because of the security issues with its operating systems. Microsoft lost a contract in the early 2000s with the US Navy to Red Hat, simply because the Navy didn't trust the Microsoft Operating System. So Microsoft had to do something, otherwise it was going to lose its market dominance.

And so Microsoft established the Trustworthy Computing Initiative in 2002. The Trustworthy Computing Initiative was a major change in the way Microsoft wrote code. It took the traditional waterfall methodology that was used for the delivery of their applications and then integrated a **Secure Development Life Cycle (SDLC)**, to ensure that security was embedded into the process of creating code. Not tacked on at the end, but rather integrated into the day-to-day activities of code writing and creation so that the products output by Microsoft would no longer have so many embarrassing attacks.

There were four areas that were identified as part of the trustworthy computing initiative; security, privacy, reliability, and business integrity. And so application security architecture was born. The concept of hardening operating systems became paramount, as did establishing an understanding of what group policies could do and how a security architect needs to consider these things as well.

Not only that, but interest in the access of the platforms started to take off. At that time, domain controllers were used and were provided with primary or secondary designations. But to access different domains, there needed to be some way of crossing domains. Enter the concept of federation. **Single Sign-On (SSO)** had existed for a couple of years and Federation was just a logical extension of SSO.

Provisioning, on the other hand, came about because of a consolidation in the identity market. Originally, there were products meant to propagate identities into the various domain controllers to alleviate the lack of a federated solution. Remember, domain controllers were relatively recent inventions and a lot of applications were still using their own identity stores rather than a central repository. So, the infrastructure had to be put into place to drive down the cost of help desk calls and the cost of putting hands on the various platforms.

But there was a second area that was standalone at the time, and that was the workflow products. The concept still stands today, where there are standardized business processes that can be replaced by automation. No need to send documents around for approvals if you already know who needs to approve what. The same goes for hiring – if you know what the role is and what access they need, then you can automate those activities.

The two markets merged and created today's provisioning solutions, which have a combination of pure provisioning as well as a business workflow engine.

Now, as a security architect, you need to be aware of the various infrastructure layer components that you can use in your various security zones. These tools allow the security operations group and their associated security officers to secure the security assets from threats and compromises.

There were other advances in security architecture around this time that should be understood. There were intrusion detection systems, antivirus solutions, and a monster security solution called an **SIEM**. But they were focused on infrastructure situations. So, like what happened when network controls got too hard, attacks shifted from infrastructure to applications.

Security in application architecture

All the lessons that were learned when Microsoft created its SDLC through the Trustworthy Computing Initiative were passed along to the creation of applications. But by moving up this one layer, you start to see way too many application developers. Creating applications is much easier than creating a piece of infrastructure with machine language and the associated lower-level languages. The creation of graphical user interfaces, the simplification of code writing, and the variety of languages meant that almost anyone could start to write applications.

And creating an application that doesn't have vulnerabilities? Well, that became a situation where there wasn't a return on investment. So, security people started to take an insurance approach to developing or implementing applications. What would happen if this happened or that happened?

Plus, you had project management offices that were using waterfall methodologies to deliver projects, including projects around application development. So solution architects had to figure out how to deliver their projects quickly in order to meet schedules or improperly determined costs for projects. Using an SDLC? That would take too long and the company was demanding more and more return on investment.

SDLC approaches work for companies that see the ROI associated with it. But, by and large, architects are technical people and not used to talking business. With the push to deliver applications quicker and quicker, a new framework for developing applications came into being – the Agile approach. And IT managers loved it because it was delivering application components faster than ever before. But there was one problem: Agile requires a fair bit of discipline to ensure that what is delivered meets certain quality standards. And that can't happen if Architects don't truly understand how Agile works.

So now you have applications being written quicker than ever but without the discipline to ensure that the code written didn't have any bugs or vulnerabilities in it. Applying SDLC to Agile is difficult because the two approaches are diametrically opposed. Agile is about building small components quickly. SDLC is meant for working with a waterfall methodology and inserting controls. In short, SDLC imposes structure and guidelines that the Agile methodology doesn't.

The security architect had to start taking a bigger picture approach. They had to look at the way applications where being written and provide guidelines around how it should be written and how the code should be checked. In short, they had to start looking at application development more along the lines of quality control rather than insurance or from an ROI perspective.

Now you have various tools that are used for checking code. But the original code scanners could only check maybe 10-20% of the lines of code. The rest had to be reviewed manually. Can you imagine manually reviewing an application with 100,000 lines of code? Not really possible. But reviewing small snippets each time they are written is something that is much more feasible. Security started to become embedded into the application development process.

To this day, I still have an issue with the Agile methodology. I've found far too many projects where Agile is code for develop quickly without any checks and balances and results in having to go back and rewrite the code.

For the security architect, code review is something that is done by those that do a lot of code writing. But most security architects by this time had come up from the networking and infrastructure areas and weren't that aware of how to code. Sure, they could write scripts to automate specific processes, but write in Java or C++? Not going to happen. So what did they do? They reverted to what they were good at, which was network-level and infrastructure-level solutions.

Along comes the application gateway, the XML accelerator, and the web proxy. Security architects decided that, with so many applications being written and being put into place, it wasn't feasible to check all that code. And, besides, many companies were buying applications off the shelf without any guarantees that the applications were written securely. So a "bump in the road" approach became standardized.

By putting something like an application gateway between the users and the application itself, you now had a way of protecting the application from itself. You started to look for known good patterns rather than patterns of malicious intent. The vulnerabilities were still there but the ability to exploit them became harder simply because of the bumps in the road that were implemented. Infrastructure was used to protect the applications that were sitting higher up in the OSI stack.

Are you starting to see a pattern? Basically, an architecture is created and then a security architect must come along and figure out how to protect it. Network architectures created? Great, let's look at network level tools. Infrastructure architectures being created? Okay, let's figure out how to protect them now. Applications being developed? Can we use something a little lower to figure out how to protect them?

It's always the lower levels that are used to protect the levels above, simply because of learning curves. But what happens when all those levels are thrown out the window and the company comes up with something called virtual solutions?

Security in virtual architectures

Have you ever heard of Moore's Law? It's an observation that one of the co-founders of Fairchild Semiconductor came up with in 1975. Gordon Moore noticed that the power of the semiconductor doubled every 18 months. He changed that to every two years but people never forgot the original 18-month time-frame.

But, over the last decade, the power of processors has been slowing down and you started to have to think about how to decrease costs more and more, rather than think about how to increase productivity more and more. Remember, to get a true return on investment, you have to either decrease costs or increase what you can do with your expenditure.

Well, IT people started to look back at what they had done before. Back when Microsoft released their first operating system, MS-DOS, a lot of applications were being built to run on DOS. But more and more people wanted simpler computers, so Microsoft came up with a GUI-driven operating systems called Windows. But what do you do with all those applications written to run on DOS? A company isn't just going to throw out perfectly good applications when a new operating system comes out. There needed to be some sort of backward compatibility. So Microsoft came out, in their first set of Windows, with something called a **Virtual Machine**.

Basically, it was a version of DOS that runs inside Windows. It fakes that it's a DOS machine so that software that runs on DOS can keep on working. But, at the end of the day, this was the birth of the virtual world.

A little earlier, we talked about VLANs and VPNs. Both are logical extensions of virtualization. You use VLANs to fake a logical LAN that is isolated from other network segments. A VPN will fake an extension of a private network. But, in both cases, they're a virtualization of IT concepts.

Around a decade ago, virtual servers started to show up. And these, as you may guess, fake that they are standalone servers. You have the ability to assign CPU, memory, I/O, and other resources to this virtual server, but all these virtual servers could sit on a single machine. There's a bus that runs between each virtual server and the end result is a mini-network all in one contained unit.

Virtualization brought along a number of challenges, though, for the security architect. All security devices are meant for physical networks: real networks, if you will. So how do you, for example, put an IDS in place in a virtualized platform? Well, you virtualize, naturally. The various vendors started producing either virtualized versions of their security devices or they would provide software and you would put the software on a virtual server. This allowed you to have a small, self-contained network complete with security devices.

But what about security concepts? Take, for example, administrators. In a normal, physical network, you would have local administrators for individual servers and platforms. As the concept of security domains expanded, so did the role of the administrator. Then, there was the role of a domain administrator, who had rights over all boxes in their domain.

Virtualization changed that. You then had shrunken networks and security zones, to the point that you could place them on a single platform. There would be multiple servers sitting on that platform. A new role emerged, which can be called a virtual administrator. This is a role that manages the backplane of the virtual network (predominantly called the HyperVisor) as well as all the resources. The god power of a domain administrator, but limited to the virtual network.

Security architects had to start adapting again. When we look at virtual environments, we should take the same view as we would of the controls in an entire domain, but compressed into a virtual environment. The concepts and the principles are the same; it's the technology that has changed. We started to create architecture patterns. What is placed into the ESX? How do you manage the devices on the ESX? Do you have the management traffic out of band or in band? We had to think about how to manage these environments efficiently and still maintain a level of security.

This was extended to **Enterprise Service Buses (ESBs)**. Back when people started expanding application architectures, they started to have to think about how they could do things more efficiently. Many applications were asking for the same pieces of information, just for different purposes. Or, there were common communication patterns that were emerging between applications because of the movement towards XML. So how could you make communication more efficient?

The first thing they did was limit the amount of wiring that was necessary. The ESB just made communication more efficient by applying the same rules to every application's input and output. They all had to make use of the same roles. They had to use encryption. They had to communicate either across HTTPS or SFTP. Standardized architecture patterns started to be put into place and security architecture was no different.

Virtualization has changed a lot of things for IT. For security architects, virtualization has actually allowed us to enforce strict patterns of behavior, simply because the other architecture towers wanted to have consistent patterns of behavior for their applications. The beauty of this is that security architects just had to review one interface and then that pattern could be reused over and over. Much more efficient.

Security in the cloud

So now we have virtualization, the concept that allows IT to be as efficient as possible with limited resources. But what was the logical extent of this? If virtualization allowed IT to consolidate resources and become more efficient, what would happen if multiple companies started to consolidate? Wouldn't that make the entire IT industry that much more efficient?

And so began the movement to the cloud. **Software as a Service (SaaS)**, **Platform as a Service (PaaS)**, **Infrastructure as a Service (IaaS)**; as a service came into vogue. Everyone was trying to figure out how to leverage products that everyone already had across multiple organizations. Companies such as SalesForce came up with their CRM that was available to everyone. The catch was that there was little in the way of customization. Google and Amazon came out with their IaaS so that you could make use of the massive efficiencies of a large data center but for your small company—economies of scale made available for the little guy.

The same is starting to occur for security products. You can get **Identity as a Service (IDaaS)**. There's **Federation-as-a-Service (FaaS)** from Ping Identity. Multiple companies provide IDS as a service. And the various SIEM vendors have SIEM as a service.

Here's the catch, though. How do you, as a security person, ensure that you have security in place when you don't have control of the infrastructure, networks, or applications that are being used by your organization? Sure, you have a lot of cost savings associated with putting servers on the **Amazon Web Services (AWS)** cloud, but at what risk? And are the security capabilities that AWS enough to protect what you are designing?

The cloud has a lot of capabilities but it's still in its nascent stages when it comes to security. Like all that has come before, a wonderful new capability emerges and everyone rushes towards it. And then they realize, "uh oh, maybe it has some gotchas. Better call security and get something designed".

Security architects must always work to catch up to where IT is going in general. The best way to deal with it is to look to old architecture patterns to see if there's a way to protect the new environment. But keep an eye on this space because, unlike yesteryear, the borders of the enterprise are changing. And if they change, how do you deal with a lack of borders?

It means moving away from protecting boxes (such as servers, routers, firewalls, and so on) to protecting information. It's the information that is important after all.

Security architecture

Let's break down security architecture by starting with the architecture component. To create a good architecture, you must have a structure in place that allows you to deal with all the details. Typically, the best way to put together an architecture is from the network layer up. This means understanding networks, infrastructure, applications, information, and business architectures. Each one of these layers has a security component and, as a result, needs to have a security architecture component.

But that's only part of what an architecture does. At the end of the day, an architecture is meant to communicate a future state. It's meant to take information from the business and translate that into technical terms for IT people. It is also meant to take information from IT people and communicate it to non-technical individuals.

What we've learned about IT projects is that, if there hasn't been any planning (both short term tactical planning or long-term strategic planning), most projects will either fail to be fully implemented or, when implemented, only a fraction of the capabilities of the solution will be used. Architecture is meant to change that. It's meant to provide the plan to implement a solution specific to a project and it's meant to provide a strategic vision so that the IT project, once implemented, moves the organization down the road to fulfilling. Architecture is probably the most important function that an IT organization can have and, without it, IT becomes nothing but a black hole for expenditures on technology.

Now, let's talk about security. Security is meant to reduce risk. It's meant to consider vulnerabilities and the potential for those vulnerabilities to be exploited. As a result, often, people who work in security are viewed as roadblocks to moving forward. This is an unfair characterization that comes about because people want to move quickly. But by moving quickly, risks and issues can be introduced into a project. A better way of characterizing security people is as individuals who` specialize in a specific type of quality assurance.

The problem security people have is that they typically come from a technology background and are not able to communicate security risks to non-technical individuals. That, combined with a lack of understanding of the business, results in conflicts with other departments. The other issue with security people is that they often come up with problems without a corresponding solution. And this is where the security architect comes in.

The security architect should understand the risks that a security person will find and then be able to come up with solutions that will be acceptable to the business. They should create architectures by looking at each layer and understanding how those individual layers will deal with risk. Dealing with risk needs to be done at different layers within the IT organization as well. The security architect must understand the importance of governance, the creation of strategy and program management, the various security activities, as well as architecture activities, in project delivery, and the role that operations play in creating architectures.

People tend to misunderstand what security architect is and, as a result, mischaracterize the role they play with the roles of other positions. Often, security organizations will view a security architect as someone who determine risk levels. But that's not what a security architect does. Determining risk levels is only a small component of what a security architect does. Remember, a security architect is an architect that specializes in security, not a security person who can do design. This is a very important distinction.

What's important to understand is that there are different types of security architects just as there are different types of IT architects. Each security architect has an important role to play but they must balance different amounts of business and technical communication.

Now, when you combine both security architecture, you have a function that is meant to provide a strategic vision to reduce the security risk of an organization over a 3-5-year period and a tactical vision to implement IT security projects that will move the organization down the road of reducing the business's security risk.

This book is meant to talk about how to create the various security architecture deliverables in the importance of each. My recommendation to you is to take each of these areas that the book will talk about and create standardized templates. It's with the use of templatization that you can improve the quality of your work, as well as improving the architecture return on investment.

Architecture layers in an organization

There are many architectural errors that must be thought about in an IT organization. Each one builds on the one above it. Those layers are the following:

- **Governance**: When you start talking about security, you must be coming from a place that the entire organization agrees with. That place is governance. This can be things such as policies, organizational oversight, and the principles that are used to ensure an organization is secure. The moment you start talking about security without referencing a governance framework, you are opening the door to disagreements within an organization.

- **Strategy and program management**: Once you have governance in place, you want to have a vision of what the security of your organization is going to look like. Any architectures that you build must be in alignment with that vision and that's when security architecture strategies come into play. A security architect must be thinking about how to create strategies or how to align their projects with the strategy of the organization. The projects that security architects work on will come from a program driven by the strategy.

- **Project delivery**: It's in project delivery that most people think security architecture work occurs. It's important to understand that there are two types of projects: security projects and non-security projects. When you're talking about a security project, the security architect is also the solutions architect. When you're talking about non-security projects, the security architect just plays a supporting role to the solutions architect. But, in both cases, the security architect plays an important role.

- **Operations**: This is security architect typically is involved in higher level one time activities. But operations play an important part in a feedback role. They see how well a project is implemented, since they're the ones that must manage the end result, and they see the risks that an organization has that need to be addressed. Security architecture needs to have operations as an input into everything they do.

And that brings us to the different types of security architects.

The different security architecture roles

The type of architectural role depends on a combination of the amount of business interaction and the amount of technical interaction. Remember, security architecture is about communicating with both the business and technical people. But this is a balancing act, and the amount that you deal in one area will dictate what type of security architect you actually are.

The more business focused you are, the higher up the food chain you become. The more focused on technology an architect is, the more closely they are aligned to the actual operations and activities that person deals with. So, for example, if an architect is primarily focused on the business side of things, they are typically up where the CIO or the chief architect is, whereas if they are very technically focused, they're typically going to be a technical architect.

The same goes for the degree of experience. If you've just started, you're going to be a student architect, and maybe even need some sort of certification. But as you gain experience, the need for certification starts to disappear and you start to be referred to as a master architect.

The three primary architects that we'll talk about in this book are the enterprise security architect, the project security architect, and the security engineer.

- **Enterprise security architects**: Enterprise security architects tend to deal more with the strategy and program management layer. They have a big picture view on how the enterprise needs to look from a security point of view and will put together a program toward move to that end vision.
- **Solution security architects**: Solution security architects are the security architects who focus of projects, whether as the solution architect themselves or in a supporting role. Needless to say, such projects are typically security technology focused.

- **Security engineers**: Also referred to as a technical architect, the security engineer is someone who slowly focuses on the technology for implementing the technology on looking at ways to optimize the technology and to support the technology. They're different from solution security architects simply because they deal with just a technology and not the surrounding business processes.

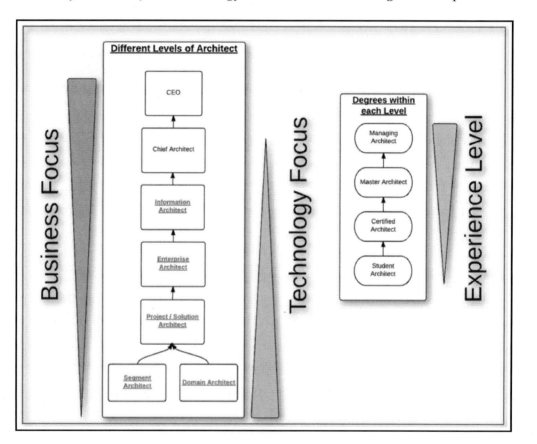

The one other role you should think about and understand is that of ` the chief security architect. This role is the most senior of all security architects. It is found in much larger organizations, where there are multiple security architects and there needs to be a lead in the security architecture domain. In most organizations, you're talking about a chief architect, and then the Enterprise security architect will report to the chief architect. The chief security architect is a leadership role, deals more with the administration associated with running a group of security architects, and will often be involved at the governance layer.

It will that has been discussed benefits by providing standardized approaches to security architecture, whether that's a standardized template for deliverables or a standardized process for creating those deliverables.

The importance of templatization

Back in the 1990s, ISO 9000 became something of a fad among organizations. The point was to try and standardize your approach to doing activities so that you could have a continuous, consistent level of quality. This resulted in organizations having standardized processes and using standardized templates for their activities. This is very easily ported to security architecture and allows security architects to dramatically improve the quality that they deliver, as well as provide a return on investment, simply because they're able to do things quicker. The more you do something, the more quickly you get at it.

With each of the layers that we've talked about (governance, strategy and program management, project delivery, and operations), it becomes very important to look for ways to create a standard approach to security architecture activities. One of the biggest issues that organizations have is trying to understand why they should have architecture in the first place. The tendency is to just go out and do something, without thinking first, without planning, and that approach often causes issues and problems delivering projects, but does have the appearance of doing things quickly.

The need to go quickly is the reason why we've seen the rise of the Agile framework. Today, people have come to expect to have things right away. They typically have a lack of patience, and that lack of patience can drive poor decisions. One of the things that I learned a long time ago was that, sometimes, the best decision is no decision. But people tend to want to have the appearance of doing things. Doing is viewed as better than not doing.

So, to provide that faster process that organizations are looking for, using a template and using a standardized process helps speed everything up. It allows you to show what the end result will look like and will allow you, as the security architect, to look for ways of speeding things up and improving what you deliver.

In most of this book, we'll talk about standard deliverables and what should be in those standard deliverables, but the best recommendation to you is to create what works best for your organization. This book will give examples, but you know your organization best and, like with any framework, you should adopt and adapt what best suits your organization. Remember, your purpose is to communicate and people will have a level of trust in you if you are consistently doing the same thing.

Security architecture principles

Security architecture principles are those beliefs that should drive your approach to solutions. They are something that are higher than policies and standards because they drive how to enact and respond to the requirements of policies and standards. They are, in fact, a characterization of the personality of your role.

When you start working with an organization, it's important to understand that organization's personality. By talking to stakeholders, you can get an understanding of how they view their organization and how they would like to see solutions implemented. Are they open to cutting edge technology or do they want tried and true solutions? What do they value as their organization's crown jewels? Is there an approach that they want to take to developing solutions?

The role of a security architect should have its own principles. Those principles allow you to understand how to interact with any organization and deliver results in your architecture tower. Some of the principles that you should consider when you act as a security architect are the following:

- **Understand that security is not the core business**: This is the biggest failing of security people and organizations, and is common across all companies. Security people tend to think that their way is the right way. But a security architect must do what is best for the business, not what's best for security. Security will provide a series of risks that the security architect puts a solution together to deal with. And, with that, the security architect starts to add value to the organization and gain the trust of those around them.
- **Understand and mitigate risk**: The corollary of the previous principle is that the security architect needs to understand the true level of risk and then provide solutions. One of the common issues that comes up is that security people will point out risks but not solutions to mitigate risks. A security architect is a builder, a planner. They must come up with plans and solutions, not just problems. And it's the process of finding solutions that meet all stakeholders' needs that allows trust to be built.

- **Communication is key to success**: An architect is all about communication. If you can't communicate, you can't understand issues or requirements and you can't get people on board with solutions. An architect must be fluent in communication of all forms. They must be able to communicate verbally when in person, providing presentations, or on phone calls, they must be able to communicate in text form, whether that is in emails or memos, and they must be able to ensure that their communication is available whenever a solution needs to be understood, which means ensuring that designs are documented clearly and concisely. This goes for a security architect as much as for any other architecture tower.

Make sure you communicate continuously through the architecture process, don't wait until the solution is done to do a grand reveal. You want to be floating trial balloons or talking about direction with your stakeholders as you create your architecture artifacts so that, when the work product is completed, no one is surprised and the end result is rubber stamped.

- **Don't preach**: The implementation of a solution happens best when all stakeholders are on board. To achieve that, the security architect needs to talk to stakeholders at times during the creation of the various architecture artifacts. If you actually listen to your stakeholders, you will know what they are asking for in terms of requirements and will then be able to communicate a design that meets those requirements. Too often, people enter into a situation and have a preconceived view of what the solution should be. They don't listen to what their stakeholders believe and, as a result, the solution implemented doesn't meet the stakeholders' needs. And a solution that doesn't meet stakeholders' needs won't be used.
- **All solutions are a combination of technology, people, and processes**: Too often, people are sold on new, shiny toy. They want to put in technology for technology's sake and not consider that there are different components to a solution. If you put in technology, who is going to maintain it? What are the business processes that the technology is going to support? Is there integration of other solutions already in place?

If you gathered your requirements properly, a solution will come together naturally. Maybe a lower cost option is to realign business processes. Maybe a better solution would be to offshore to a cheaper country. There are all sorts of solutions that can be found, so make sure you are driven by requirements and be open to solutions that cover technology, people, and processes.

- **Governance drives what must be done, not personal opinion**: Always be driven by organizational policies and standards, because they are meant to represent what the organization believes and how the organization would like to move forward. If there aren't any policies and standards, make it a point of creating them with the help of stakeholders so that the organization has a common view on how to move forward. If you try to put forward a stance that is not based on organizational policies and standards, then it's your own personal opinion and has the exact same validity as the opinion that is opposite to yours, and no one wins that fight.

There is a view that there is one other area of a solution besides technology, people, and process, and that is governance. It may be that a solution will need a governance component such as a new policy or a review board, or some other governance activity. That means that governance should be thought about when putting together solutions.

- **Repeat back to your stakeholders what you are hearing in your own words**: Nothing gains trust more than repeating back to your stakeholders what you have been told. It shows to them that you have heard what they are saying and, more importantly, understand them. Most importantly, it ensures that you actually have heard them and understand what needs to be done. Once you've done that, then you can start talking about solutions.

When you work as a security architect, make sure you are completely aware of the principles that you will be following and, if possible, communicate them to your stakeholders. That way, your stakeholders will know what to expect and it will allow you to improve the trust level with your work products.

Summary

At the end of the day, it's important to remember that security architecture is an architecture activity that focuses on security and is not a security activity that happens to deal with architecture. There is a big distinction between the two that should be understood simply because of how security architecture came about.

Originally, architects would create their IT solutions and then add security on afterward, once they understood what they were doing. But, as technology has evolved, it's come to be understood that architecture has to include a security component in each layer and not just be added on afterwards. It's the add-on effect that will cause vulnerabilities to be included in any solution.

Fortunately, this is being understood more and more. As a result, it's getting harder to find old school vulnerabilities, such as those at the network layer, because those issues have been understood and dealt with. That doesn't mean that architects now automatically build security into their solutions—that will never happen as long as people take shortcuts to design and implement solutions. But the frequency of incidents and vulnerabilities is decreasing on a per-solution basis. But here's the problem: the more that technology changes and evolves, the more solutions there are and, as a result, the more vulnerabilities there are. The number of vulnerabilities per solution is down, but the number of possible solutions is up, so you see an increase in total vulnerabilities. And it depends on the organizational personality that is creating the solutions as well.

So how do you deal with that? The solution has to start at the organizational level. It can't start with a single manager but, rather, from an executive directive. And how do the enterprise executives direct? With the use of governance capabilities. Very few organizations have built security holistically into all aspects of solution creation and implementation by starting from the bottom and moving upward. Top companies have had direction from executives with the use of governance, forcing the organization to meet executive requirements.

The next chapter in this book goes into governance and how security architecture is involved in governance within the organization and within an architecture itself. All architectures have three components, technology, people, and processes, and it's a poor architect that doesn't consider each one of those components. But, I've come to realize that there is actually a fourth component that all solutions have: governance. Remember, an enterprise is typically a business solution for an industry problem. Executives should quite properly be viewed as business architects. The only difference between them and an IT architect or security architect is that the amount of technology in the mix of their solutions is typically minimal.

Questions

Question 1: What is the key capability that a security architect possesses?

Question 2: What type of security architect deals with strategy?

Question 3: What was the first architectural framework?

Question 4: What are the three primary components of a solution? Is there a fourth and, if so, what is it?

Question 5: Does a non-security project have a security component?

Question 6: Which layer did security issues start showing up in first?

Question 7: What is the purpose of architecture?

Further Reading

Add additional references to useful Packt resources, or other information that might help explain a particular concept in further detail.

2
Security Governance

Security governance is the foundation of anything and everything that a security architect does. It provides the direction that a security architect will take and provides a framework for whatever a security architect designs. Without governance, architecture in general, and security architecture specifically, becomes very individualistic and can lead down a path where solutions do not meet the needs of the organization.

One of the biggest complaints that security people get are that they are obstructionists. They are always saying no without providing any guidance. As a result, others in an enterprise will start to avoid and go around security, and that typically comes down to issues with governance.

If a security person, including a security architect, says that something can't be done or that a project can't do something without the backing of governance, it becomes a conflict situation. The security person doesn't have a leg to stand on. They are only talking from their own point of view, which, no matter how well-meaning it is, just can't represent the organization.

Governance is meant to ensure that the approaches to security are reflective of the organization's personality. It reflects not just security's view on issues but how the entire organization sees issues and approaches. It strikes a balance between security and other areas without being a situation where a single person stands on a mountaintop and preaches a set of values.

Remember, security is not the core function of an organization. The core function of an organization is whatever the Board of Governors says the core function of the organization is. So when security gets in the way of the core business, other individuals in the organization will go around security. Here's my primary rule for security: DON'T PREACH!

The other thing to remember, and that's regardless of what type of IT professional you are, is that there isn't any such thing as an industry standard. I have yet to read a book with the title industry standard. Sure, there are technical standards such as TCP/IP, or XML, or DOC (or any number of other technical standards) but there isn't anything called an industry standard. The only things that exist are the philosophies that are popular at any moment in time.

To be truly successful, you must approach governance within an organization strategically. You should look at the personality of the organization and the longer-range goals, and then create a governance model that reflects where you are, as well as where you want to go. Take technology out of the equation and look to model patterns of behavior. If you do that, your governance model will be much more successful.

This chapter will talk about the three primary artifacts that are used in security architecture from a governance point of view: security principles, security policies and standards, and security architecture guidance. Each of these artifacts builds on the previous one and, as a whole, allows the organization to truly understand where the organization wants to go.

As a result of this chapter, you will learn the following:

- What security principles are and how to create them
- How to create security policies and standards, as well as which policies and standards tend to be the focus in security architecture
- What a security architecture guidance document is and what should be in it
- How each of the artifacts talked about build on each other

Security principles

Security principles are the core of the personality of the organization that you are doing design work for. They talk about the approach that you should take and how to interpret lower governance artifacts, such as policies and standards. They are higher-order by nature and are almost philosophical in nature.

In order to properly interpret security architecture activities, it is important to come to an agreement as to the approach that needs to be taken. This is commonly called a philosophy or a set of guiding principles. In any case, documenting them provides architects the ability to view the environment, and their activities within that environment, with a common view.

Typically, these principles are written with security architecture in mind. That said, it is often possible for other architecture towers to leverage these same guiding principles in their work. This allows for a more cohesive approach to architecture, considering no single solution has just one architecture tower in it. For example, a new application implementation will need the appropriate underlying servers to be placed in the appropriate network segment, use the correct identity and access management mechanisms, and store the information in the correct structure in its databases.

Each of these areas goes into different architecture towers, so the approach to one will have an impact to another. If you are using bleeding edge technology for the application, but the approach from the server level is to use an older, deprecated technology, then you will have a conflict.

Developing principles

Never, ever just write principles (or policies and standards) on your own, even if you are the chief security architect or the CISO. Remember, this is all about reflecting what the organistaion is all about, not what the security group or the security architects are. There will be a much more in-depth approach documented in the security policies and standards section, but the best way to approach creating any sort of governance artifact is to use an iterative approach. In other words:

Talk to people.

Consolidate what you hear.

Feed it back to them for correction.

Finalize and communicate.

First, talk to multiple different stakeholders in your organization that you will be dealing with on an ongoing basis, and don't limit it just to security people. Ask other architects about their approach. Talk to operations managers, to people in the PMO. Talk to the executive level. They all have a vision as to the personality of the organization and it's your job, as the security architect, to document what the stakeholders believe that the principles of the organization should be. Then, and only then, do you add your own view. But if you go in just with your own opinion as to how a security architecture should be created, you are setting yourself up for conflict within your organization.

When you talk to the stakeholders, do it in a one-on-one setting. Do NOT do it in a group setting because if you do, there will be a dominant personality who will want to force the conversation in a direction. That wallflower over in the corner may have a very valid opinion but just won't speak up when the dominant personality is in the room. So, don't be lazy and try to do this in a group setting. Talk to the stakeholders individually. You can bring them together later.

When you talk to these stakeholders, ask them open-ended questions such as how would you like to see the security architectures created? What type of vision do you have of how an architecture is created? When you ask open-ended questions, the stakeholders may just give you responses that you weren't expecting. And that's a good thing, because it means that you are learning about your organization. If you ask a Yes/No question, all you are looking for is a validation of your own opinion and you won't be doing yourself any service.

Once you have collected comments from the various stakeholders, consolidate and prioritize them. There may be disagreements between stakeholders and it's good to identify those disagreements right off the bat so that you can guide the organization to being on the same page. Try to consolidate the principles into no more than ten principles that are a single sentence in length. More, and you risk people not reading them. Too few, and you won't have enough to guide how you put together your designs.

The same goes for the length of the principles. These are principles, not policies and standards. You want them to be one sentence in length and be something that you can mention in an elevator pitch, in an argument, or on a marketing poster. Again, if they are too long, people won't read them or bother to reference them.

Once you are comfortable with the consolidation and the structure, circulate them to the stakeholders to make sure they agree. If the original interviews of the stakeholders brought out disagreements, bring those stakeholders together in the same room and have them review the principles. At this point, everyone should have provided feedback into your draft principles and you should feel fairly comfortable that they will be accepted. But bringing all the stakeholders into the room at this point allows for everyone to realize that the organization is determining the principles, not just one individual. They will feel that much more ownership and will communicate it to their own groups.

Principles signed off now? Great! Communicate it. Trumpet it to the entire organization and make sure that everyone knows who was involved in the creation of the principles. By doing that, you are showing everyone in the organization that the leadership in the organization believes in this approach and it will encourage others to follow these principles.

Sample security architecture principles

Principles should be very simple to read and understand, and shouldn't be more than one sentence in length. They should speak directly to the character of the organization and how the organization feels they would like to approach security architecture. And try not to have more than ten principles. This ensures that they will actually be read and understood.

To create these principles, it's important to remember that solutions deal with three or four core components. Most architects will tell you that these components are people, process, and technology. I believe that there is actually a fourth component: governance. The solution of principles is dealing with the problem of alignment of an organization so you should keep those three or four components in mind as you create your principles.

Let's start with the people component. Remember, you want to be talking in very broad terms. The people component will talk to the *who* aspects of the principles. Some approaches from a people point of view might be:

- Who are your primary stakeholders going to be?
- Who is ultimately responsible for security architecture? Sure, you may be creating it, but is it owned by the CISO or the Chief Architect, or someone else?
- How do your customers fit into it? Who are your customers?

Sample principles associated with the people component might be:

- All security architecture is owned by the Chief Architect with input from the CISO
- We view our customers as the end users of any system we are designing for
- We will always take into consideration the requirements of the sustainment teams

Short and simple. No longer than a single sentence. But, they clear indicate exactly what the organization is thinking when it comes to security architecture.

Okay, now let's look at the next component: the process component. The process component should talk to *how* you do things or how your solutions will impact others. Answer the question how, and you start to get the process principles. Some approaches to the process principles might be:

- What framework will you be following in developing your architectures?
- Is there a focus that you will have from the outset of your design efforts?
- Are you looking for a speedy implementation or will you be looking to balance the business needs with risk?

Sample principles associated with the process component might be:

- We will use comprehensive architectural planning based on the TOGAF framework
- We will focus on enterprise-wide solutions rather than local solutions that are enhanced for specific business groups
- We will carefully balance the business need to quickly offer new products against the security risks it might pose to our customers, company brand, or employees

Technology principles were left for last because people always jump to technology first and ignore the other two components. So, for technology, look to answer the *what* component of the principles. To that end, never specify a technology. This is simply because technology changes rapidly, so while the technology may be applicable today, it may not be in use in 3 years. And principles are what describe the organization, and they shouldn't be changed more than every 5-7 years. Re-validate them regularly, but don't change them just because it's convenient.

Some of the technology questions you want to be asking are:

- Are you comfortable with bleeding edge technology or do you want to be looking at more stable solutions?
- How are you going to look at refreshing the environment? Are you going to be driven by business need, or are you going to be driven by architectural risk?
- Will you take solutions from the various business groups that may have been sold the shiny new object, or are you going to push solutions back to the business groups?

Sample technology principles may be:

- We will adopt proven security technologies that will protect our company and customers. To that end, we want to see examples of the technology in use within our industry.
- Solutions will be driven based on requirements gathered first. We will view any product-based solution that hasn't had requirements collected first as a flawed solution to be rejected out of hand.
- We will take a *Best Suite of Products* approach rather than a *Best of Breed* approach to allow for a more efficient management of assets.

Finally, let's talk about governance itself. Governance principles answer the *why* aspects. Remember, there should always be checks and balances so even governance should have a set of principles. Now, some people think of governance as just another process but you can't call a policy and standard a process. They are artifacts. Make sure you talk about governance in your principles.

Some of the governance questions you may want to be looking at are:

- How are you going to measure what you have accomplished? Are you meeting the requirements of your organization?
- Is there a way you want to make sure the security architectures are meeting the needs of the business?
- Who has oversight over all security architecture?

Sample governance principles may be:

- We will benchmark ourselves against other organizations in our industry. We want to be in the top quartile in stakeholder satisfaction.
- All solutions will be reviewed by stakeholders after requirements have been gathered, designs have been put together, and the build environments have been implemented.

If you notice, each of these principles are simple and one sentence in length. If you were to limit yourself to 10 principles, you could put all these principles onto one sheet of paper and hand it to any new employee for them to post on their cubicle wall. But, they talk to the character of the organization while still allowing plenty of design creativity moving forward.

Oh, and one more thing. Please keep security principles and security architecture principles distinct and separate. Remember, security architecture is architecture focused on security. It's not security that brings in solutions.

Security architecture policies and standards

Security architecture policies and standards are the foundation that a security architect uses to build any solution or to provide guidance to any projects they are supporting. Like principles, the policies and standards of an organization must be something that are signed off and agreed to by all stakeholders, not just security stakeholders. If they aren't signed off by all stakeholders, then it becomes a situation where the security architect and the client will not be able to come to an agreement.

But, and this is very important, the security architect can't just say the policy says this, so you can't do it. The entire purpose of an architect, regardless of whether they focus on security or some other architecture tower, is to provide solutions, not to throw up roadblocks. If all you say is *no because the standard says X*, then you aren't building, and hence you aren't an architect.

There are three terms that need to be understood as part of this chapter. They are the following:

- Policies
- Procedures
- Standards

Many people use these three terms interchangeably or use the definition of one to describe a different term. For the purpose of this book, policies are stances that indicate the intent or goal of what an organization is aiming for. They are stances that are the core values of the organization and are not meant to be changed for convenience sake.

Procedures are the methods that are used to implement the policies. So, for example, a policy may say something like passwords need to be changed every 30 days, whereas the procedure would outline the way that the IT organization can force those changes to occur.

The final term that is quite commonly used is standards. Standards are measuring sticks that are used to compare where an organization is in an area compared to where they want to be. There isn't typically any enforcement involved in standards, whereas policies are meant to be enforced.

Often, organizations will create standards so that they do not have to deal with the internal politics involved in creating policies. By calling a document a set of standards, it allows an organization to avoid getting board-level approvals. The problem with not going through the process of getting board-level approvals is that the organization itself doesn't see that the uppermost level of management is buying into the process and, as a result, may believe that the standards don't need to be followed. This ends up completely defeating the purpose of putting together a policy or standards document.

How you make your security architecture policies and standards is probably more important than the end working product. Being inclusive with various stakeholders will improve the quality of your security architecture policies and standards.

Policy development process

The primary problem with creating policies is getting the necessary buy-in from the appropriate people within an organization. If they don't agree with the policies, the policies aren't even worth the paper that they are written on. It is necessary to get individuals together so that the diverse opinions can be discussed and developed to the point that policies can be agreed upon:

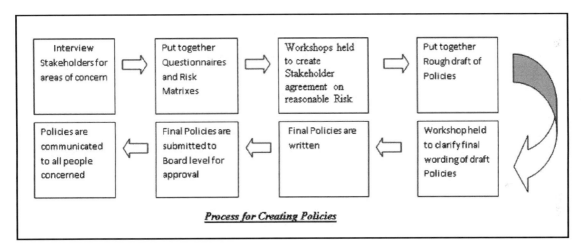

Process for Creating Policies

The best solution for this is a series of workshops that are done in several stages. They are as follows:

1. Interview individual stakeholders
2. Agree upon areas for policy development
3. Discussion of the different options within individual policies and the selection of policy requirements
4. Review of draft policy documents
5. Final sign-off of policy documents

Each stage is important. They allow for the proper flow of discussion about the policy areas and allow the group to come to the point where there is buy-in from the different members of the organization.

Interview individual stakeholders

Over the years, I've found that trying to get individuals to agree while in a group setting is both frustrating and a massive source of time wasting, both for you and for the stakeholders involved. The best way to start the entire process is to interview each stakeholder individually, much the same way that you would gather requirements from individual stakeholders.

Arrange to meet each stakeholder at their location in a one-on-one setting. This way, the stakeholders will feel free to mention areas that they are looking to get policies or standards written up on. What one stakeholder believes is important may not be the same as a separate stakeholder. Plus, that wallflower that is sitting in the back of the room during a group session will now be able to provide their input, and that input might actually be really valuable.

Once you have interviewed each stakeholder about the areas that they think policies and/or standards should be written for, you consolidate them. These will be the areas that you present to the stakeholders in a group so that there can be consensus moving forward.

Agree upon areas for policy development

The next stage is usually developed in an atmosphere designed to allow the areas of concern of individuals to be documented so that policy options can be developed for later on.

One example might be where the IT manager has concerns about the ability of individuals to have physical access to servers. Another example may be that a teachers' representative is concerned about the privacy of student records. You now have two individuals with completely different areas of concern.

By getting everyone together, you can create a common consensus as to the areas that need to have policies and standards developed. Some of the policies can be compiled into a major policy area. By discussing the various areas of concern, the bare bones of the policy or standard document is created.

Discuss policy options

Once there is a common agreement on the various areas that need to have policies, the security architect will go off to research the different areas within the policy or standard area and provide different options for each individual governance area.

For example, imagine if an organization wants to have a password policy. Some of the individual areas that could be discussed with regards to a password policy might be:

- Length of time between password resets
- Password composition
- Who can administer passwords
- Number of times a password can be reused

The security architect would put together an options document for the individual areas that tries to give three options for each policy area (with different degrees of risk being considered), and describes the pros and cons of each option.

An example of the policy area of *length of time between password resets* is shown here. The security architect would put together something like the following:

Policy area	High risk	Medium risk	Low risk
Length of time between password resets	**Option**: Never reset. **Pros**: The end user never has to remember passwords and the help desk doesn't have the cost of password resets. **Cons**: If a password is ever discovered, the unauthorized person would have permanent access to the account.	**Option**: Reset monthly. **Pros**: Limits the amount of time that an unauthorized person could use an account. Increases overall security of the account. **Cons**: Users may have a tendency to write down passwords, which can be discovered by someone else.	**Option**: Reset daily. **Pros**: The amount of time that an unauthorized person can access an account is extremely limited. **Cons**: A great deal of administration problems come about since users will have a greater tendency to forget passwords and require help desk support.

Some of you reading this may say that the high risk option should never be used. But that's your opinion and it may not be held by all the stakeholders. Our job as security architects is to understand what the requirements are and then provide solutions. In this case, the requirement is to put together a specific password policy statement that meets company needs. Besides, each one of these options may have valid areas. The high risk option may be perfectly acceptable for a location storing nothing but publicly available documents. Why force authentication activities if there's nothing of value there?

Each area of a policy would be laid out like this for the workshop discussion. Ideally, the options document would be delivered to the workshop attendees prior to the workshop so that they can review the document and determine their own stance on the individual policy areas. Most areas will actually have consensus right off the bat.

The workshop would hash out the risk levels that the group will accept for the individual policy areas and the security architect would go back with the direction laid out by the workshop attendees.

Review draft policy documents

Once the security architect has direction from the individual workshop attendees, he/she puts together a draft policy/standards document. The draft policy documents are submitted to the workshop attendees prior to the next workshop so that they can determine how they would like to see the wording of the policy document changed. Often, the wording of the policy document can have as much discussion as the actual decisions on the direction of the policy areas. Be aware, however, that seldom do people read documents that are provided, so don't expect much feedback; hence the reason for the second workshop/meeting.

Because there will be a discussion about wording, I would suggest that there be two workshops scheduled to finalize the wording of the documents. The first workshop would go over the draft's wording and the second workshop would get everyone's agreement on the finalized policy document wording. You may receive some additional requests for changes, so you may have to arrange for a third workshop.

Final sign-off of policy document

This final stage involves presenting the finalized policy document to the workshop attendees for final sign-off and then communicating it to the organization as a whole. The presentation to the organization is necessary to ensure that the entire organization understands that there is buy in from the appropriate people and that the policies have the effect of law within the organization. Putting together a policy document will not have any effect if the people within the organization don't even know that it exists.

There are many ways that the presentation can occur. There can be a large meeting with the entire organization at once. There can be a series of seminars with smaller groups so that the policy document can be discussed. The policy document can be disseminated to the different groups within the organization with a sign-off sheet that is signed by the employees to indicate they have read and understood the policies. Or, the policy document can be presented during the onboarding process for new employees. Any number of ways can be followed to ensure that the organization is aware of the new policy.

The last thing that needs to be done to ensure that the policy document is finalized is to ensure that the document is in a location that's easily accessible by the employees. It can be in a common room, in the company library, or on the corporate intranet website. As long as it is easily accessible, the policies and standards can be followed by the organization.

The policy document

There are two common problems that people make for themselves when writing a policy document. They tend to make it too long and without any clear structure. By making the document excessively long, it puts employees within the organization off and tends to discourage them from reading it. The wording should be short and concise, and the individual policies should be broken out in sections that clearly indicate what they are for. The ideal case is that the policy or standard is no longer than two pages. Any longer and you are not clearly communicating direction.

One other thing. There is a tendency to go into great detail about specific areas in a policy or standard. What is being created is something that would normally be called an architecture pattern. The intent of that document is to take any decision making away from the policy reader. Remember, the policy or standard is meant to provide guidance in such a way that the reader can find a solution that meets their needs, while keeping a solution's risk at an acceptable level.

The following is a good template to use for the creation of a policy:

<NAME OF POLICY> Policy

1.0 Purpose

The purpose of this policy is to `<REASON FOR POLICY>`.

2.0 Scope

The scope of this policy includes `<DETAIL ALL PERSONNEL AND SYSTEMS THAT ARE AFFECTED BY THIS POLICY. ALSO DETAIL OUT OF SCOPE AREAS>`

3.0 Policy

The policy that applies to `<POLICY AREA>` within `<CLIENT>` is as follows: `<SHORT BULLETED SENTENCES RELATED TO POLICY AREA>`

3.1 <POLICY AREA> Guidelines

- `<DETAIL GUIDELINES THAT GIVE EXAMPLES OF POLICY>`
- `<MAKE SHORT BULLETED SENTENCES>`

4.0 Enforcement

Violations of this policy will be subject to `<POLICY ENFORCEMENT ACTIVITY/HR ENFORCEMENT POLICY>`

5.0 Definitions

Terms	Definition
`<TERM TO BE DEFINED>`	`<DEFINITION OF TERM>`

Language of policies

Another common problem that people make when writing a policy document is that they mix up the wording used in policies with those used in procedures. Procedures are used to explain how to do something, whereas policies are used to say what the end result must be. Two completely different purposes.

For example, a policy may say that all passwords must be changed every 30 days. A procedure will say that the IT Administrator will go into Local Security Settings when an account is created and set the password expiration to 30 days. The difference is that the policy doesn't care *how* it is done. A well-written procedure will write out, step-by-step, how to implement the policy.

The other thing to remember when writing a policy is that you want to be as independent of specific technologies as possible. Because the IT industry changes so much, it is important that policies not refer to specific technologies. An example might be something like access control lists.

Access control lists (ACLs) control what services are allowed in and out of a machine (commonly by using a router, firewall, or HIDS). A poorly written policy might say something like *SSL are to be used in all internal client/server connections*. The problem is that SSL might not be around in 5 years, having been replaced by TLS. A more appropriate policy would be something like *encrypted communication must be used between endpoints and servers*. This second statement covers not only SSL, but also things like TLS, SSH, SFTP, and any other encrypted communication channel.

The point of writing policies is to try to ensure that you don't have to rewrite them every year or so. You want to review them for relevance but rewriting policies shouldn't occur because then the tendency is to change them to make life easier for individuals. People tend to want to change policies whenever meeting the policy or standard makes their designs more difficult. Simpler is not necessarily better. It's just simpler.

Policies are the bedrock of an effective security architecture. Without them, each successive security architect can change the setup of the security measures in solutions to suit their own beliefs. Where one security architect believes in a much more stringent set of security measures, another might be more lax. Plus, either's beliefs might not be the same as those held by the organization. Policies and standards are meant to ensure that the organization's core beliefs are communicated to all employees at any time during the life of the organization.

Security policy and standard areas

Many organizations try to align with the ISO 27000 series of security standards. In this group, there are several policies and standards areas recommended for those that follow the standard. These are represented in the following diagram:

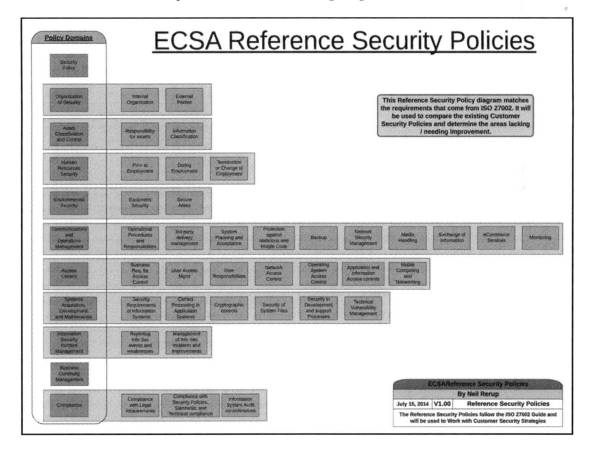

To understand this diagram, realize that it is a compilation of both policy domains and supporting standards. The column on the left, titled **Policy Domains**, are all the areas that ISO 27000 calls for an organization to have higher-level policies on. All the boxes to the right are considered supporting standards and they are meant to support the policy document.

For security architecture, it's important that a number of these policies and standards are more about security than they are about security architecture. Typically, security architecture will focus primarily on the following policy domains and their supporting standards:

- Communication and operations management
- Access control
- Systems acquisition, development, and maintenance

The other domains are primarily about security management. That said, there are some components of architecture that you can find in the business continuity management policy domain if you are looking for security architecture requirements associated with disaster recovery environments.

Security Architecture Guidance (SAG) document

One of the common problems that keeps coming up in various projects is the lack of understanding of what needs to be included in a security architecture. It is important to understand that security architecture has touch points in every individual architecture component within a design. As a result, a security architecture needs to be a component of an architecture/design, and not viewed as a separate tower. By taking this approach, the solution architect can ensure that each architecture is designed in a manner that reduces risk to the organization.

The SAG is meant to describe the various areas that need to be thought about and addressed in a design. You could almost view this as a primer to security architecture. If you look at each of these areas in your design, you'll greatly improve the security posture of the solution and simplify the process of getting security architecture approvals for the various gates in the PMO process.

Each section of the SAG should have requirements stated. Address these requirements as follows:

1. As part of the business requirement documentation activities, you need to gather the appropriate requirements for your project. Collect the appropriate standards for the project and add your security requirements.
2. Use the requirements to put in the appropriate security controls in your **Architecture Design Document** (**ADD**). It will help in making sure your solution has the appropriate level of security applied.

Also, if there is a security risk, you want to have mitigations for that risk. If you can't mitigate it with one method, then show how to do so using a different method. For example, say an application doesn't have the ability to log security events. Show how security events are then logged using infrastructure logs and network device logs. Security is applied in layers and is never one specific component.

Security should always be based on the risk levels and the business requirements, never based on industry best practice. There has yet to be a document that someone can point to that is the assigned industry best practice.

Security architecture guidance for projects

When looking at a solution, a security architect really only looks at the areas shown in the following diagram:

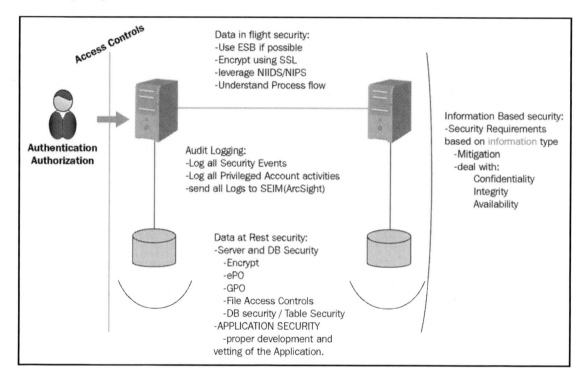

Information-based security

The first thing to understand is that the security levels for a solution should be based on the information that is being handled. Without understanding the information, the associated risk levels can't be understood. So, for example, if a solution is working with information available to the general public, it doesn't make sense to secure it as if it were highly confidential information. Conversely, if you are dealing with confidential or personal information, you don't want to post that information on the internet-facing web portal. Understand the information you want to secure.

Once you understand the information that the solution is handling (and there's normally a number of different types of information, such as information in files, authentication information, and so on), you can indicate the various confidentiality, integrity, and availability requirements.

Each area of your solution should always reflect back on the first two areas in this section. Please note that these requirements are tied to the business requirements associated with the solution. Good security is based on business requirements and is NOT done for security's sake.

Authentication/authorization controls

Once you understand the information that you are handling and the requirements around that information, you can start looking at the individual components of the solution. The most common one looked at is the authentication and authorization controls. Many people will refer to this area as **Identity and Access Management**, or **IAM**.

Authentication is the act of proving that someone is who they say they are. This is commonly done by identifying them through who they are (for example, username), what they know (for example, password or answers to secret questions) and, for more secure requirements, what they have (for example, RSA tokens), which is often referred to as **two-factor authentication**.

Once you've authenticated the person, you should state what that person can do within the system. This, by the way, also applies to system accounts where there is automated communication. You want to clearly state what an account can or cannot do. Often, this is done through the use of roles.

Access controls

Another common area that is looked at are access controls. This is tightly aligned to authentication and authorization controls because you are stating how the authorizations are managed by a solution. A coarse-grained example of this may be firewall rules, which basically talk about computer-to-computer communication control. But access controls are also things like file permissions within the solution or, if you are talking at the application level, the controls that are in place when someone interacts directly with an application.

Data in flight security

The focus of security architecture must always be on the information itself. To that end, it's important to realize that information has two states, data in flight and data at rest.

Data in flight deals with data that is in transit from one system to another. This is a base requirement of pretty much all distributed solutions, since this means that there are two or more servers of some sort involved in a solution. When you look at your solution, think about the confidentiality, integrity, and availability requirements associated with the information and then put in controls to support those requirements. Those controls could be things like these:

- **Process flow**: Communication should always be initiated by the higher security posture device to the lower security posture device and not the other way around
- **SSL**: This is meant to ensure that the channel that information is passing through is encrypted.
- **Certificate exchange**: This is meant to ensure that the solution components are communicating to authenticated components
- **Network IDS/IPS**: Intrusion Detection Systems/Intrusion Prevention Systems generally look for patterns of behavior that are inappropriate with regards to data in flight

Look at how you can mitigate your solution away from data in flight risks.

Data at rest security

Data at rest security deals with the how to secure data while it resides in one place for any length of time. Often, people think in terms of files that are stored on a server, but there are multiple locations that data can reside for any length of time. If you think about it from the point of view of the data, you can start to see where it will reside. It can reside in memory for a period of time prior to being transferred to a hard disk. It can reside on the hard disk or in a database (SQL, Oracle, or some other form). It can reside on a tape drive used for storage of data. Always look at where the data can reside before looking at the controls you can put into place to deal with data at rest security.

Some of the data at rest controls you can use are:

- **ePO**: ePO allows for the actions being done on a system to be monitored and acted on by the security operations center.
- **GPO**: **Group Policy Objects** deal with what policies are applied to a server through central policy management.
- **Antivirus**: This is used to prevent malicious code from acting within the system.
- **Encryption**: The favorite panacea, encryption works to support confidentiality requirements. Just remember that there is a performance hit with encrypting and decrypting.
- **Hardening**: The only things that a system should be doing are those that are absolutely necessary. Hardening removes unnecessary services, removes unnecessary accounts, and generally improves the baseline security posture of a device.
- **Database security**: This is where most data being acted on by a solution is stored. As such, the database has specific needs, such as ensuring all the other sections of this document are also applied to the tables within the database and not just at the database OS level.
- **Application security**: At the end of the day, it doesn't matter how secure all the other components of a solution are if the application has vulnerabilities built into it. Always ensure that the application, if custom built, is written without any vulnerabilities built in, or if a **Custom Off the Shelf** (COTS) application is used, it's been vetted appropriately so that you don't inherit the vulnerabilities created by someone else.
    - Performing an **Application Vulnerability Scan** will often show what the application security posture of a solution (either custom or COTS) is.

Audit logging

Something will happen. It always does. To ensure that improper actions are caught either while in process or for doing investigative work after the fact, it is important to have logging turned on in all components of your solution. Without that information, Security Analysts can't stop something from happening while in process, or determine what happened so that it can't happen in the future.

Typically, ALL privileged account activities should be logged, not just the normal security events.

Summary of requirements in an SAG

As you can see throughout this section, there are a number of areas that need to be commented on when putting together your **Architecture Design Document** (**ADD**). Those requirements are as follows:

Req.#	Requirement description
1	Document the type of information that the solution is handling
2	Document the confidentiality, integrity, and availability requirements that the business has
3	State what your authentication mechanism will be
4	State what the authorizations are within the solution
5	State what you access control mechanisms are from a network perspective, a host perspective, and from an application perspective
6	State what your data in flight controls are
7	State what your data at rest controls are
8	State what your logging controls are

Summary

At the end of the day, governance is probably the most important component of any security architecture. You use it to create a foundation for all your architectures while, at the same time, remembering that it is a component in any solution.

When you deal with governance, remember that you have a phased approach to setting up your foundation. You have your principles that describe your organization and how you will approach all architecture activities (you can probably think of principles as the "art" to the policies and standards "science"). You will have your policies and standards, which are the rules that all architectures will have to meet, while still allowing the architect room to creatively design. And the SAG document is something that can be provided to non-security architects to "guide" them in how to include security in their designs.

Keep all governance activities in mind while you are pulling together your architecture and you will be able to avoid any conflicts within the organization. And, most importantly, make sure you take an iterative approach to developing your governance model. If your stakeholders aren't directly involved and providing input into your governance, then they have every right to just say that they don't agree with it. So, which would you rather do - have a fight every time a design comes up or set the foundation for a successful architecture practice for the long haul?

The next chapter will go into security architecture strategy and program management. These two areas build on your governance and provide the "glue" that pulls all your security architectures together. Hopefully, by now you have begun to realize that security architecture isn't just about a short-term, tactical project, but about what is best for your organization over the long term. And governance, with strategy and program management, deals with a 3- to 5-year time frame.

Questions

1. How long should a single principle be?
2. What areas should principles cover?
3. When you put together either principles or policies and standards, how do you involve people outside your security or architecture group?
4. What is the difference between a policy and a standard?
5. What policy domains do a security architect focus on?
6. What areas does a security architect focus on when looking at architectures and designs?

3
Reference Security Architecture

The **Reference Security Architecture (RSA)** is probably the most important weapon that a security architect can have in their arsenal. The RSA is a reference that the security architect will use whenever that person does anything architecture related. The reason behind this is that you don't want to forget some component in a solution, strategy, or program that you are responsible for, so you need to reference some standard.

Now, to refresh your memory, solutions always have three or four components: technical components, people components, process components, and governance components. Each of these components needs to be thought of during your design process, so reference your RSA as often as possible.

There aren't many reference security architectures out there currently. One of the few that I've been able to find is an RSA that has been published as a component of a TOGAF book titled the **Open Information Security Management Maturity Model (O-ISM3)** (`https://publications.opengroup.org/c102`). The problem I have with this book is that I find it is missing security architecture areas and doesn't go into sufficient depth for my purposes. It doesn't include physical security technology and it doesn't break down **Identity and Access Management (IAM)** in a manner that I found appropriate. I have also found that it doesn't deal with processes, people, or governance components sufficiently.

Another guide that you could use is the TOGAF security guide (`https://sabsa.org/togaf-security-guide/`), which was created by TOGAF in collaboration with SABSA. I haven't looked too much into it simply because it was written after I created my own **Reference Security Architecture (RSA)**.

The RSA that will be described in this chapter is something that I have created for my own use and that I provide to my clients and anyone that asks for it. That said, take it and adapt it for your own use. You may find a better way, in your mind, to communicate what you need to have done but, at the end of the day, it's your RSA and it's meant to trigger questions and thought processes.

Reference security technology architecture

The first iteration of the RSA that I created focused primarily on the technology areas with some overlap into the process areas. This layer of the RSA has nine primary areas:

- **Border protection**: This area basically deals with the network layer security architecture components.
- **Detection services**: Detection services goes into solutions that are meant to detect security events in process. They aren't proactive by nature and tend to deal with incidents.
- **Content control services**: These services are technologies that are related to controlling files that come into and leave the enterprise. They take two views of files being moved: when the transfer is externally initiated coming internally and when the transfer is internally initiated going externally.
- **Configuration management**: Most security people would view configuration management as something akin to hardening, but there's so much more to ensuring that devices are configured appropriately.
- **Auditing services**: When you think of security, you think of activities associated with pre-incident, during incident, and post-incident. Audit services are those solutions that are done pre-incident to ensure the appropriate levels of risk mitigation.
- **Physical security technology**: Most cybersecurity professionals don't think about physical security, but physical security has technologies that have to be considered and go a long way to correlate within security analytics.
- **Identity and Access Management (IAM)**: This is probably the area that can be termed as the only area in security that has a true **Return on Investment (ROI)**, so ensuring that IAM is part of your RSA is very important.
- **Cryptographic services**: Encryption. It's the first thing people say when they think of cybersecurity, and that's great and all, but what components make up cryptographic services? This section deals with cryptography.

- **Application security**: At the end of the day, all the other areas are developed in order to deal with vulnerabilities that are created at the application level. So, if you remove the vulnerabilities before you put an application into production, doesn't that alleviate the costs in the other areas?

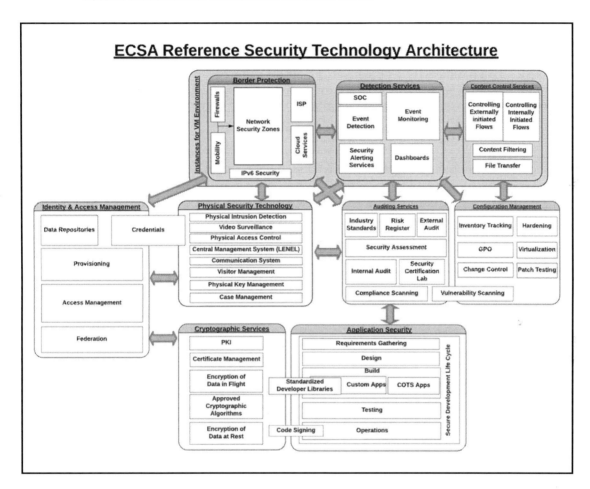

One of the interesting things about some of these different areas is that you normally think in terms of physical components. But, with the advent of virtualization (which leads into cloud solutions, which we are going to talk about later in this book), some of these sections have a different impact depending on whether they are in a virtual environment or a standalone physical environment.

Take, for example, a virtual server farm and configuration management. When you talk about a virtual server farm, you talk about individual virtual server instances connected to a backplane, all within a physical device. As a result, there's hardening associated with the virtual server instances as well as the hardening of the ESX backplane that hosts the virtual servers.

Virtualization has also impacted IAM with administrative roles. Originally, there were just local administrators when you had standalone servers. But when the concept of domains was created, then the role of a domain administrator was invented to manage the common aspects of devices across an entire domain. But, with virtualization, isn't there now what I would call a virtual administrator that is responsible for all common services across a virtualized environment?

Each of the areas in the reference security technology architecture has specific components that should be thought about, regardless of whether you are talking about tactical project solutions or you are thinking in terms of a long-term strategy. Let's delve into them a little more deeply.

Border protection

As mentioned in the previous section, border protection can legitimately be thought of as those security components that make up security at the network layer. The individual components that you should think about in border protection are:

- **Network zoning**: Whenever you create a network level security environment, you want to logically group components of a similar security classification. You don't want to have devices classified as public mixing with servers classified as highly classified because, if a public server is compromised because of lower security controls, then it can be an easy jumping off point to attack the server with the more sensitive classification. You also want to have a consistent set of security controls based on security classification simply to make management easier.

  As a result, several common security zones are now in use. Think about how you want to control your:

- **Test/Development environment**: This area should be used for any test or development activities and should not have traffic leaving the environment. Test/Dev has the highest capability to disrupt the production environment, so there shouldn't be any traffic flowing to and from Test/Dev.

- **QA/Mirror environment**: The QA environment (also called the Mirror environment) is typically a copy of the production environment. It is used to test solutions that are thought to be complete, whether that's just a patch or whether the solution is more complex. If the solution works seamlessly (in other words, there isn't any negative impact), then you can put a solution into the production environment with a higher confidence level that the solution will not impact production activities.
- **Production environment**: The production environment is where the devices and solutions that do the day to day work reside. If you impact this environment, you will negatively impact the operational activities of the business itself. This is why you test out solutions in the QA environment and make sure that the Test/Dev environments are segmented from production.

  Many organizations will segment the production environment into logical groupings based on security classification, just to make sure that each have their own consistent security controls and to ensure that one area doesn't impact a higher security classification area. I've seen data centers with 26 production zones just to isolate traffic since traffic flows from one zone can impact the traffic from another.

- **Corporate desktop environment**: Many architects forget that the desktop environment should be isolated as well. The one zone that will end up having the most malware activity will be the corporate desktop environment. You also have to remember that a lot of issues in an IT environment are caused, not by malware, but by simple human area. If you want to ensure that the activity of people does not impact your production servers, you want to isolate the corporate desktop environment from the other production environments.

Some organizations will also have a wireless security zone. In today's world, you have multiple wireless devices that are used to do business. These devices that can range from laptops (which have been around for a while), to tablets, smartphones, and other wireless devices. Separating this environment from the corporate desktop environment may be a good idea for your organization.

- **DMZs**: A common interpretation of the DMZ is a buffer zone between the outside world (some call that the internet), but you will definitely want to control the traffic moving from one internal zone to another, especially if you have multiple production zones with different security classifications. To do that, you want internal DMZs, or a policing layer that monitors traffic flowing from one zone to another.

There are a few devices that you can use for creating the DMZ or policing layer. The best is probably a virtual firewall environment. This way, you have all the firewalls that are separating individual zones sitting on a logical backplane, and the backplane becomes the policing layer, ensuring that traffic flows from one firewall to another.

Design Rule #1: When you design your network zones, always logically group your devices based on security classification. Don't intermix them.

Design Rule #2: When you design your network zones, always have your traffic initialize in a higher-security zone and go to a lower-security zone. Do not let traffic be initialized from a lower zone and go to a higher zone.

Other devices that you want to think about when dealing with the Border Protection capability is the capability for central firewall management, individual firewalls and what they need to be able to support (for example, externally facing versus separating internal zones), Mobile Security capabilities (since the concept of a border has changed with the advent of mobile devices being connected internally), **Virtual Private Networks** (**VPNs**) (which allow you to have encrypted traffic tunneling from one zone to another), and proxies (which can be used to isolate or mask what is going on internal to a security zone).

One more word on mobile devices and border protection. The traditional concept of network borders was that anything behind a firewall was considered internal. But with the use of mobile devices, including the entire concept of **Bring Your Own Device** (**BYOD**), the border of the network became the phone and not the firewall. Shift your design concept away from protecting **devices** to protecting **information**. Once you understand that it's information that you are protecting, your design concepts change. This is true, especially if you think about cloud-based solutions and that the Cloud will just be another security zone.

Detection services

Detection services are those capabilities that are put in place with the specific focus of trying to detect incidents that are in the process of occurring. While there are plenty of security technologies, most technologies are meant for protection while in incident. Detection services, on the other hand, are meant to determine if an incident is actually occurring.

Some of the technologies that are logically grouped into detection services are:

- **IDS/IPS**: Remember, the entire point of the IDS/IPS was originally to detect incidents that were happening at the network layer or inside the host itself. These have evolved into the **Intrusion Prevention System** (**IPS**) where the device will also protect, not just detect.
- **Network Access Controls (NAC)**: NAC are controls that are placed on the actual network ports associated with hard-wired connections. With the rise in wireless networks, NAC is shifting to wireless NAC, but remember to consider wired-based NAC controls as well.
- **Event monitoring**: Event monitoring is primarily centered around the security incident and event monitoring solutions, or SIEM. With the intent of all devices having security logging capabilities, there needs to be a centralization activity, because there's no way any organization can review logs manually. Therefore, the SIEM is meant to be a consolidation of these logs and make use of an alerting system. As Security Orchestration improves, you will see SIEMs start to react to the alerts and then send automated corrections to various devices.
- **Dashboards**: Often referred to as GRCs, dashboards are something that every security organization asks for. It's a way of having a central status location where someone can go and find out what the exact security situation is within the environment. A security architect will design one in order to answer the age old question, *How secure is the company's environment?*

There are non-technologies that get included in this area, such as **Security Operations Centers** (**SOCs**), security alerting services (which services that alert your organization when there's an issue in the wild that you should be aware of), and incident response. These will be talked about more deeply in the *Reference security process architecture* section.

Content control services

Security technologies aren't just about dealing with malware. They're also about controlling the flow of files such as intellectual property into and out of the organization. That logical grouping is called content control services.

This area can be more logically grouped by the direction the flow of files is moving relative to the organization itself. Externally initiated is the flow of documents from outside the organization into the organization. Internally initiated is about controlling the flow of documents from inside the organization as they go outside. Some of the solutions you want to think about in this group are:

- **Antivirus**: Malware will most often move into the organization in the form of files from outside the organization, so you would use AV for malware file control.
- **Anti-spam filtering**: A solution that combines with your email solution, anti-spam filtering will reduce the amount of waste email that the employees in the organization need to deal with. You may be able to leverage your ISP's capabilities in this area and not have to actually design and implement a solution yourself.

- **Web-based antivirus**: With more and more solutions being made use through HTTP and HTTPS, you have to worry about malware coming through things like web-based mails systems such as, Gmail. Gmail may not be something that your normal AV can deal with, so you want to ensure you have this area covered.
- **Web activity monitoring**: For those organizations that want to ensure that their employees aren't doing any web surfing or going to any improper websites, web activity monitoring is something that can allow you to monitor and control website accesses. It's useful for limiting access to sites for illicit purposes (for example, porn sites) or from using non-approved solutions such as Dropbox, where your employees can place files without permission.
- **Whitelisting**: A traditional method of protection within your environment was to use blacklisting approaches. These are approaches where you list activities or actions of files that are not allowed. This is how AV typically works—by looking for specific malware signatures. But, with zero-day attacks being much more prevalent, you'll want to consider putting solutions into place that allow known good patterns of behavior, and only allowing those known good patterns of behavior. Now, instead of having to deal with updating AV signatures continuously, you just allow good activities instead. But this solution typically is best used in environments where you can predict what a known good behavior pattern looks like (for example, in a data center). Putting this solution in a desktop environment becomes very difficult, because many organizations cannot or will not limit what their employees put on their desktop. So, as a result, they can't say what a known good pattern of behavior looks like.

- **Data Loss Prevention (DLP)**: DLP was very popular for a while. It's a technology that controls the flow of documents based on the meta data of the documents themselves. It's dependent on documents actually having been given a security classification so that the solution knows if the document is allowed to flow from one security zone to another. The problem with this type of solution is that there is a dependency on employees actually classifying data, and that seldom occurs because it's an additional burden on employees.

- **Content filtering**: Content filtering is similar to web activity monitoring, except that it's more specific to the information that is being accessed rather than just the websites. This type of technology works by searching for specific patterns in the files and then denying the content. An example might be looking for a certain amount of skin tone in pictures to indicate if a porn site is being visited.

- **File transfer**: Good old FTP! One of the original TCP protocols, FTP is meant to move large files to and from specific folders on specific servers. But, as files get larger and larger, more efficient solutions need to be found. So many organizations have shifted to Managed File Transfer (MFT) solutions. FTP is also a solution that can be used for transferring files to and from partners as part of some sort of electronic communication.

Configuration management

Configuration management tends to have just a few technologies and is dependent on more manual processes. It is meant to ensure that the configuration of a solution, while in production, stays in the configuration that it was originally intended for. Image standards will fall into this area, as will processes such as change control and information classification. Some of the technologies you want to consider in this area are:

- **Group Policy Objects (GPO)**: GPO is something that is typically pushed by your domain controllers. It is the technical policies that determine what the configuration of logical groupings of devices within a specific security zone should look like. Often, security architects will mix the concept of a security zone with a domain because of the use of Active Directory for authentication but, remember, you can have multiple security zones within a domain and, as a result, you can have different GPOs within that domain.

- **Hardening**: I've placed hardening here rather than the common term of **Gold Image** because you can have different base configurations for different servers depending on the purpose of those servers. Each application that resides on a server may need different services. But hardening means having to ensure that non-essential services are removed from your end point. Creating a Gold Image will create your baseline and you, as the security architect, will want to make sure the Gold Image meets your design.

- **Virtualization**: Just as you want to harden a server or endpoint, you'll want to make sure that the virtual environment is configured appropriately. So, look at the ESX and how it's configured to ensure that you have integrated security into its design.

- **Patch management**: Patch management isn't really thought of as a security architecture component, but your solution has to think about how patching will occur, both from a process point of view as well as how those patches will get into the environment in the first place. And, remember, the patches may impact your production environment, so make sure it's been tested in your QA/Mirror environment first in order to minimize their impact if they have to be rolled back.

- **Vulnerability scanning**: You could logically group vulnerability scanning either in configuration management or in audit services since it has a purpose in both areas. But, at the end of the day, you want to have some form of vulnerability scanning capability to ensure that all components are configured appropriately without having any vulnerabilities. This may be a laptop with Nessus installed and then you put the laptop on the network next to the device, or it may mean a vulnerability scanning solution that can scan all devices within the environment.

> **Design rule #3**: Make sure that the scanning solution isn't scanning through a firewall. Otherwise, you may not see all the configuration elements of your targets and you'll also load up your firewall with traffic. Agents placed in each security zone with the management traffic going back to a central console is a good design concept.

Auditing services

Auditing seldom has anything to do with technology unless you take into account that organizations often have standards that your architectures have to meet. If that is the case, you need to ensure that your architectures are in alignment with your organization's standards.

From a technology point of view, though, there are a few solutions that you want to think about to include in your overarching security architectures. Those solutions are as follows:

- **Risk registers**: There are different types of risk registers that you should be aware of. Most security people think of risk registers as those solutions that record security risks. If you talk to a project manager, that person will think about the risks associated with project delivery. But, for an architect, a risk register should be focused on architecture risks, not security risks or project risks. Create risk register solutions that allow you to document your architecture risks, whether from a strategic or program management point of view, or from a project point of view.

  For those of you that don't understand what an architectural risk is, these are risks associated with the implementation or continued use of a specific solution. For example, once a technology is no longer supported by a vendor, there is an elevated risk of being able to deal with that technology if it fails. Another example might be to use a technology that is not an accepted internal technology standard. If, for example, you typically use Active Directory for authentication but a new solution wants to make use of internal authentication mechanisms such as a flat file, then there's an elevated architecture risk if that flat file becomes corrupted. Architecture risks are not necessarily the same as a security risk or a project risk and it's important to differentiate between them.

  Your risk register solution can be as simple as a spreadsheet or as complex as a SharePoint solution. But try to make sure that the risks are measured using a methodology that is acceptable to the entire organization so that you can provide a consistent level of risk description, regardless of the architect that is doing the documentation.

- **Security certification lab**: While not a specific piece of technology, a security certification lab is something that you use for testing new technologies in order to ensure that you know what the security flaws may be. You don't necessarily have to have this lab internal to your organization—you can make use of an external organization to test solutions that may be critical to your organization. An example of this is the testing that occurred on many of the smart meters when the utility industry started moving to the smart meter infrastructure. The labs that this work was outsourced to would look for both known as well as *unknown* vulnerabilities. There is a standard that you'll want to look into called **ISA-99** (https://www.isa.org/isa99/), which is meant to define how to look for the security posture of industrial devices, and it's perfect for any device that fits into the **Internet of Things (IoT)** realm.

- **Compliance scanning**: Compliance scanning is different from vulnerability scanning because a compliance scanning solution will look for compliance to specific standards whereas a vulnerability scanning solution will look for vulnerabilities. Remember the old saying, *You can be in compliance but that doesn't mean you are secure*. Compliance scanning solutions will only measure your environment against specific areas of standards.

- **Industry standards**: While industry standards isn't a technology, many of them call for specific technologies to be in place. So, in order to make sure your organization is in compliance with those standards, you need to be aware of them. For example, the **Payment Card Industry** (**PCI**) standard calls for the use of a SIEM. For the purposes of this book, the SIEM is described in the *Detection services* section, but understanding that there is a standard calling for it means there is an overlap between the two sections.

This is probably the limit of the technologies in the audit services area, but I'm going to take the time to talk about one area that will be covered in much greater depth later in this book, and that is cloud services.

Cloud services isn't just about making use of AWS, Google data centers, or Microsoft's Azure. It's about making use of an application or solution that resides outside your organization's control. So, while cloud services may be the direction your organization is moving to reduce costs, realize that there are few controls that you can have. One of the few is contractual agreements with that vendor.

 Design rule #4: Make sure you have the ability to audit the technological configurations and controls of cloud solutions that are in use, otherwise you have to completely trust those solutions.

Physical security technologies

One of the things that I've come to learn is that we, as security architects, cannot ignore the physical security aspect of an organization. When you view physical security, remember that there are two views of this area: if you are in corporate/physical security, you view physical security as one of two areas — physical versus cyber security. But if you are in IT security, you view physical security as one of many disciplines. It's almost like the Canadian discussion where Quebec views itself as one of two countries, whereas the rest of Canada views Quebec as one of 12 provinces. Both have their points and you have to remember them when you work on your designs.

Physical security makes more and more use of technology as time marches on. Gone are the days of just using security guards. People have become viewed as an expensive resource that can be inaccurate. So, like in many areas, people are replaced by technologies and it's those technologies that you, as a security architect, have to keep in mind, and in ways that you may have not thought about.

Take, for example, video surveillance cameras. Traditionally, we have viewed cameras as just lenses that record what is captured to a tape. But nowadays, video cameras have an operating system built into them. So, when you are dealing with your patch management solutions or with your vulnerability scanning solutions, you have to make sure you are considering the IT components of the physical security technologies. It's just the expansion of the IoT into the realm of physical security. Ignoring physical security technologies is a danger to your environment.

You also have to remember that physical security is important to the overall security of your solutions. If your solutions have higher security requirements, for example, two factor authentication, what's the point of putting that in place if someone can just walk up to the server and unplug it?

There was a story that I was told when I first moved over to IT design. The person that told it to me talked about how he was supporting a smaller company remotely from about two hours travel time away and, one Monday morning, he got a phone call from the company's general manager saying that nothing worked. The person tried to log in to the company's infrastructure but wasn't able to connect. He talked to the general manager, indicating that he was going to have to travel the two hours, and charge for that time to come out. After getting permission, he travelled to the company.

Once he arrived, he tried to connect to the infrastructure from the general manager's computer thinking that, since the general manager was inside the network, there shouldn't be a problem. But, again, the person wasn't able to connect. So, he went into the server room (remember, this was a smaller company, so they didn't have dedicated data center and this was before cloud services) and discovered what the problem was.

All the servers had been stolen over the weekend.

Design rule #5: You can have all the fancy technology in the world that you want, but if someone is able to just walk up to the solutions, what's the point?

Some of the areas of physical security that you want to think about in your security architectures are:

- **Physical access control**: You are going to have physical access panels and controls throughout your company's environment. That means there will be things such as card readers, motion detectors, door contact sensors, and electric locks. Each of these components need to be monitored in some way and, since you have Identity and Access Management solutions, physical access controls will have an overlap with your IAM capabilities.

- **Video surveillance**: I mentioned previously about the need to consider cameras and their operating systems. Keep them in mind when you are looking at cameras that may be external to your company's buildings. Many video cameras now make use of wireless technologies and, if they don't have a hardened operating system, what's to stop someone from parking on the street and just jumping onto your wireless network through an unpatched camera?

- **Physical intrusion detection**: These are solutions that are used to monitor if an intrusion is in process. They can be glass break detectors, door contacts, motion detectors, sounders, gate contacts, and fence post sensors.

- **Visitor management**: Visitor management solutions are meant to track when someone enters and leaves an environment. If someone enters but you don't see that they have left, there is a high probability that the person is still in the environment. Make sure you have a zero-sum situation when it comes to people entering and leaving an environment, especially into your data center/server room.

- **Communication system**: For organizations that are more spread out, you need to ensure that you have a communication system in place that allows you to reach people remotely. You'll have dispatch systems, either for security guards or for maintenance people, or you may have a service maintenance system that will provide some "ticketing" capability for the upkeep of the environment.

- **Central management system**: This is probably the core to your physical security environment. All the other physical security solutions mentioned so far will be communicating to your **Central Management Systems (CMS)**, but you also want to make sure that the logs of the CMS are going into your SIEM so that you have correlation between physical security issues and cybersecurity issues. Often, you will have a physical security alert that is a precursor to a cybersecurity incursion. Why worry about trying to bypass a firewall if you can walk into a company and plug directly into a network port? It's that walking in component that you want to know about.

At the end of the day, you don't want to forget about the physical security technologies. They need to be considered when you are putting together a design, simply because you need to understand what the protections of the environment are that you are putting your solution into. Plus, physical security technologies will provide you with an understanding of any precursors to attacks since it's often easier to physically access solutions for intentional tampering rather than going through firewalls.

 Design rule #6: Integrate the logs from your CMS into your SIEM so that you can correlate physical security logs with cybersecurity logs.

Identity and Access Management

Identity and Access Management (IAM), is probably the one and only area in security that you can actually point to and say that it provides a return on investment to your organization. It can be used in several ways for a ROI:

- You can use it to provision accounts across multiple systems and, as a result, you can have cost savings associated with system administration.
- You can implement **Single Sign On (SSO)** solutions on multiple applications so that your employees only have to remember one password, making them more efficient and reducing your help desk costs for password resets.
- Federation allows you to extend your single sign on solution to cloud solutions, allowing those same benefits from SSO to be applied to the cloud.
- Self-service administration can be set up so that things like forgotten passwords can be dealt with automatically, reducing your need for help desk support.

There's also an overlap with physical security when you talk about IAM. Normally, for elevated security, you could use things like smart cards and tokens or biometrics. But those solutions can be extended to physical security accesses which then allows for a reduced cost associated with managing accesses into the physical space as well.

IAM can be logically broken down into five different areas:

1. **Credentials**: The credentials you specify in your architectures can range from anonymous access, through Usernames and Passwords, all they way into 2 factor authentication (typically identified as who you are, what you know, and what you have). 2 factor authentication will typically involve a key fob, smart card/token, or the use of biometrics. However, I don't think biometrics will ever truly take off, simply because of the physically intrusive nature of those solutions.

2. **Data repositories**: Data repositories can often overlap with the non-security area of infrastructure architecture and it all depends on what the contents of the repositories are. Common repositories that user credentials are stored in are Active Directory, LDAP servers, and databases. This area will also logically contain database security.

3. **Access management**: Access management does just as the name implies — it manages the accesses into systems. If you were to look at a system, access management would be considered the solution that is put as an interceptor to the system itself in order to control if a user is allowed to actually make use of the system. SSO, remote access, citrix access (that is, use of thin clients), and **Digital Rights Management** (**DRM**) are all solutions in the access management space.

4. **Provisioning**: Going back to the example of looking at a system, while access management deals with accessing the frontend of systems, provisioning deals with the setting up of accounts in the backend of systems. Most systems, if standalone, will have a data repository on the backend where user credentials are stored. Provisioning will connect to the backend repository and automate the creation of new user accounts and the associated credentials. Provisioning will also include workflow engines so that rules are applied as to what the order is of getting approvals or work done flows. A common solution that would fall into provisioning is **Role-Based Access Control** (**RBAC**). Be very careful when looking at RBAC solutions, simply because most organizations are not consistent in how they grant accesses to systems and, as a result, there can be a long lead time and high cost in implementing a RBAC solution.

5. **Federation**: Federation is the creation of a trust relationship between domains, whether those domains are within one organization or between enterprises. There are a number of web services that are the focus of federation and those would include protocols such as SAML and SPML. There are other federation protocols such as OpenID, WS-Trust, WS-Federation, and OAuth, but the grand-daddy of them all is SAML. SPML is used for provisioning users across domains but is seldom used in cloud solutions.

Design rule #7: While IAM is viewed as a solution that can provide a ROI to your organization, remember that there is an elevated risk associated with centralizing these activities. Therefore, consider the risk level of your solution before committing to integrating IAM with it.

Cryptographic services

In this day and age, when you talk about cybersecurity, people will automatically think of encryption. You are connecting to a website? Make sure it's making use of a SSL connection. Interested in Bitcoin? Blockchain technologies are highly dependent on encryption. Want to make sure no one reads a document? Make use of public/private key pairs.

Encryption is an extremely complicated component of cybersecurity, and most security architects barely have a handle on it. So, let's start off by breaking down what your confidentiality and integrity requirements are for two areas:

- **Encryption of data in flight**: Most compliance standards require that there be protection of data while moving from one resting point to another. This is because you don't want your data to be intercepted and easily read. Therefore, you can deal with securing data in flight by encrypting either the path the data is traveling in, encrypting the data itself while in flight, or both. If you are talking about encrypting the path, you are most often talking about using some sort of **Virtual Private Network** (**VPN**) tunnel. This will make use of the IPSec protocol. The other instances of using encryption will be using certificate-based communication such as TLS, SSL, or SSH. If you ever see HTTPS, the S in HTTPS means secure and is using HTTP over a SSL or TLS connection. The same goes with SFTP – Secure FTP connections over SSL or TLS. TLS is becoming the dominant form of encrypted connection as a result of known vulnerabilities that have been found with SSL.

- **Encryption of data at rest**: When you have data resting or residing in a database or file share, you may want to consider using encryption to protect it. If a database, that may mean encrypting the entire database, encrypting just a single column in the database tables, or just individual cells within the database. For file shares, encrypting the files will allow for a level of assurance that the file isn't going to be manipulated or read if someone is able to access the server itself.

One thing to keep in mind is the growing area of big data. Big data is the use of data spread across multiple repositories. In essence, this is a multi-location database. What you should keep in mind is that there may be individuals that have access to data in one database but maybe not in another. You now have to consider if your encryption will cause a problem across big data lakes.

While you are considering securing your data, regardless of whether it's in flight or at rest, you need to consider what the encryption algorithms are that your company is going to approve the use of. Again, it comes down to the risk level associated with the data you are talking about. The higher the risk level, the more stringent the encryption requirements should be. But whatever the requirements, make sure you document them in your security architecture standards so that you have consistent application of your encryption standards.

Design rule #8: Most organizations don't have the time to keep up with the different standards. I would recommend that you tie your encryption standards to what is recommended by NIST. Let it be NIST's job to stay on top of evolving encryption standards and then tie your approved algorithm list to them.

One last area that you should think about when it comes to encryption is how you are going to manage the keys and certificates within your organization. There will come a point in every organization where they have so many keys and certificates in use that it's time to centralize the management of them. If you make use of self-signed certificates (certificates generated by the systems themselves), you will run the risk of not having a consistent application of your encryption standard as well as losing track of when your certificates will expire.

To deal with this situation, you will start to look at **Public Key Infrastructure** (**PKI**) solutions. PKI solutions will centrally create certificates that are then used when your server teams set up servers. The PKI will then centrally manage the encryption standard and track when certificates and keys are going to expire. Some of the components that are involved in PKI solutions are:

- **Certificate Authorities (CAs)**: This is the workhorse of your PKI solution. It's the server that does all the work, will generate the keys, and will be the interface for your PKI Administrators. There can be different levels of CAs where the Root CA is the proverbial keys to the kingdom and is often taken offline unless a new Subordinate CA is needed to be created. The **Subordinate CA (Sub-CA)** does all the work in the PKI solution and you will typically have one Sub-CA for each domain that you are creating certificates for.

- **Certificate validation**: Certificate validation is the process of validating that the certificate that is communicated by a server is actually a valid certificate. Think of it as a third-party validation of certificates found on the server. The user of the server may want to ensure that the server is safe, so they will reach out to the CA that created the certificate and ask whether the certificate is still valid and real. Your PKI solution should have a central location where the certificates can be checked (typically, this will be your Active Directory server for the domain).
- **Certificate Revocation List (CRL)**: The CRL is a list of all the certificates that have been revoked prior to their expiry date by their issuing CA and should not be considered trustworthy. A solution will read the CRL to see if a certificate has been revoked.
- **High Security Module (HSM)**: The HSM is a solution that you will use if you want a higher level of assurance level that the CRL and the certificate repository isn't tampered with. These are specially designed components that typically require multi-factor authentication just to be accessed for administrative purposes. They can be quite expensive and some organizations may just make use of a file server that they keep offline except when there needs to be checks of certificates and public/private key pairs.

Many organizations will make use of Microsoft's certificate authority server configuration and it will do the job quite well for most organizations. But if your organization is larger, look into solutions from companies like Entrust, Verisign, and many others since they are much more robust and focused mainly on the business of encryption.

Application security

Application security is an area that far too many architects, regardless of tower, don't focus on enough. The application layer is where the vast majority of vulnerabilities are created and it's the area where reducing vulnerabilities comes into play the most. From a security architecture point of view, though, you have to focus on the tools and components that go into application development rather than on external devices such as **Web Application Firewalls (WAFs)**. WAFs are great for dealing with existing vulnerabilities, but they do nothing to actually remove the vulnerabilities, which is a much better solution for dealing with problems.

The *application security* section of the RSA is focused on what is called a **Secure Development Life Cycle (SDLC)**. This is the process of integrating security into the **Software Development Lifecycle (SDL)**. As you may have noticed, the two acronyms are very similar and, as a result, many people will mix up the two life cycles. The SDLC is an attempt to integrate security into each stage of the SDL so that you can reduce the cost of rewriting applications and blocks of code.

When you look at dealing with vulnerabilities introduced during the application development process, take the approach that vulnerabilities are specific types of application defects and that you are performing quality control looking for these defects. The cost of correcting code that has a bug in it goes up exponentially the further into the application development process you go. The following diagram shows how the cost of repairing a defect goes up the further you go in the development process. Most defects are introduced in the design and coding stages, but they aren't found until the application is being readied for production. So, to correct the defect, your costs will go up because you have to go back to the design and code stages to rewrite the code:

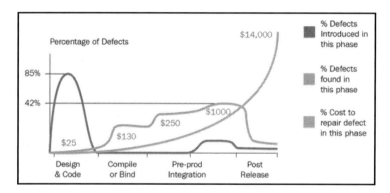

For a security architect, there are a few things you can do to improve this situation and this goes back to your typical project delivery process. At each stage, you have tools that you can make use of to ensure the overall improvement in the security of the application. Let's look at each development stage:

- **Requirements gathering stage**: Most projects fail simply because requirements aren't gathered properly. If you talk to your stakeholders and ask them what their security requirements are, they'll probably say something simplistic such as, *well, it has to be secure*. But this tells you nothing. Make sure you gather the requirements properly (this will be talked about at greater length in a later chapter). If you do this stage properly, you will have a greater degree of success.

- **Design stage**: The design stage is where the security architect can have the most impact. What you'll want to do is introduce a couple of concepts to your Application Architects to ensure that security is built directly into the solution.

    First, have a checklist of appropriate design patterns that you expect to be used, depending on the language. If you are not big on application languages, find a checklist that has already been created and make use of it. I have an Architecture Checklist that I provide for Java, C (and the different derivatives), and a couple of other languages. I provide that checklist to the Application Architects for them to make use of.

    Have a set of design rules and patterns that you know are good and available. For example, if you know that the architecture from a conceptual level is meant to communicate across different security zones, have a design rule that states that communication must be initiated from the higher-security zone and flow to the lower security zone. Never allow lower-security zones to initiate communications.

    Finally, make use of Threat Modeling tools. Microsoft has a Threat Modeling tool that is very good and focused on the .NET suite. Threat Modeling tools will look at the environment and the requirements gathered and then provide recommended strategies associated with what will probably be the threats the application will see.

- **Build stage**: When you build, keep in mind that there are typically three types of applications: Custom applications built specifically for your organization, COTS Applications which are bought off the shelf and then implemented, and Hybrid Applications, which are typically COTS applications that are then customized for your organization's use. There are a few things you can provide to ensure that vulnerabilities aren't introduced at this stage:
    - **Standardized developer libraries**: People are generally lazy. I'm definitely lazy (I'm pulling from a lot of material I've written in the past to create this book), and that's no different for developers. Rather than write their own code, they will often pull down development libraries from somewhere online. As a result, you will inherit the vulnerabilities that are built into those code snippets. Make sure you have a set of approved and standardized developer libraries so that you don't have to deal with someone else's flaws.

- **Provide coding best practices**: Remember, you aren't doing the coding. The developers are. So, make sure your developers have some form of approved coding practices. Make use of checklists so that your developers know what to do and what not to do.
- **Code reviews**: Most organizations will have unit or integrated code reviews occurring by QA or, at a minimum, by peer developers. Again, make sure the people doing the code reviews know what to look for in terms of what is good practice.
- **Service-oriented architecture**: Probably one of the biggest trends over the last decade has been the move to Service Oriented Architectures, or SOA. This allows for the standardization of interfaces between applications and, as a result, you can spend more time on the initial interface and then reduce the time you spend every time that interface is reused. SOA has also introduce the use of the Enterprise Services Bus (ESB) because of the use of standardization in application development.
- **Enterprise services bus**: The ESB is a concept that takes a bus but makes it available for multiple applications to connect to. It allows for the reduction in the number of interfaces that have to be managed with each application and allows for an improved speed of deployment of new applications. As a security architect, definitely promote the use of an ESB, because it allows you to ensure that approved security architectures are made use of, which includes the use of encryption, the centralization of authentication/authorization mechanisms, and the control of application communication flows, since rules can be put into place saying which applications can talk to other applications.

- **Testing stage**: The testing stage is where either unit code or integrated code is tested to determine if there are any defects. This is the ideal stage to also introduce security testing of application code. There are four types of security testing that you should consider at this stage:
  - **Static code reviews**: Also called Whitebox testing, static code review is testing of code BEFORE it has been compiled. This allows the testing tool to actually read the code itself and look for improper code practices or the vulnerabilities themselves. But don't expect the tools that you use to catch all security defects. Whitebox testing tools have come a long way from the days when they were catching only 10% of defects but they aren't yet coming close to 100% success.

- **Dynamic code reviews**: Also called Blackbox testing, dynamic code reviews is the testing of code AFTER it has been compiled. This type of testing will look for the behaviour of the application by itself without being impacted by the underlying infrastructure configurations.
- **Vulnerability Assessment**: Vulnerability Assessment is typically for looking at infrastructure configuration. Some tools will look for flaws in the application itself, but these tools typically look for known flaws rather than looking at coding behavior. For that type of testing, you want to look at fuzzing.
- **Fuzzing**: Fuzzing is testing where you look at the inputs of an application and then put all sorts of different possible information into those inputs to see what the results are. Fuzzing takes time and can be expensive but, at the end of the day, it's very well worth it simply because fuzzing is looking for unexpected behaviour rather than known flaws.

- **Production stage**: Most people don't think about the Production stage because it's not viewed as an area where application development is actively being done. But this is often the stage in which you can catch improper Quality Control and Change Management practices going on. Remember, just because you have an approved application ready to be put into production doesn't mean that someone won't tweak the application without going through change management. Those tweaks can introduce vulnerabilities. At this stage, you definitely want to perform **Code Signing** (taking the hash of an approved application) so that you can do regular checks of the application once it's in production. When you check the applications periodically, create a hash and then check it against the pre-production hash. If the hash has changed, then you know someone changed the application without going through change management.

Design rule #9: Make use of checklists for every stage in the development life cycle. This way, you can encourage the use of standardization, which will reduce your workload in the long run.

Reference security process architecture

Unfortunately, too many people jump immediately to technologies to find solutions to problems. By doing that, they ignore a number of the different possible solutions to problems and ignore the fact that ALL solutions have a technology, people, *and* process component to them. This section will talk about security processes and the **Reference Security Process Architecture**.

The Reference Security Process Architecture is meant to provide an outline of the different security processes that may or may not be involved in your solution. They wrap themselves around any technology that you are planning on making use of and are typically leveraged by the roles identified in your Reference Security People Architecture (see the next section).

One thing to remember about processes is that, because they are concepts rather than real world physical items, they can change quite a bit over the duration of the solution if you don't apply some sort of governance to them. In fact, some people view governance processes as part of your security process architecture. At the end of the day, you need to keep in mind that processes have to be as flexible as possible based on the way the organization changes. A new person comes in that is used to doing things a certain way will mean that the processes associated with your solution will apt to be changed.

The best way to deal with security processes is to identify what the end goal is meant for each process and let the specifics of the way the process works change over time. That way, you'll at least provide the flexibility for your organization to adjust as it needs to. Create the changes or additions to the processes when you create your solution, but expect the process to change over time.

The other primary reason why you have a Reference Security Process Architecture is the same reason why you have the Reference Security Technology Architecture — you want to make sure you don't miss anything in the various architecture activities that you are involved in. Your processes can be identified for a current state assessment, processes can be included in any strategy work that you are doing, and you definitely need to consider processes when you are creating solutions that need to meet some sort of industry compliance such as PCI, NERC, or something else. Remember:

Security is not a technology, it's a process.

There are 11 different logical groupings of processes that you should consider in your Reference Security Process Architecture (remember, these are specifically associated with your security personnel), and they are shown in the following diagram:

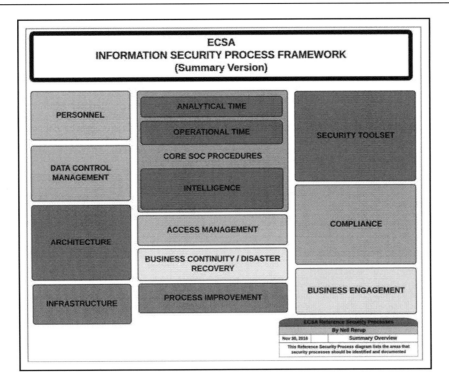

The process areas that you should be thinking about are:

- **Personnel**: Personnel processes are associated with the training and scheduling of security personnel.
- **Data control management:** How do you deal with security classifications and the associated information? If you are looking at the different compliance standards, this may include disposal of media, management of encryption keys and certificates, or just the specific processes associated with the various classifications.
- **Core SOC processes**: Remember, your SOC has operating processes and procedures and your solution, if specifically a security solution, should fit into what the SOC is doing.
- **Intelligence**: Since there are three different time frames associated with an incident (before the incident, during the incident, and after the incident), one of the major areas you should be considering is processes that identify issues *before* an incident occurs.

- **Architecture**: There is going to be bleeding over between your security organization and the architecture group, so be aware that there are architecture activities that need to be adjusted as required. This book is all about architecture processes, specifically security architecture.
- **Access management**: This is probably the most well known of the process areas because most enterprises have identity and access management solutions that have processes wrapped around them.
- **Compliance**: The compliance processes will be the most impactful of all the processes because they can impact any potential fines that your organization ends up paying if they don't meet compliance.
- **Infrastructure**: Sometimes, you have to wrap your security processes around those of other groups within IT. Infrastructure processes tend to wrap around those activities that your IT Infrastructure group perform.
- **Business Continuity/Disaster Recovery**: Not all organizations put BCP and DRP into the security realm. If they do, you need to think about these specific processes.
- **Business Engagement**: Probably the most neglected of the areas, your security organization needs to engage with the business to make sure that security is supporting the business.
- **Process Improvement**: Remember that I said that the processes you put into place will change over time? Well, if you are proactive, you can make sure the changes to those processes is done effectively and supports the metrics that you are using to guide your organization.

Again, keep in mind that people will change processes on their own if left to their own devices. So, focus on the end goal of the processes that you include in your solutions and not on the specifics that make up your process.

Personnel processes

Personnel processes have more to do with how you manage your security operations personnel once they have been on-boarded than they have to do with human resources processes. Think in terms of how your SOC personnel come onto shift and leave their shift. There are four primary processes that are included in this section:

- **Shift scheduling and staffing**: How are the SOC personnel scheduled and staffed? Are they in-house personnel or has the SOC been outsourced?

- **Shift turn over**: If there are different shifts, how are the primary tickets and alerts communicated to the next shift? Hopefully, your SOC personnel don't just get up and walk away at the end of their shift. Remember, communication is key to a successful organization.
- **Daily operations call**: This can be for just the SOC or in alignment with the other operations groups (for example, NOC, or an Infrastructure Ops group). These calls should be dealing with cross-functional issues that may or may not include security issues.
- **Training**: Whenever you have a new solution being put into place or an update to an existing solution, the SOC personnel should be trained up on what the changes are so they can make as much use of the solution as possible.

Personnel are the key to any security group, and you should really take the time to understand who they are and what their needs are. Remember, they will be able to provide you feedback for your strategies and/or solutions, so they are a stakeholder in any of your security specific solutions.

Data control management

Data control management processes get down to how you deal with data. Not information, but data. Typically, this will mean dealing with the containers of the data as well as the classification of the assets associated with that data. The primary processes you should think about in this area are the following:

- **Data classification**: How do you classify data? Once data is classified, how is it treated? Sounds like something from a policy perspective, but this is more the practical, day-to-day handling of data.
- **Computer and media disposal**: If a computer is being decommissioned, how is the hard drive wiped? If it's being repurposed, how do you ensure that the data that was once held on the computer isn't still accessible by the next user?
- **Media library management**: Remember, it's not just the computers and servers that we have to consider. There's also the media that the data is backed up onto. Where is it stored? How is it tracked?
- **Anti-contamination**: This goes to how you deal with a device that may be needed for criminal charges or forensic purposes. Where do you keep that component? How is it handled? If it's going to be needed for criminal investigations, how are you going to ensure that the evidence hasn't been tampered with?

- **Encryption and certificate creation**: You can view this area as the creation of keys and certificates for end users. But you should also keep in mind that, when you set up a Root Certificate Authority, the keys associated with the Root CA are the keys to the kingdom and needed to be handled appropriately. So. how do you support your organization's key and certificate needs?

Remember, and this was said in a previous chapter, if you focus on protecting the information and data, it becomes much easier to create your solutions. It's call INFORMATION security for a reason.

Architecture

This entire book is about architecture, so not much be written about architecture processes. Just remember that each of these chapters is talking about artifacts that an architect creates and how those artifacts are created. But there are always processes wrapped around what the architect does.

For example, the architect is always involved with the Project Management Office (PMO), an organization that has nothing to do with cybersecurity and is primarily focused on bringing solutions into implementation, so you need to consider how your architecture processes are integrated into the PMO.

Keep in mind that there are different business units that you need to integrate your processes into and, if you do that, then your work load will be easier.

Infrastructure processes

Just as architecture is integrated with a number of different business units, security is integrated with multiple different areas. One of those areas that there is a heavy integration with is the Infrastructure group.

Whenever the infrastructure group (for example, The Wintel team or the Networking group) are creating or implementing something, they really should have a touchpoint with the security group to ensure that the quality of their work meets the organization's policies and standards.

Yes, I said the quality of the work. Remember, you'll get much further talking with groups from a quality control point of view than from an insurance point of view. While we may be involved with reducing the enterprise's risk profile, people in general are much more aware of things like improving the quality of their work than they are with the checks and balances associated with risk. They understand what they are doing and that you can help improve what they are doing. But if you talk from a risk point of view, most people will get glazed eyes.

So, based on that approach, here are the two primary conversations that the architect will often get involved in when they are the support security architect rather than the solution architect:

- **Hardening**: Infrastructure groups will have a gold image that they will use when they implement a new server or network component. But the solution being put into place isn't going to make complete use of all the services made available through that gold image, so there is going to be a need to harden the underlying infrastructure and the security architect will need to understand what is needed in the solution and what can be removed.
- **Configuration Management**: When the solution is put into place, there will need to be the basic configurations that need to be changed and this has nothing to do with hardening. For example, there will be local accounts that an application is going to want to make use of. But if you have a RBAC solution that you are trying to move the organization towards, you'll want to make sure that the solution architect is configuring his solution appropriately. This is all process oriented.

You are going to work side-by-side with the infrastructure groups because you are two sides of the same coin. Taking a quality improvement/quality assurance approach will definitely improve your relationship with them.

Core SOC processes

At the end of the day, the SOC is more about monitoring and watching for incidents than they are about all the other day-to-day activities in preparing the organization for an incident. The moment an incident occurs, they have to act. So. understanding what their incident-based processes are is really important.

These activities can be broken into two logical groups. Those processes can be organized as those associated with a crisis (like Operational Time processes) and those associated with an incident (that is, Analytical Time processes). A crisis is something that has to be dealt with in a rush (for example, a web portal has just been taken down, or a DDoS is occurring in real time) whereas an incident is defined as something that doesn't impact the immediate operation of the business but needs to be acted on. A crisis and an incident can turn into each other (for example, a crisis can be downgraded to an incident once under control, or an incident can be upgraded to a crisis if the incident starts to impact the business).

The one truly important aspect of all the processes that a security architect needs to support is providing what the impact of any crisis or incident will have on the rest of the organization's IT environment. Remember, you don't want to make a change that will make things worse. So, the security architect needs to provide guidance as to how to improve the situation from a holistic point of view.

Operational Time processes are as follows:

- **Crisis response**: How do you react to a crisis? Who gets called? Is there a crisis response team that is set up automatically?
- **Triage**: How do you go about fixing the crisis? What normal operational processes are bypassed?
- **Callout**: Who do you call for specific action items? For example, if a new windows server needs to be commissioned, who do you call?
- **Case Management**: During the actual crisis, how do you document what is occurring? Who is responsible for managing the crisis? Who is reporting to whom?

The Analytical Time processes are as follows:

- **Incident Response**: These are the actions that are normally taken in association with an incident. There are a number of organizations that can provide incident response actions, but understanding how an organization will respond to an incident is important.
- **Incident Summary**: Once an incident has ended, there needs to be a summary of the actions that occurred. Who is writing that summary and who receives the summary report? Are there recommendations that come out of the incident summary? How are those recommendations tracked for implementation?
- **Incident Monitoring**: You'll want to monitor incidents as they are being resolved as well as for a period of time after the incident is concluded just to ensure that nothing additional occurs. If that's so, who is monitoring it, where is the information placed, and who has access to the incident information?

- **Incident Research**: How did the incident occur in the first place? How do you determine a fix for the incident? Who is doing the research (often called Forensics)?

- **Change Management**: Many organizations have Change Management processes, which typically include a Change Advisory Board (CAB) group meeting to inform all IT groups of upcoming changes. But there is typically an emergency process for making changes. All of this is managed by a Change Coordinator. Who is that person and what are the processes for making changes to the environment?

- **Problem Management**: Problem management is associated with an unplanned issue that needs to be dealt with. For example, a server is falling down and needs to be replaced right away before it becomes a crisis, or maybe a planned implementation of a solution does not go smoothly and the change has to be backed out. Again, there is usually a Problem Coordinator (often the same person as the Change Coordinator). Who is that person and how do you handle problems?

The SOC should have standard operating processes/procedures (SOPs) that they follow so that things go smoothly. Look for those documents so that you know how to hook the processes of your solution into the SOC's standard processes.

Intelligence

Intelligence processes have to do with understanding your environment and are typically tied to the detection services section of the Reference Security Technology Architecture. They are wrapped around your detection technologies such as the SIEM and IPS. But, remembering that technologies have to actually be used, the question then becomes, *what do you do with the information that the technology provides?*

The processes that you want to think about here are as follows:

- **Monitoring**: How do you define what severity something is in the SIEM? If you put in a new solution, how do you want the SOC to react if there are changes to the underlying configuration? Or a number of failed login attempts? Or alerts that come up from your AV solution?

- **Event analysis**: In this day and age of data analytics, how do you view a series of events taking place? If a server has failed logins followed by changes to the configuration followed by the IPS detecting a ping sweep occurring from that server, what does that mean? Maybe it's an indication that a server has been compromised. Or maybe it's someone trying to figure out how to make a solution work correctly and they just forgot their password. Part of your solution has to talk about how to deal with correlated events.

- **Modeling/Baselining**: When a solution is put into place, you'll want to provide the operational groups a baseline of how the solution should be working. That way, if it's not working properly, alerts will occur. How do you communicate with that baseline? And what information do you include in that baseline that is relevant to the different operating groups?

- **Vulnerability/Compliance Scanning**: Scanning a network can impact devices as well as network load, so you don't just start scanning without letting people know about what you are going to do. It's part of the reason why you don't want novice people interested in hacking to test some tool that they found on the internet. What will happen if your solution is scanned? Do you want your solution scanned? If so, how frequently (dependent on the criticality of the system)?

Access management

Pretty much every solution in place will have roles and identities set up for accessing the solution. Some may be making use of Active Directory, some will make use of a database that is associated with the solution, and some may be using local accounts. But, in all cases, there is a group that is responsible for providing access to your solution. For smaller solutions, it's probably the business group that owns the solution. But for more enterprise wide solutions, it's probably your central help desk or a IAM Operations group. You can plan for people to come and go, so there's going to be a need to provision and deprovision accounts. Your solution needs to be included in what they are doing.

Access management processes will include:

- **Account provisioning/deprovisioning**: How do you get people provisioned in a solution? How do you remove an account within 24 hours of them leaving your organization (pretty standard with all companies that are looking to be compliant to some standard)?

- **Account reviews**: How do you review the accounts in a solution? How do you check to see if there are stale accounts and, if there are, how do you get them removed? It's not as simple as just removing them — there will be people that have to approve the removal of accounts.
- **Physical access**: Remember, there are physical technologies that you need to consider as well, so access management isn't just cyber but also physical access to systems. Who gets to put their hands on your solution?

Identity and Access Management is probably the most well known of all the different technologies, but there are all sorts of different processes that you have to think about as well.

Business continuity/disaster recovery

Most people that put together solutions always forget to think about how to deal with the solution when a disaster occurs. They don't design in a disaster recovery environment and they don't consider what the RPO and RTO needs to be for bringing the solution back up. But that's associated with the technology itself. If people don't consider the technologies, they definitely don't consider the actual processes associated with enacting the BCP or DRP.

The BCP/DRP processes that you need to consider as part of your solution are:

- **Process triggered updates**: What triggers the updates to the plan(s)? Are there some sort of approval mechanism to get the solution included in the BCP/DRP? Is the BCP/DRP only for high criticality systems?
- **Scheduled review**: Is there an annual review of the BCP/DRP that occurs? Is that when the systems get included? If a review determines that a solution should be in the DRP but isn't, what do you have to do to change the systems?
- **Incident/disaster simulation**: Your organization is going to want to simulate a disaster annually to ensure that the DRP and BCP can be used properly and that the systems actually do transfer over to the DR site. Have you included your solution in that simulation package?

Don't ignore the importance of the BCP and DRP for your solution. You'll have to include the DR capability in your solution, but remember that:

> *The "P" in BCP and DRP is defined as PLAN and that is all about processes.*

Security toolset

For a security professional, their toolset is of the utmost importance and there are going to be processes around them. But all solutions, regardless of whether they are security tools or something from a non-security space, all have multiple layers to them. Every tool that is connected to the network needs network support. If a solution is placed on a server, then the Wintel or the Unix team will need to support the Operating System layer of the solution. It's not until you get to the actual application that the security team typically gets involved.

As a result, many of the same processes that were talked about previously also apply for the security tools. It's just that those processes talked about previously are now talked about at the application layer, and the support team is the security group rather than a different support technology group. Taking that into consideration, here are some of the processes that are at the application layer for security tools:

- **Vendor management**: Do you realize how many security vendors there are? And they all want to talk to either the CISO or the security architect. Who talks to them? Are there rules that your Procurement Department has put out as to how Vendors are engaged? Are there discretionary spending limits that you can spend with them?

- **Procurement and licensing**: How do you get the licenses from the Vendors? How do you engage support for the tools? How long will the support contract run for? If your solution is going end of support but your organization hasn't yet implemented a new solution (or even decided on what the new solution is), can you pay for support from the Vendor even after the solution has gone end of life?

- **Maintenance**: Who is going to maintain and administer the solution? Not all security analysts have the ability to do this, so is there a specific role in your group that will support the toolset?

- **Usage:** Are there rules that need to be applied as to who uses the tool? How the tool is checked out? When it can be run? Remember, security tools can be very invasive, so you need to make sure that you have control over the use of them and that it is process driven.

- **Backup**: For more critical solutions like Firewalls or IPS's, how do you back up the findings? Is that the role of the Backup team? If so, how do you monitor that the solution is being backed up properly?

- **Software/firmware revision control**: Vendors very seldom will create a solution and then not issue patches or revisions to the tool. How do you get the updates to the tool? Who does the install? Do you need to go through Change Management (remember that other process section?)?

Once you've answered these process questions about your security toolset, look at the other section. Each of those areas also applies to security tools.

Compliance

Compliance will, most of the time, fall to the security group. When you put together your solution, you also need to ensure that you have included the appropriate areas into your compliance processes. That way, when it comes time for your preparation for audits, you can ensure that your solution is ready for the poking and prodding that comes from being audited.

Compliance processes that you need to consider are:

- **Internal scheduled audits**: Many organizations will schedule internal audits of systems either as a dry run for an external audit or as part of compliance with internal policies and standards. These audits are often run by the Chief Risk Officer or the Chief Financial Officer rather than the CISO. Make sure that you understand if your system needs to be part of these internal audits.
- **External scheduled audits**: These are going to be audits run by professional auditors, either brought in as independent arbiters for measurement against internal standards or, more likely, for independent measurement against an industry compliance standard. Understand if your system will need to be part of these audits and what information needs to be provided as part of those audits.
- **Privacy Impact Assessments (PIA)**: Privacy is becoming more and more important in today's world, especially after the use of Facebook to gather individual's information. If you are part of a government organization, it is very doubtful that you can put a solution into place without having it go through a PIA. Understand what that process is and where the personal information is that is residing in your solution.
- **Security/Threat Risk Assessment (STRA)**: Very seldom will a security professional be allowed to review their own solution. In fact, this is a big part of what a security architect does for non-security solutions. Understand how your organization wants to have STRAs done and how you are supposed to communicate this to your stakeholders. This topic will be discussed in a later chapter.

- **Vendor Risk Assessments**: This is different from a STRA. The Vendor Risk Assessment is specific to the vendor and it's product, whereas the STRA is about the overarching STRA. Every solution will have a network component, an infrastructure component, a process component, and so on. The STRA will look at everything whereas the Vendor Risk Assessment will only look at the Vendor's product. You do this when you are first evaluating a vendor's product for being brought into your organization's environment.
- **Security Policy Management**: In the governance chapter, we talked about how to set up policies and standards as well as how to set up governance associated with your architecture. Refer to that section on the different processes that you need to deal with.

Business engagement

Very seldom does a business unit not engage with the rest of the business. That definitely goes for security because you will have tight scrutiny over security and security solutions by the executive level of your company. However, you also want to be communicating about security risks and changes to the security solutions that you are designing. So, to that end, think about the following processes as part of your solution:

- **Corporate communication**: When you make a change to a solution that will impact the entire organization, you'll want to communicate what those changes are and how they will impact people. While this typically will fall to the Project Manager for a project you may be working on, you need to consider what information your PM needs to communicate.
- **Operational requests**: Communication is a two-way process. While you may be communicating changes to the company, the company may have requests that your solution needs to support. For example, how will someone ask for changes to a Firewall's ACL? Or how do people get to have their baseline configuration of a server changed and approved by the security architect? Think about how you will receive requests and act on them.
- **Reporting**: What's the most asked question that CISO will receive? *"How secure are we?"*. Your solution will have reporting capabilities and you need to understand who the consumers of those reports are and how those reports need to get to them. There are solutions that don't make use of RBAC for read-only access, so you may have to export reports and then ensure that they get to your stakeholders. How do you confirm that those reports have been received?

- **Physical security**: Most physical security teams are in separate groups from the cybersecurity team. How do you engage them? What information do they need and what do you need from them?
- **Privacy officer**: This is another group that cybersecurity will engage with but will not necessarily be part of the same group with. How do you engage the privacy officer for PIAs? How do you communicate to the privacy officer if you have questions about what is defined as private information?

Make sure that you know how to engage with groups outside of your cybersecurity group or architecture group.

Process improvement

Back in the early 1990s, ISO 9000 became a very hot topic. ISO 9000 was all about continuous improvement and was meant to instill quality and quality control into business processes. This concept is something that should be highly valued by the security architect because you always should be looking for ways to become better at what you do and providing better solutions to your stakeholders.

This is typically done by providing ways to measure how things are done. There's a business saying that goes like this:

If it's important to you, measure it.

For process improvement, you want to have a few different processes that look at how things are going and that provide you with feedback on solutions. You'll want to incorporate this information back into your strategic plans so that you can plan for improvement. Some of those processes are:

- **Information metrics**: Metrics and KPIs are not the same. A KPI is a metric but a metric is NOT a KPI. The difference is the alignment with the business or strategic objectives. For example, the number of servers in an organization is a metric. It's a number that tells you information, but it doesn't tell you anything about your strategic alignment. When you collect metric information, it tells you how is it used and what processes need it.
- **Key Performance Indicators (KPIs)**: If your organization is strategically driven, you should have a number of KPIs that tell you how you are doing associated with your strategy, and your strategy should have driven a project. So, how has your project moved your KPI and who to do you communicate that information to?

- **Reporting:** At the end of the day, we need to communicate to our stakeholders how we are doing. We can't do that in person every minute of the day, so we need to provide reports. Make sure that you understand how your solution or strategy is doing and be able to provide a report associated with that information.

Reference Security People Architecture

By nature, people are lazy. And that's not necessarily a bad thing. It's that laziness that results in standardized processes and templates, and ensures that we do things the same way on a regular basis. You can leverage others work and build on it, resulting in that old saying of standing on the shoulders of giants. If you have to recreate all the time, it takes longer and won't have the same quality results that would happen if you haven't corrected the flaws in previous results.

I bring this up because the Reference Security People Architect that I use is something that I have taken from somewhere else. The market research company, Forrester, came out with a research paper in May 10, 2010 titled "Security Organization 2.0: Building A Robust Security Organization" and it was made available by Symantec. It's a really good paper that, while a little older today, provides insight into the various functions that a security organization typically provides to enterprises.

The core for their paper talks about their proposed organizational model. This is important because, rather than talking about the titles that the CISO organization would have, it talks about the logical grouping of responsibilities that need to be covered. As a result, rather than talking about titles (for example, Security Engineer versus security architect, Auditor versus Risk Analyst, and so on), you start to talk to the activities that need to be dealt with inside the CISO organization.

Their proposed CISO organization looks like the following diagram:

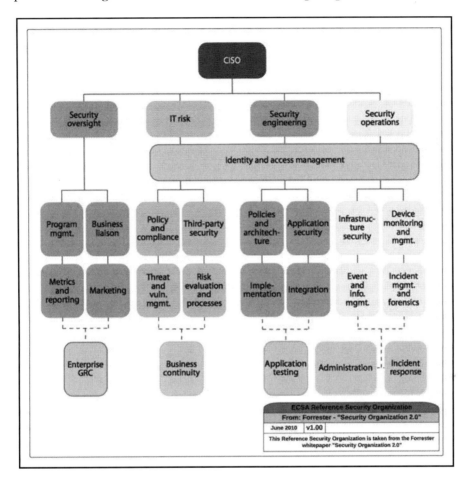

The diagram has logically grouped the responsibilities within the CISO organization into the following:

- **Security oversight**: This is, in essence, the functionalities that are associated with managing the CISO organization
- **IT Risk**: These functions deal with the cybersecurity risks that the CISO organization needs to be aware of and acting on
- **Security engineering**: I actually would call this Security Architecture but a rose by any other name would smell as sweet—except if it's called "engineering" *grin*
- **Security operations**: Here's where your SOC responsibilities would fall into

Now, it's important to understand that these security functions don't necessarily have to be part of the CISO organization. These are capabilities that can be in many different locations. For example, there's a train of thought that the IT risk capabilities should be in a separate group from where the operations group should be due to the entire "separation of duties" approach. In fact, a number of organizations are moving towards placing the actual management of boxes in the Infrastructure Operations group and keeping the risk aspects in the CISO area, and there's a lot of good reasons for doing that.

But the actual functions and responsibilities still exist. The same goes for individual capabilities such as Policy and Compliance or Architecture. Utilities tend to have their Compliance Officers lined up in their OT environment, whereas the CISO is typically in the corporate environment. As a result, there isn't any lines for reporting from the Compliance Officer to the CISO, but the function still exists. The same may apply to the security architect. You, as the security architect, may be reporting to the Chief Architect rather than the CISO. In smaller organizations, all architecture functions may be reporting to a Director of IT. But, again, the function still exists, but it just doesn't exist in a CISO organization.

When you use your Reference Security People Architecture, understand where the individual responsibilities are and what their lines of reporting are. This will typically show up in your Reference Security Process Architecture since specific processes will fall into specific areas of a business.

To understand what each function means and is responsible for, let's break them down in the rest of this section.

Security oversight

As I said previously, security oversight is primarily about the management of the security organization. This means not only internally facing management but also interfacing with the rest of the enterprise. The functions that reside in this grouping of functionality are as follows:

- **Program Management**: Program Management goes into the entire concept of the security initiatives that need to be put forward to move the security of the organization to a strategic future state. This is talked about at greater length in the Strategy and Program Management chapters later.
- **Business liaison**: As I mentioned in the Reference Security Processes Architecture, there is a need to interface with the rest of the business. While the Business Engagement set of processes talks to HOW to interface, the question of WHO still needs to be thought about.

- **Marketing**: You can think of the marketing functionality as the security awareness aspect of the CISO organization. Who is responsible for making sure that people are aware of things such as phishing attacks or malware infestations?
- **Metrics and Reporting**: If the CISO is responsible for the security organization and the security of the organization, how do they know how they're doing? If it's important to an organization, it should be measured. The how is the process, but who does this? Is this done by an executive assistant? Is it something that is provided by the outsourcer that is providing SOC services to your company?

IT risk

IT risk goes to those functions that measure the cybersecurity risk that the company is dealing with. The responsibilities for dealing with the risk are found in the Security Engineering and the Security Operations groups, but the actual measurement and monitoring of risk is dealt with in this logical grouping.

The breakdown of these responsibilities are as follows:

- **Policy and compliance**: Who is responsible for measuring compliance and ensuring that policies are being followed? What is the lines of reporting for this person?
- **Third party security**: This has nothing to do with having third parties actually doing security but, rather, everything to do with monitoring and measuring the risks that are inherited by working with third parties. For example, if your company is using Cloud Services, how do you know what risks are inherited from those companies? More importantly to the Reference Security People Architecture, WHO is responsible for monitoring and measuring the risks from third parties?
- **Threat and vulnerability management:** This became a very clear hook with the Reference Security Technology Architecture and the Reference Security Process Architecture. In each of those two reference areas, we talked about vulnerability management through scanners and processes. In this reference area, you have to ask the question of WHO is responsible for this?
- **Risk evaluation and processes**: Who is responsible for risk evaluations? If a project is being worked on, who is doing the Threat Risk Assessments? Is it the security architect or is it a Security Analyst? It's not important about the role title, it's important to make sure the activity has someone responsible for it.

Security engineering

I'm a security architect and I view engineering as too narrowly focused on technologies and not broadly enough to look at solutions that have all three components: people, process, AND technology. But, that said, since I'm leveraging the Forrester model, let's talk about the Security Engineering functionalities. This entire book will break down what a security architect does, but this will give you a logical breakdown of these functions:

- **Policies and architecture**: This is where you logically group the actual functions associate with architecture and with policy development. But, in this area, we are talking about the security *architecture* policy rather than security policy.
- **Application security**: Who is performing static and dynamic testing of the code that is written by your AppDev group? Who is monitoring the actual SDLC that your organization uses? Who is responsible for ensuring that application security is integrated into any of your application development activities?
- **Implementation**: There are a number of ways to implement security technologies. The architect could create the plans and then provide oversight of the individual operations groups that implement the associated components, or you could have a security engineer that will implement each and every aspect of a solution.
- **Integration**: Where implementation is the responsibilities for the security specific projects, the integration is the integration of security technologies into non-security projects. For example, who will implement your AV agents into a non-security project like a Web Portal? Remember that security is not something that lives in isolation — it is something that should be integrated into everything.

Security operations

Security operations is probably the most flexible of security areas simply because, over the years, organizations have played with numerous ways of assigning people to deliver security operational activities. Many organizations have outsource security to Managed Security Service Providers (MSSPs). It's one of those areas that have changed in individual organizations a lot based on how they view the importance of security. As the importance goes up, the more security operations are brought back in-house.

The functions that the SOC deals with are logically grouped into the following areas:

- **Infrastructure security**: If you were to go back to the *Reference Security Technology Architecture* section, you would align these functions with the Border Protection services and the Configuration Management services. Who is responsible for, for example, managing the firewalls? Many organizations will give firewalls to their Networking groups. But the SOC will monitor the rulesets and their changes as well as the alerts that the firewalls generate. The same goes with your PKI solution. Often, the Certificate Authorities are managed by the Wintel group (if the CAs are Windows-based), but the SOC will have oversight on the generation of the keys and certificates.
- **Device monitoring and management**: This goes to the security devices such as IPS' and anti-virus solution management. Who is managing these devices?
- **Event and information management**: The SIEM is the core technology for all SOCs. It provides the alerts to security events that are occurring and will kick off investigations. Who is monitoring the SIEM output as well as the alerts from those solutions that are not integrated into the SIEM?
- **Incident management and forensics**: So, your SIEM has issued an alert. Who is looking into it and dealing with the incident (or crisis, if it's that big)? After the incident is over, who's dealing with the forensic activities? Sometimes, this will go to the CSO simply because physical security is often staffed with former police officers that understand the legal requirements for evidence handling.

Identity and Access Management

There is one logical grouping that runs across IT Risk, Security Engineering, and Security Operations, and that is **Identity and Access Management (IAM)**. IAM is one of those groups that can fit into a number of different areas. In fact, IAM is often something that isn't even considered part of security at all simply because it has a ROI ,whereas the rest of cybersecurity is considered an insurance play or a cost to the bottom line.

Keep in mind that IAM will often be split into a number of groups, all on its own, because it integrates so well with other non-security areas. Password resets or account management is often put into the help desk area. SSO is often put into the Wintel team because of the close alignment with Kerberos and Active Directory. Federation? Often put with the networking team because the integration of two organizes often requires VPN and/or dedicated leased lines connectivity. So, each of the functional areas in the CISO organization are touched by IAM.

At the end of the day, it doesn't really matter who owns the functions in your Reference Security People Architecture. What's important is if these functions actually exist. There are arguments that can be made to centralize them, and there are arguments to keep actual device management away from security personnel. It all depends on your organization's principles and approach to delivering solutions, including the personnel components.

Just keep in mind that your solutions need to be considering the impact to your security organization. If a non-security solution is being put into place, there are responsibilities that need to be integrated both during the creation of the solution as well as after the solution has gone into production. So, don't forget to find a solution and document the impacts on your organization. Don't forget your organization has stakeholders into your solutions.

Summary

A Reference Security Architecture is a great way to ensure that you don't forget some capability or service that can be used in any solution. You can create it and use it for communication in any number of different ways, and also leverage it for your checklists in different areas of architecture, ranging from strategies to project delivery, to project support and through to operational support.

It's a living document, simply because technologies change over time and security architecture solutions change over time. When I first created my RSA, it was just one page and it focused on security technologies, which is what we have talked about throughout this chapter. But, because all solutions have four components (technology, people, processes, and governance), I have grown it and adapted it to provide a Reference Security Process Architecture, a Reference Security Organization, Reference Security Policies and Standards (built on ISO27000 series), and a Reference Security Architecture Strategy Development.

Questions

1. Aside from this book, what other sources are available for providing a reference security architecture framework?
2. How can you use network zoning, even though it's not really a security technology for improving your security posture?
3. On which side of a firewall should you be placing your scanning solution? On the target side or on the management side?
4. Should you consider physical security technologies in your reference security architecture? If so, why? If not, why not?
5. Why do most projects fail? And where are most vulnerabilities introduced?

4
Cybersecurity Architecture Strategy

In this chapter, we'll talk about the creation of the cybersecurity architecture strategy. The cybersecurity architecture strategy is typically the domain of the Enterprise Security Architect and should focus on ensuring that all security architecture components are supporting the direction that the business goes in. Remember, very seldom is a company's core business cybersecurity. This is a mistake that a lot of security people make: thinking that the company will bend over backwards for their requirements without taking into consideration that their FIRST responsibility is to support the business.

A lot of security people will argue that risk mitigation is their first responsibility. But let me put it to you this way—if you take cybersecurity away from the business, will the business still run? Probably, though the risk level will rise for the company. But if you take the core business away, will the business still run? No. So, make sure that your strategies are focused on supporting the business first and then mitigating risk as a way of supporting the business.

Cybersecurity architecture strategy

The cybersecurity strategy is the central focus of any person working as an Enterprise Security Architect. It drives the organization forward with regards to what security technologies need to be in place and is typically driven by the risk that the organization needs to manage. It takes a long-term view (typically 3 – 5 years) and needs to take into consideration a number of things:

- The direction the business wants to go in from a corporate point of view
- The direction that the IT division wants to go in from a technological point of view in support of the business

- The security risks that need to be managed to support the business direction
- The architectural risks associated with the existing security technologies in place

Again, and I've said this previously in this book, it's important to understand what the core function of the business is. Very seldom is its focus on security. As a result, the Enterprise Security Architect needs to be creating strategies that are focused on supporting each organization above it. That means supporting the business, supporting the IT department that cybersecurity is part of, and then dealing with risk.

Risk has been mentioned a couple of times so far. But risk of what? We, as people that work in the security field, tend to focus on cybersecurity risks. But there are other risks that need to be considered as an Enterprise Security Architect. There's the risk of using ageing equipment and that the equipment will fail or go out of support. That is called architectural risk. There's the business risk that the business is manages such as the risk of a competitor gaining an industry advantage or that the customers of the business are going to shift to another solution, or the risk associated with SEC filings where it will impact the share price of the company.

Risk needs to be managed long-term for the good of the company, and it's the role of the Enterprise Security Architect to plan for that risk. This is where the cybersecurity strategy comes in.

When you create a strategy, regardless of whether it's a cybersecurity strategy or a business strategy or some other strategy, you must always determine these four core components:

1. **Where you are**: What is the current state of the area that you are creating a strategy for? If you don't know where you are, you can't know how to get to your end state. Try to make sure you understand all components of your current state which, like all solutions, will have people, process, technolog, and governance.
2. **What's the future state?** Where do you want to go? What does the end state look like when you get there? Remember to think 3 – 5 years from now and don't just extrapolate what is currently in place (unless that's your strategy—to maintain the status quo—which is perfectly acceptable).
3. **What resources you have to get there:** Moving from point A to point B means taking advantage of any resources you have or plan to have. It could mean money, it could mean existing infrastructure, it could mean people. It could even mean projects of other architecture towers that you can leverage to move in a direction. There are lots of different resources available to you and they don't have to mean using a pool of money.

4. **How are you going to get there?** This is, in essence, the list of initiatives that you have created to move from the current state to the future state while making use of the resources you have. A logical extension of this is the roadmap which ties together initiatives into a logical order.

The cybersecurity strategy can be created for different layers and you should use your RSA to make sure you don't miss any areas. It can be an overarching strategy that goes into the various different sections of your RSA, but not too deeply. It can be for individual sections (for example, you can create a strategy specific to **Identity and Access Management (IAM)**), or you can create a strategy for a very specific technology within one of your sections (for example, a strategy for upgrading firewalls over a five-year period).

Just make sure that your strategies support the strategies above it. You can visualize strategy layers using the following diagram:

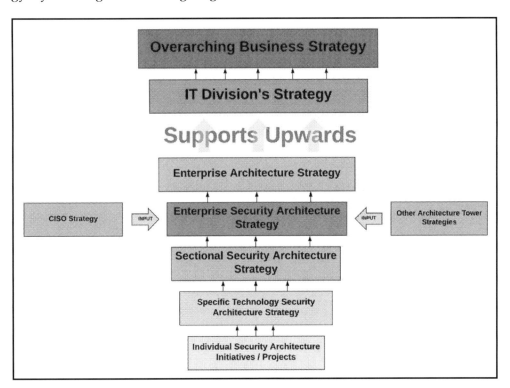

Figure 1: Support strategies through layers

All the components that go into creating a strategy can be shown in the following diagram, and the rest of this chapter will explain these components in more detail:

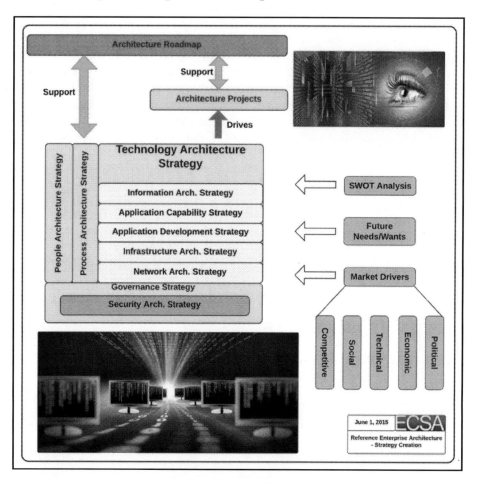

Figure 2: ECSA strategy creation process

Leveraging the Reference Security Architecture

One of the reasons why you want to make sure you have a RSA is that you want to use it as a structure or framework for everything that you do, including the creation of your security architecture strategies. Use your RSA to structure your strategies. There are a number of different areas where you can use your RSA in your strategy creation, so let's talk a bit about them as an overview before we go into them in depth.

First off, think of the creation of a strategy as just another project. The very first step in any project is gathering requirements. Use your RSA as a framework for gathering requirements, what is expected to be accomplished, and what should be going into that future state. The requirements are typically a component of the future state/vision that the strategy is trying to create.

Next, you want to understand what the current state is for the area that you are creating the strategy for. Again, break the area down into its component parts by leveraging your reference security architecture. This can work for a higher-level strategy or when you create something for very specific areas, but make sure that your RSA can give you structure as you gather the current state, otherwise you are going to forget an area.

Strength, Weaknesses, Opportunities, and Threats (SWOT) analysis can be logically grouped into your RSA, though you may have to start looking at architecture strategies outside of the security architecture space. If you limit yourself to looking for solutions to moving your strategy simply based on your own RSA, you may miss some opportunities to leverage other people's solutions.

When you look at your future state, again, make use of the RSA. Ask questions around what that particular area is going to look like in 3 - 5 years. Understand how those individual components are going to support each other. Again, the RSA provides you with a framework in which to have your vision.

Requirement gathering for strategies

When you gather requirements for a strategy, or for any solution, you need to consider all the different parts of a solution. Requirements can be found from the people, processes, technologies, and governance. Let's break down how you go about gathering those requirements and what you do with them from there.

Let's start with the obvious source of requirements—people. Whenever you are creating a strategy, it's a poor security architect who just creates a strategy in isolation. Since a security architecture strategy is meant to support the IT organization's strategy and the larger enterprise business strategy, you need to gather requirements from those stakeholders, which means talking to the following roles:

- **CIO**: The CIO will own the overarching strategy for the IT department. Traditionally, the problem is that most CIOs focus downward, looking at the technologies. But that has started to change so that they are now looking at the core businesses and are trying to figure out how they can make the technologies support the business, not the other way around. As a result, the CIO is becoming more and more a partner at the table with the rest of the company executives. What are the weaknesses that IT has that needs to be addressed? What technology directions are needed to support the business direction?

- **The chief architect**: This person will have an overarching vision of what they want to the architecture for the organization to look like. Do they want to move to the cloud? Do they want to upgrade the company's data center? Do they want to move to a SOA-type architecture? Understand what their "big picture" architecture looks like and figure out how to support it.

- **CISO**: Since one of the two words in security architecture is security, you need to talk to the CISO to understand their vision for the security of the organization. Are they looking to insource or outsource security? Are they getting the metrics that they need to monitor the overarching security of the organization? Are they comfortable with being able to answer the question, *How secure are we?* when the executives ask?

- **Operations team lead**: No-one understands what the environment needs more than the operations team that manages all the various infrastructure components. Talk to them and find out what they would like to see. What solutions are hard to use? What areas are labor intensive? Is there a risk in the environment that they think needs to be addressed? Very few architects talk to their operations teams, which boggles my mind considering they are the heaviest users of all the solutions.

- **Help desk**: The help desk will be the first line of reaction when a normal user has an issue. Can't reset the password? Call the help desk. The network is down? Call the help desk. Want access to a file share? Call the help desk. Talk to the help desk to find out what trends they are seeing and where they would like to see things move to.

- **Finance**: When you talk to people about requirements, one of the things very few people ask about is the money. If you ask someone how much money they want to spend, very few people will have that answer. Talk to the finance department. Find out what the budget is for the next number of years for the IT department from a capital point of view and from an operating budget point of view. That information, combined with the information that you get from the CIO, will give you a rough idea of what the budgets will be for any of your security architecture projects. But it will also give you an idea of what budgets are put aside for other architecture towers. Can you leverage other people's budgets?

Now, let's jump to the requirements that the technologies will tell you about. When you are looking at technology, it's important to remember that they have requirements, just as people do. What you have in place will have the following types of requirements that you need to keep on top of:

- **Age of solutions**: Vendors tend to like to update their solutions and move them from support models to out of support. This allows them to charge new fees for upgrading to the latest solutions, so keep on top of how long until it is your current solutions go out of support so that you can understand when you have to plan for replacements.
- **Underlying infrastructure**: Different applications require different types of infrastructure. Some applications work really well with Oracle databases, but not so well with SQL databases. Other applications may have been written for WebSphere, but your company is looking at focusing on IIS. The support infrastructure that your applications need will dictate the requirements of what infrastructure needs to be in place.
- **Patching and updates**: Some solutions, such as antivirus/malware protection need to be able to reach out to the vendor's master servers for regular updates of signatures. Other vendors have regular updates to their software (for example, Microsoft with their patch Tuesdays) that your organization needs to gain access to in order to make sure the solutions are as up-to-date, as required by your security policies.

These different technical requirements can all be grouped under the term architectural risk. The third area that you need to gather your requirements from is the process area. Processes are something that are very ethereal in that they can and do change based on the people or groups of people that are responsible for an area. It's important to remember that you have to be flexible in adapting to process requirements. Rather than focus on the specific process requirements, shift your focus to how adaptable those processes are in terms of your solution. Look at:

- **Compliance requirements**: Compliance with standards often requires that certain process must be in place. That doesn't mean that processes have to occur in a certain way. Understand what processes need to be followed, and those are your requirements. Let the "how" of the process take care of itself.
- **Users of the process**: The more users of processes, the more fixed the processes become, simply because it's hard to train more and more people on a new process. If there's a process that affects the entire organization, there's less likelihood that the process will change.

- **Workflow**: Often, a solution will have the ability to integrate processes into their capabilities (for example, provisioning solutions will have the ability to be triggered based on workflow events). Some organizations are trying to become process-driven. Determine if there is any workflow engine requirements that you need to build your strategy around.

And, finally, there are the governance requirements for a strategy. Typically, an enterprise will have a series of security policies and standards. These are overarching and are security architecture standards. As such, these standards should be longer-lasting than a strategy and be viewed as an input into the standards. For this section, I'll refer to ISO27000 simply because it is a standard that many organizations have tried to align themselves with. Some of the ways that governance can impact a strategy might be:

- **BCP/DRP**: ISO 27000 series has a recommended policy tower associated with business continuity plans, which will drive disaster recovery plans. This policy will likely drive how DR sites are set up and used.
- **Access controls**: There is an entire policy domain associated with access controls in ISO27000, which includes coverage for user access management, operating system access control, and application and information access control. This policy domain will impact any strategy a security architect has in relation to IAM.
- **Communications and operations management**: Just as an operations group, from the people perspective, will have requirements for strategy, the communications and operations management policy domain will impact strategy because it is a codification of what the operations group should be doing. There will be governance points about protection against malicious and mobile code, network security management, and third-party delivery management (which can impact the use of the cloud or outsourcing vendors).

Over and above policies and standards, governance requirements may actually call for a governing body for a specific area. For example, years ago, I created an encryption standard for a customer that wanted to make sure that the appropriate guidance was being provided for which systems did or did not need encryption. This called for the creation of an oversight body that exceptions had to be approved by.

Requirements are needed to create your strategy, just as they are needed to create your project solutions. Just think of a strategy as a specific type of solution and you'll be successful.

Current state assessment

Keeping in mind the four components of a strategy (where you are, where you are going, what are your resources?, and how are you going to get there?), probably the most important component of the strategy is the current state assessment. Again, this is where your Reference Security Architecture comes in.

A current state assessment is something that many organizations want, but few actually have. That is because most organizations grow organically without any plan or strategy in place. As a result, they don't have a complete picture of what they have or the state it is in. Several years ago, I was working with an organization that asked me to create an Enterprise Security Architecture strategy that included what should happen with the firewalls. The Chief Architect wanted to move towards a virtualized environment and that included moving to a virtualized firewall solution. When I was doing my discovery of the current state, I discovered that the network team was in the process of upgrading all the physical firewalls because they had either come to the end of their life or were literally failing because of over-taxation of the firewall resources. It was an opportunity lost and an example of what happens when you don't forecast and plan for system replacement.

To perform a current state assessment, you need to make use of your RSA. With your RSA, create a spreadsheet similar to the following diagram. In one column, itemize the different components in your RSA. In the next column, label it your current state technology, and use this column to document the current state architecture component that you have and, if possible, try to discover what your versions and the state of the resources are. The next set of columns should be dedicated to the architectural risk associated with the architecture element and should indicate, ideally visually, when the element is due for change. What flows out of this is a natural component of the roadmap of activities:

	Current State Technology	Current State Situation					KEY	
		Year 1	Year 2	Year 3	Year 4	Year 5		New Investment / Major enhancements
Border Protection								Asset Enhancement (minor enhancements)
Central Firewall Mgmt	Cisco's Mars							Operate only
Firewalls	Cisco (multiple), Fortinet, Juniper							Retire
Mobile Security	not applicable							
Web Application Firewall	Imperva							Eliminated
Test/Dev Environment	only for application development							Investigate
QA/Production Mirror	yes							TBD (based on outcomes of investigation)
Production Environment	yes							
Corporate Desktop								
DMZ between zones								
T&D / Generation Environment								
VPN								
Proxies								
IPv6 Security								
IPv4 / IPv6 Bridge								
Wireless security								
ISP								
External Services								

By making the spreadsheet visual in nature, it becomes easier to determine when actions should occur. Have different colors for the different categories and use the output of this worksheet as an input into your roadmap.

This can be done for non-technology areas as well. Do the same for the RSA associated with your people, processes, and governance.

By this time, you should start to see your strategy starting to be created all on its own. One recommendation for creating strategies is to NOT go into strategy creation with pre-conceived ideas about what the output should be. If you go in with an open mind, you will start to see the solution come together on its own, with its own rationale for doing the individual activities. If you start off wanting to justify a strategy, you will run into all sorts of issues and road blocks.

To provide a parallel, how successful are projects when the business comes to you with a technology that they have chosen without looking at requirements? Seldom is the solution that's successful, plus there is typically a misalignment with the rest of the businesses requirements. The same goes for strategy creation. An open mind will come up with the best results.

Environmental variables

Another component of the current state is indirect elements. Sure, you've documented what your current state solution components are (technology, people, process, and governance), but you also have to anticipate the drivers that are moving the organization in a certain direction. These drivers are described as environmental variables and are things that you do not have any control over but have to take into consideration. Current state assessment provides you with what you have control over. Environmental variables provide you with what you don't.

Your typical **Masters of Business Administration (MBA)** program will lay them out in a number of different ways. Some of the more popular sets of environment variables are the following:

- **Political variables**: Political variables are those that are driven by political entities or, in the case of larger organizations, internal politics. I've found that the larger the organization, the heavier you have to understand the internal politics. These variables are not social in nature but, rather, driven by politics or business. There may be a team in your organization that has more power than a different group, so aligning with their efforts may improve your strategy's ability to deliver.

- **Economic variables**: Economic variables talk to financial variables, and this is where the macro and micro economic picture will be going. It talks to variables that will impact budgets which will, in turn, impact the capital and operational budgets available for projects. You may find that you don't have the funds available directly for your projects. But, maybe, you will leverage the budgets for other non-security projects and get them to implement one of your strategy elements. That's money saved.

- **Technical variables**: Technical variables are those that are driven by changes in technology in the market or potential changes in technology direction within your organization. Two major examples over the last several years the move to **Service Oriented Architectures (SOA)** back in 2000 – 2010 and, more recently, the move towards cloud solutions. Both are trends that make use of standardization but in different ways.

> By the way, don't forget that technology doesn't mean information technology. There are numerous other technologies that you should consider. The entire **Internet of Things (IoT)** is an example of technologies that now have IP addresses. I was creating a strategy and completely forgot that video cameras used in physical security are now both wireless in nature and makes use of a Unix kernel. So the question that I have to start asking myself is, How do updates get to IoT devices? And who manages that? Is that an IT function or is it the function of some non-technology group (for example, smart refrigerators have IP addresses. Is it the janitorial staff that deals with it or IT?).

- **Social variables**: Social variables are those that deal with the way people act or react to situations. These variables are often mitigated by communications but, because people are involved, can be extremely volatile variables to deal with. Examples of these variables are the shift towards social media and, more recently, the hyper-partisanship that people have taken towards various topics (For example, the Me-Too movement, gun control, and so on). Within an organization, how the various groups within the organization communicate and organize will impact the social variables of your strategy.

- **Competitive variables**: Most people think of competition as companies that your organization competes with, but that ignores the fact that there are competing groups within any organization that may want to take over a certain area. I once worked for EDS global in their security and privacy portfolio group, but the internal CISO organization felt they were better able to deliver on solutions. Plus, there was a dedicated government support group that was supporting the NSA and CIA in Virginia that felt they were better for certain things. Remember that you can have competition both within and outside the organization.

Understanding that the things that are out of your control can help you anticipate and create backup or contingency plans if something happens that is out of your control.

Future wants and needs

Many of the future visions will come from the requirements gathering exercise that you went through earlier. There will be the requirements that the individuals need to meet, the requirements that are needed to support the organization's business plan and the IT organization's strategic plan, and there will be architectural needs that the current state assessment determined. But, at the end of the day, a strategy is about what you want and need to have in place.

There will be many times where you will have a list of "wants" that you want to get fulfilled. Maybe you want to move to a new technology platform, one that truly meets your vision for the future. Maybe there is a series of changes to the environment that you want to make to ensure that the network zoning meets your vision of what the security structure should look like. Regardless, what you want may not be what you actually need, and that is the reason behind pulling together these requirements.

So, let's start off with the practical. Look at your current state and analyze what the architectural risks are associated with what you found in relation to your Reference Security Architecture. Are there components there that need to be upgraded or replaced because the vendor won't be supporting the solution much longer? What about where your organization is going? Is there a need for some supporting security infrastructure that needs to support that direction?

When you start to list your future state vision, make use of the four-quadrant decision-making process. You'll find this approach very relevant when you are looking at time management. The decision-making process is shown in the following diagram:

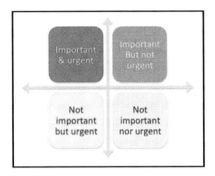

Figure 4: Four quadrants of decision-making

The four quadrants are as follows:

- **Important and urgent**: This is the top left quadrant and it is where many of us live in our day-to-day lives. Working in this area means we are putting out one fire after another and, overall, behaving very tactically. While it may feel that we need to be in this quadrant because of the urgency, it's actually an issue that results in us not being able to act strategically. You would place items that are literally about to fall over into this quadrant.
- **Important but not urgent**: This quadrant is where we create our strategies. We are looking longer term and, by dealing with the important items but not with the ones that are urgent, we can actually reduce the amount of activity in the important and urgent quadrant. Focus on items you would put into this quadrant as your primary strategic activities.
- **Not important but urgent**: These are the items that continuously pop up on our desks that we need to deal with, but they aren't timely. You place any "want" items in this quadrant. You may "want" to go into certain areas, but it's the two previous quadrant items that you need to prioritize.
- **Not important and not urgent**: These are those items that are the "nice-to-haves". If you have spare resources or can figure out a way for a non-security project to push these items forward, then go for it. Otherwise, push these to one side for another year.

To use these quadrants, make a list of all the items you have in your future vision. Then, honestly put them into the various quadrants to determine their priority. The priority that you should have them in is as follows:

1. Important but not urgent
2. Important and urgent
3. Not important but urgent
4. Not important and not urgent

Like with all things, make sure you are being driven by the requirements that you have gathered. If you do that, your strategies will have that much more buy-in by your stakeholders.

Strengths, Weaknesses, Opportunities, and Threats (SWOT)

Now that you know your current state and what your future vision is, you need to know what resources you have available to make use of. A lot of this may come out of your current state assessment, but the most common way of determining what resources you can make use of comes from the SWOT analysis.

Strengths, Weaknesses, Opportunities, and Threats (SWOT) analysis breaks down a number of elements and allows you to understand what you can use and what you need to be aware of. Similar to environmental variables, SWOT information is more along the lines of what you can or cannot leverage for your strategy, whereas the environmental variables are things you need to be aware of but are out of your control. When you look at the different elements of a SWOT analysis, look at them in the following manner:

- **Strengths**: Strengths are the things your organization is good at. You may have a really robust IAM solution in place that you can leverage or a SOC that is well-trained and responsive. These are items that you can easily take advantage of in your strategy. And remember: not all solutions have to be technology-based. Sometimes, a change in process or leveraging people can be as effective, if not more effective, than buying a new shiny toy.

- **Weaknesses**: Weaknesses are things that you can't depend on. For example, you may have older legacy solutions in place that can't make use of new security technologies (for example, utilities have SCADA devices in the field from the 1970s that work perfectly well, but can't support security standards created in this century). You either have to ignore these areas or you have to think of ways to improve your weaknesses.
- **Opportunities**: Opportunities are things that people continuously overlook. Most people inexperienced with creating strategies automatically look for a pool of money to spend on initiatives, but there are often other ways of getting things done. For example, and this example was brought up earlier in this chapter, maybe you can leverage an existing project that is underway and has financial approvals. Put forward your security requirements in such a way that it will advance your strategy. There have been numerous data center migrations, for example, that have been leveraged to create new security zones or implement new security technologies such as virtual firewalls.
- **Threats**: This is really similar to environmental variables in that you need to be aware of things that are going to occur and that may impact your strategy negatively. For example, say a major project that you want to leverage is not going to get underway for at least a year after you need your strategic item put into place. Can you adjust your strategy in some way to still take advantage of it?

A SWOT analysis is the last step you take before you put together your initiatives, and it can have a major impact on how your initiatives come together.

Initiatives (both direct and indirect)

At this point, you should have a pretty good idea of what initiatives you want to have in your strategy. This is the core of your strategy. Your initiatives will have been sorted and will have real weight behind them because you did your research and planning. If you included your stakeholders to get their requirements, it's at this point that you want to present your initiatives to them in order to get their buy-in and see if you missed something.

Invite your stakeholders together in a group meeting and present your initiatives. Start off by talking about the process that you took to create the initiatives and then tell them the reasoning behind each initiative. If some of your initiatives are going to leverage other architecture tower initiatives, talk about what effect your requirements will have on those projects so that there are no surprises for those people.

Also, get feedback on your initiatives to make sure that you are in alignment with the people that you are trying to support. Remember that others are going through the same process, so they may be making changes to *their* initiatives. Those changes may impact your initiatives, and you want to know about them before you finalize your security architecture strategy.

Roadmaps

Roadmaps are where you put timeframes around your initiatives. Seldom will your strategy have enough resources for all initiatives to be done all in the same fiscal year. You want to spread your initiatives out through your timeframe (make use of a 3 - 5 year timeframe so that you are giving your organization enough time to change) to make effective use of the resources available to you.

But, prior to assigning timeframes, understand what the relationship is between each initiative. There are going to be some initiatives that have to occur prior to other initiatives can occur — dependencies, as it were. If you know which initiatives are dependent on other initiatives, it allows your roadmap to flow properly. And these dependent initiatives aren't just security architecture initiatives. It also includes the initiatives from other architecture towers and other business units, and those initiatives will have their dependencies on you just as much. There is a give-and-take that occurs in planning the order that initiatives take.

Annual review

One of the nice things about having a 3 - 5 year strategic plan is that, once you have created it, you just have to maintain it. You don't have to create it from scratch every year. You do have to understand what has changed in the organization but, if you have done your current state assessment for your original strategy, you just have to keep an eye on the components rather than discovering them all over again.

Every year, review your strategic plan to see how your initiatives have done and what changes you have to make. Seldom do strategies go exactly according to plan. You'll still have your planned initiatives, but some issues may have arisen that have pushed some initiatives back. For example, maybe a project didn't get implemented as smoothly as it could have been and resulted in taking longer than expected. Maybe some unknowns came up when projects were being implemented that changed the organizational priorities, or maybe a PM decided to de-scope certain requirements for a project initiative in order to meet financial and timeframe requirements.

One word of caution about allowing a PM to de-scope requirements is that project managers are typically focused on the budget and the timeframes for delivering a project. But remember that those aren't the only requirements in a project, and different requirements have different priorities. If a project has it's scope shortened, that doesn't make the requirements go away. All it does is push the rest of your initiatives out that are dependent on the requirements not met. Be very aware of what impact missed requirements will have on your strategy. These will have a longer-term impact on budgets and timeframes that the project manager may not be aware of since they are focused only on their one individual project.

So, review your strategy every year, ideally about a couple of months before your fiscal year ends. This way, you can make adjustments to the budget you propose and the initiatives you propose to have acted on.

Metrics

There's a saying in business — if it's important, you measure it. A strategic plan should be important to you and your organization. You need to measure it and how it is doing in supporting the organization, and that means picking the appropriate metrics.

Picking metrics isn't as simple as asking, *How many initiatives were completed?*, though that can be one of your metrics. Ideally, you are looking to see how your initiatives impact the performance of your organization in support of the business plan objectives. That way, if an executive asks you what you've done to support the company's business plan, you can easily turn around and say "Metric A has done this, metric B has done that for your business plan."

Don't choose too many metrics to measure your strategic plan with. Remember that every solution has the elements of people, process, technology, and governance. So, pick two or three for each area and then track them. Some of the sample metrics you could use are as follows:

- **People metrics**: What was the satisfaction with the new solution by end users? Are there fewer incidents occurring? Are fewer people having to support an environment? Is the administrative costs supporting a solution going down?
- **Process metrics**: Are processes occurring faster? Are your end users getting responses quicker? Are you able to provide metrics faster to executives?

- **Technology metrics**: Are your outages going down? Are there fewer vulnerabilities available to be exploited? Are the supporting systems more effective?

- **Governance metrics**: How many non-compliance items do you have? Are you able to answer the question, *how secure are we?* when the executives ask?

Summary

At the end of the day, a cybersecurity architecture strategy is meant to move you from a current state that is not appropriate for where the business wants to go to a vision of what the future should look like. You want to make sure that you think about all aspects of your organization, both in your company's control and outside its control, as you plan. Then, you want to create your strategy so that you are able to move forward with where the company should be by using some sort of roadmap for leveraging your assets and strengths while mitigating your weaknesses and threats.

In the next chapter, we will start to talk about all the strategic and programming activities that a security architect gets involved in. Remember, strategy is not the only thing that the Enterprise Security Architect gets involved in. There is also the documentation of your key decisions, there's the documenting and monitoring of risks (which are components that impact the creation of your strategies), and there's the evaluation of the current state. It's that last one that is probably the first activity that every Enterprise Security Architect does when they get involved in an organization.

Questions

1. When you are creating your strategy, what are the four core components that you need to include?
2. There are five environmental variables that you need to consider when you create your strategy. What are they and are they within your control?
3. From a time management point of view, where should you live and where do most people actually live? What's wrong with that?
4. Why are metrics important? If you were going to measure your strategy, what (in your mind) would you be focused on? Is that a strategic measurement or a tactical one?
5. If your financial department tells you that they don't have enough money for all your initiatives, how can you get around that?

5
Program and Strategy Level Work Artifacts

As an enterprise security architect, you have to focus on activities and deliverables that are more strategic in nature than individual projects. The previous chapter talked about the creation of strategies but, at the end of the day, there's much more to being strategic than just working on strategies. If you are looking 3 – 5 years into the future, you actually have to start thinking about how to communicate and manage your strategies. And that, after all, is what architecture is all about—communicating ideas.

Strategy and program artifacts have to, by their nature, revolve around strategies. That means that the enterprise security architect needs to be able to provide work products, such as **key decision documents (KDDs)**, whitepapers, and current state evaluations. All of these revolve around your RSA, which we talked about a couple of chapters ago.

Reference security architecture

I'm not going to rewrite everything about the **reference security architecture (RSA)**, but it's really important to understand that your RSA is the foundation to everything that you do with every security architecture role that you perform.

Take, for example, the strategy work that we talked about in the previous chapter. The RSA is the structure that you use to put your strategy together. It allows you to break down the various components in your organization and realize what you have, what you are missing, where you are strong and where you are weak, and how all the various different components work together.

So, while this section isn't that big in this particular chapter, your RSA is core to who you are as a security architect. Grab it and let's use it to provide context to the rest of the strategy and program activities that the security architect does.

Key decision documents

At some point in your career as an enterprise security architect, you are going to have to go into some depth in explaining why you made a decision and that explanation has to outlive you and your activities in your organization. You may move on or you may move up in an organization but someone down the line will want to know why a certain decision was made. And that's where the KDDs comes in.

To be clear, this isn't just writing for posterity's sake. You'll often have to justify a decision to the executive level and, if you can't show that you've thought through the decision thoroughly, you will run the risk of being overruled or, in the worse case, have someone try to go behind your back and blame you for why something didn't go well.

I had a case where I went through a thorough vendor selection process and then documented the decision to go with that vendor. Later, when a project to implement the vendor's solution was taking way too long and was costing too much, the KDD was able to justify the decision to move forward with that particular solution and it backfired on the person that was pointing fingers. Sometimes, documentation of decisions is a really nice way to CYA.

Typically, your KDD should have the following sections in it. I like to have each section start on their own page just for "cleanliness" of presentation, but that's up to you:

- **Purpose**: You'll want to provide a paragraph or two as to why you are writing the KDD. Typically, it gives context as to how the KDD fits into your strategy or project activity.

 Remember, a KDD can also be very useful in the delivery of projects. It can be used to document key decisions made in the delivery of the project. More tactical, yes, but key decisions are still made in projects as opposed to the strategy level.

- **Issue**: Write down what the issue is that is forcing you to make a key decision. Typically, your issue is going to be something major like going with a certain technology focus (for example, going cloud first versus building in-house). You don't need to use a KDD to deal with an issue as mundane as the placement of a server in a specific zone. At least, not at the strategic level. The issue section should be clearly spelling out what the issue is, how the issue is affecting the organization and, remembering that this is a strategic KDD, how the issue will impact the business long term if not dealt with properly.

- **Recommendation**: The recommendation section is key to the KDD. It's meant to be an executive summary of your decision and the actions that will be taken as a result of your decision. I like to put the different options in a table and then show how each option's ratings compare. For example, the table I use in my templates (there's that lovely term again—templates) will look something like the following:

Rating System:

Low	= Not a good option short term or long term.
Medium	= Good for the dealing with the Issue over the short term but not Long term beneficial.
High	= Good option for <customer> short term and long term.

Overall Rating is determined by Averaging the Ratings for an Option, giving each Rating equal value.

Opt. #	Option	Risk Mitigation	Business Rating*	Technology Rating**	Overall Rating
1	Option #1 title	Low	Low	Low	Low
2	Option #2 title	Medium	Low	Low	Low-Medium
3	Option #3 title	High	Medium	Medium	Medium-High
4	Option #4 title	High	Medium***	Medium-High	Medium/High
5	Option #5 title	High	Medium****	High	High-Medium
6	Option #6 title	High	Low	Medium	Low

* - based on alignment of Business Strategy

** - based on alignment with Security Technology Strategy

*** - based on Gartner comment about most expensive <technology> solution

**** - based on Gartner comment about poor customer service

There are two things to remember when you document what your decision is.

Tip 1: Try to go into the evaluation of your different options with an open mind. The best thing to do is to use the KDD to make a decision rather than justify a decision already made.

One example that you will always see are those times when people have chosen a technology or a vendor long before they've even determined what the requirements are. This is related to wanting the newest shiny toy, so some organizations will want you to write a KDD to justify your decision. If someone writes a KDD and gives it to you to review, make sure that it's an honest evaluation of the options and not slanted towards backwards justification of decisions.

Tip 2: One option you will always have is to do nothing. Don't get caught in the trap of thinking you actually have to do something. Doing nothing can be a conscious decision.

People always want to do something. The hardest thing for people to do is to do nothing because they feel they aren't adding value. And this goes with everyday decisions, not just KDDs. Keep in mind that, of all the options that you will have available to you, always consider not doing something. It may actually be a better solution than some of the other options you have.

- **Assumptions**: One of the biggest problems people have when making a decision is that they try to collect too much information to make their decisions on. Most decisions have a timeliness associated with them, even ones that are related to strategic decisions. Most strategies are done towards the end of the fiscal year so that the next year will have actionable items in the business plan. At some point, you need to make a decision and can't wait any longer. Document the assumptions that you have related to this decision so that your audience has a clear understanding of what the landscape was when you made the decision, and try to logically group your assumptions based on solution components (which is to say people, process, and technology). I always add a financial aspect because I'm always being asked about the cost of a decision.
- **Risks**: When you write your KDD, include the risks associated with the decision. What are the risks that are associated with the issue? What are the risks that the decision has to take into consideration if change was to occur? And don't limit your risk to just security risks. Consider the architectural risks and the business risks in your KDD. Remember, there is more than one type of risk.
- **Constraints**: Because of other decisions in your strategy or the need to support other strategies, such as the overarching IT strategy or the business strategy, you may be limited as to the choices that are available to you, so you need to indicate some of the constraints that limit your available options.
- **Stakeholder requirements**: Whenever you make a decision of any type, regardless of whether it's a strategy or a design or some other solution (and, yes, a strategy is a solution, just the timeframes are longer), you need to reference back to your requirements. And a good security architect will always gather the requirements associated with an area. Again, make use of your RSA for identifying requirements or, if it's a more tactical solution, make use of the requirements gathered in your projects. Document the requirements that the KDD is meant to address so that you can show that you understood what needed to be met with your decision.

- **Vendor information**: If this is a decision that involves different vendors, include vendor information as well as the pros and cons of using that particular vendor. Remember that all vendors, no matter who they are, have good points and bad points, so documenting them allows you to properly understand and evaluate them.
- **Positions and arguments**: This is the core of the evaluation of your various options. This can be driven by a variety of option branches (logical grouping of decisions) and then those sub options, as shown by the following diagram:

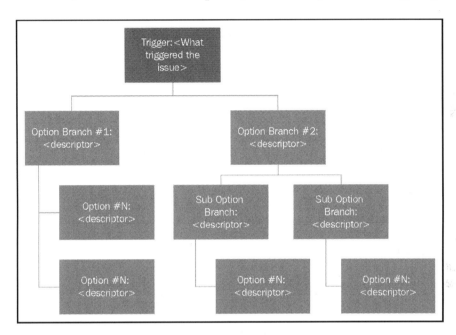

An option branch is a major grouping of options. For example, making use of a process change rather than a technology can be two separate option branches. Then the sub options become variations on the option branch. For example, say one option branch is to change a product suite from one vendor to another. Each option then becomes a different vendor. Or maybe an option branch is to stay with a specific vendor. Then the various options may be to just upgrade or to migrate to the newest solution the vendor provides. Your positions and arguments section is meant to describe each option branch and then to talk about the pros and cons of each option. Your decision will show up in the Recommendation section (as described earlier).

Your KDD is a really important document to justify a direction that you want to go. Make sure you really think through your options before making a decision rather than making a decision and then using something like a KDD to justify your decision. Like everything that an architect does, you need to build on the requirements and it's a poor architect that doesn't look at the requirements first.

Risk register

At the end of the day, the security architect specializes in security. And that means having an understanding of risk, which includes the existing risk of the current state, the risk associated with changing a solution, and the residual risk that a new solution leaves behind. But, from a strategic point of view, your strategies really need to take into consideration the risks that the current state of the environment has. And that takes us to the risk register.

Understanding risk

The risk register isn't so much an artifact that you create as much as it is a tool that you use to track risk in the environment. But remember that there are a number of different types of risk that you, as a security architect, need to consider. These include the following:

- **Security risk**: We always default to thinking about security risk. Over the years, security has had name changes. We were originally called IT security, then information security, and now cybersecurity. And those pre-cursor words indicate what we are protecting because, at the end of the day, security is about protection. Security risk is about dealing with the risks that impact whatever we are protecting.
- **Architectural risk**: Remembering that security architecture is made up of two words, security and architecture, we then have to keep in mind that there are risks associated with the architecture. These are risks associated with the architecture, or environment, that we are working with. If we make a change, how will that impact the technology environment? Will it cause other systems to fail? What about *not* making a change? What are the risks of not making a change? Or, if we are using an older technology that we know is functioning but not in alignment with strategy, what is the impact of making that change? Architectural risk is all about the risks associated with making changes (or not making changes) to the environment.

- **Project risk**: Too many times, I've seen architects view risks in project terms. That is the domain of the project manager, not the architect. Project risks are risks that will impact the delivery of a project, not the results of the solution. Anything associated with the solution itself is an architectural risk whereas anything impacting the delivery of a project is a project risk. For example, not having the appropriate person available is a project risk. Not being able to integrate with Active Directory is an architectural risk. Two different things.

- **Business risk**: As I've said previously in this book, everything we do has to support the business. But a business risk isn't necessarily a security risk. You can have a solution that improves the security posture of the business (for example, not putting in place a public-facing web portal would improve the security posture of a company) but that solution may increase the business risk (for example, not having a web portal will drive customers to competitors because of customer experience reasons). Business risks are those things that will impact the business negatively and are usually the thing that the chief risk officer will focus on.

With regards to security risk versus architecture risk, there is a distinction that needs to be understood. Security risk is typically dealing with things that happen that are outside of our control. You may have an internal user that accidentally does something to impact the organization, or you may have an external entity trying to gain unauthorized access to company information. Those are examples of risks outside of our control.

Architectural risk, on the other hand, are the risks associated with our conscious decisions. We make the decision to upgrade our servers from Windows Server 2008 to 2012. What will be the impact of that decision? Will there be applications that break? Security risks and architectural risks are associated with things that are either in our control or out of our control that impact our technology environment, and then business risks are those risks that impact the business as a whole, only one of which are impacts to the supporting technology.

Monitoring risk

Once you understand the different types of risk, you'll want to keep an eye on the risks. And that is where the risk register comes in.

The risk register is a solution that you use to document and monitor risks. It can take many forms. In its simplest form, it can be a spreadsheet. It can be more complex like a SharePoint site. Or you can purchase a rather focused solution like a **Governance, Risk, and Compliance (GRC)** solution from a vendor, such as Archer (this is not a recommendation, just an example). But all these solutions meet the same requirement—they provide you with the ability to track risks. It's just that some are more automated than others.

When you monitor and track risk, there are a few things that you need to keep in mind:

- **Time boxing**: When you track risk, you want to put a time box around those risks. You want to have an understanding of when the risk should be mitigated by and you want to have some sort of alerting capability that brings the risk back to your attention at a later date. I worked with one company that would review solutions and find residual risks that, after negotiating with the project team, would time box when the mitigation would occur. But then they wouldn't track the time box associated with the mitigation and the mitigation wouldn't occur. So why negotiate in the first place?

- **Remember the definition of risk**: People consistently mix up risk with threat impact. Risk is, by definition, an impact created by a threat versus the likelihood that the threat will occur. For example, if there's a risk that an earthquake will hit the area, the threat level might be high because of the destruction that it might occur. But if there hasn't been an earthquake in an area for hundreds of years, then the likelihood is low. What's the risk? Probably medium-low. But often, people will just look at the impact rather than the real risk.

- **Consistent measurement of risk**: Nothing is more aggravating than a security person saying that a risk is high and a non-security person disagreeing, saying that a risk is low. This goes back to mixing up the impact of a threat versus what the risk level is and it sets up a conflict between security and the people that actually own the risk. The way around that is to provide a measurement that is not based on personal experience or bias. One way to deal with this is similar to how an auditor of an industry standard works. The auditor will have very clear definitions of risk based on impact versus likelihood and that measurement of risk is something that the industry has agreed to. In your organization, this will take away personal biases and make the playing field level. Just make sure everyone agrees to the definitions you use prior to making use of your risk levels.

- **Make reporting of risk easy**: More and more, people take security seriously. It's not like it was back around the turn of the century when information security was in its infancy. They've begun to understand that security is the responsibility of everyone. Because of that, people want to continuously point out things that they view as risks to the organization. But non-security people typically don't truly understand what risk is so they will misreport issues. Make it easy for people to report risks that they see and be involved in the measurement of that risk. I would recommend that you use a SharePoint site or web interface that allows individuals to pull down pre-determined levels and their impacts. That way, they will feel like they are involved and contributing to the overall security of their organization. Those risks can go into your risk register, they can be assigned a risk level, and can be provided by those that you may not have considered having a conversation with.

The risk impact assessment and the risk register

A few years ago, I got it into my mind to create an actual flow chart for solutions in general. My thinking was that a solution was just a series of individual component risks and that, if I could create a flow chart decision tree, and an associated spreadsheet with pre-defined measurements, and then create a user interface based on something like SharePoint, I could create a situation where a risk impact assessment of a solution could be created and stored automatically in a database for tracking later.

The result was something that was really useful, and that I make available for my clients. I'll customize the measurements based on the personality of my client's company personality but, at its core, it's a way of consistently and quickly measuring the risk of a solution. I would suggest that you consider doing the same thing for your organization.

The components, without breaking it down into too fine detail, should look like the following diagram:

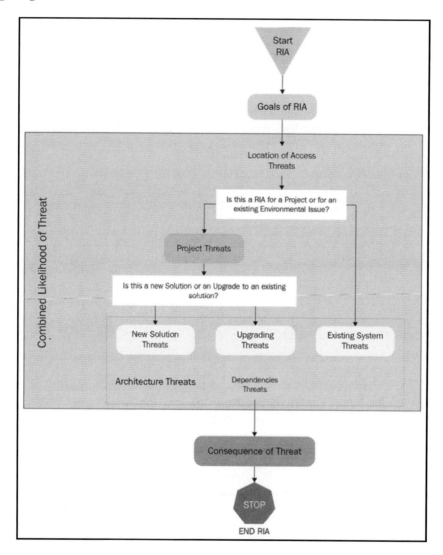

This decision tree is all about looking at a solution with all its component parts and determining what the overall risk level is for the solution. You can use this for existing solutions that are already in place, upgrades to components of the solution, or for net new solutions. But, in all cases, the purpose is to take the "interpreted" meaning out of doing a risk impact assessment to one where all the results of the RIA come from a consistent application of rules.

This particular decision tree is more summary in nature and has a number of lower-level questions that should be asked. For each answer of a question, a score is attached and then each section will be the total of those individual scores.

The decision tree is something that you can also use for determining possible courses of action for remediating risks that are in your risk register. You can tweak the various decisions that you have to make (for example, change the type of authentication from username/pwd to 2 Factor) and see how the risk changes. The end result is that you have a tool that the architect can use to determine how to improve the risk level while at the same time determining what the design is going to look like.

With your decision tree, assign ranges for each decision and seldom assign a 0 or lack of risk. All decisions are risky (getting out of bed in the morning is risky!) and keep in mind that some decisions carry the same level of risk.

Note: The following logic is something that I put into my decision tree and it's an evolving solution. Determine what logical components you want in and assign values. It's the assigning of values that allows for the consistency of measurement of risk.

When you create your RIA decision tree, make sure you include the following logic:

- **Goals of RIA**: For every solution or component, there's a factor associated with the **confidentiality, integrity, and availability (CIA)** of the solution. When you are looking at the overall likelihood of threats, you want to have a multiplication factor based on the CIA. The higher the criticality of that component, the higher the multiplication factor. I use a range of 0.95 to 1.05 as the multiplication factor where a low criticality is measured at 0.95, a medium criticality is at 1.00, and a high criticality has a multiplication factor of 1.05. When you look at them combined, take an average so that you can factor the likelihood appropriately.
- **Location of access threats**: Where a threat can come from will increase or decrease the likelihood of a threat occurring. Logically, there are two locations that access can occur: from internal and from external entities. If you have a solution that has a combination of both (for example, a web portal), then you add the threat factor because you have two threat vectors to consider:
    - **For internally facing solutions**: You are basically looking at two types of roles: the general population within your organization or specific FTEs (that is, the business unit) that will access the solution.

- **For externally facing solutions**: In this case, you have four different types of external entities: the general public, B2C, B2B, and partners.
- **Note**: In both cases, there are other types of entities but they are considered hostile. That's the reason why the factors for both don't start with 0. I build in the risk for entities that the solution isn't designed for.

- **Project or existing environment decision**: The next thing to consider in your decision tree is whether this is for a project that is changing the environment or whether this is for a solution currently existing in the environment. Remember, a RIA can be done for something that is already in place. Whichever your decision is, follow that decision path and add those risk factors together.

- **Project threats**: If your decision logic leads you to a project threat decision path, there are some risks inherent to any project, regardless of whether it's a new solution or an upgrade to an existing solution. The risks that you should include in this particular logic are as follows:
  - **When was security brought in**?: The earlier that security is involved in a project, the lower the risk will be simply because security will be tied into everything and there's less chance of missing something. I like to tie the risk levels in association with a PMO waterfall gating process.
  - **Who is running the end solution**?: Is the solution being run by a trusted partner/someone in-house? If so, the risk will be lower than if the solution is being run by an unknown entity.
  - **What is the complexity of the project**?: The more complex the project, the higher the security risk (not to mention architecture and business risks). I use ranges indicating the dollars spent but you can use things like the number of systems touched or some other measurement.

After you have looked at these variables and added them, you need to decide if the project is about a net new solution or an upgrade to an existing solution. They will take you into different decision boxes. An upgrade should be a safer situation than a brand-new solution but you still have to consider what those changes will entail.

Once you have thought about the risks that just have a project to deal with, you need to think about the actual project-specific security risks. They are logically grouped as architecture threats because they are changes to the architecture that create security risks rather than risks to the delivery of the project. There are three logical groupings of architecture threats: those for new solutions, those for upgrading solutions, and those for existing solutions that aren't being changed (that is, looking at existing solutions to understand their risk levels):

- **New solution threats**: A new solution will typically have seven areas that you should consider in your overall threat model:
    - **How are users provisioned?**: Are they done automatically? Through the helps desk? Manually by the solution team?
    - **What's the authentication mechanism?**: Break this down for either internally facing or externally facing. If both, because both sets of users will use it, take the highest risk level.
    - **Number of roles involved?**: If there are a high number of roles, there's a greater risk of misalignment of the users of the system.
    - **If there's an application, is it client/server-based or web-based?**: Remember, while web-based applications are easier and simpler to create and integrate with, client/server solutions can be more secure.
    - **Are elevated privileges needed to run?**: Some solutions have to run using elevated privileges and this can provide a way to jump from one component to another.
    - **Is there an external database?**: An external database provides two areas for risk; there are more components and the information itself is now a target. The database will end up having to be protected.
    - **Is there a QA, test/dev, both, or neither planned?**: The existence of a non-production environment will add one type of risk (for example, traffic from test/dev could impact production traffic), whereas the lack of a non-production environment could mean a different risk (for example, a poorly designed and implemented solution).

- **Upgrading threats**: Upgrading a solution means change, and change can carry risks, so consider some of the things that the upgrade may change, but also limit your RIA to just the components that are changing. If the areas asked about aren't changed in the solution, give them a zero value:
    - **How are the users provisioned?**: Just as with a new solution, there are risks associated with how a user is provisioned.
    - **Does this version have new core functionality?**: New functionality means new potential risks.
    - **Does the version include upgraded server versions?**: If the server has to change, then everything on the server can be impacted.
    - **Does the version include changes to the backend infrastructure?**: Are you changing from a server with the database included to a solution with a server and a standalone database? Or are some other backend components changing?
    - **Does this version have changes to authentication?**: Changes to authentication will impact risk.
    - **Does this version have changes to network infrastructure?**: Are you moving security zones? Changing VLANs?
    - **Does this version include moving to a new data center or service provider?**: If you are changing where the solution resides, you will have big risk changes. Think about what happens when you move from an on-premise solution to a cloud solution.
    - **Is there a QA, test/dev, both, or neither planned?**: Changes to production means changes to non-production environments. What impacts will those have?

- **Existing system threats**: There will be times where you may not understand an existing solution's threat levels. It may be a legacy solution or one that grew organically into place. Regardless of how it got there, you'll want to evaluate it. I like to look at it from three points of view; the governance processes in place, the organizational controls in place, and the technical controls in place. Remember, your organization has already accepted the risk of these solutions so, now you want to just understand quickly whether you need to look into it in more detail:
    - **Level of device management processes**: How well are the components managed? Think from an ITIL point of view.
    - **Level of security oversight processes**: How well is security reviewing the components?

- **Compliance with corporate policies**: Do you even know if the solution meets corporate policies? If you do know, how well do they meet them?

- **Key personnel dependency**: Is the solution dependent on one person? What happens if that person leaves? Or is a group looking after the solution?

- **Security roles and responsibilities defined?**: Sometimes, security isn't even involved in a solution. Is there an oversight? If not, how do you know when a security issue arises?

- **Likelihood of device failure?**: Even today, I still run into systems running on old operating systems or systems that are vastly under-designed from a resources point of view and a good sneeze could cause the solution to fall over.

- **Level of redundancy for the system?**: If the solution fails, is there redundancy in place? Is it active/passive? Or, even better, active/active?

- **Is there a DR plan in place?**: Is this solution included in the DR plan? Does it even need to be?

- **Are there levels of security controls in place?**: From a technical point of view, are there technical security components in place? Are the logs being sent to the SIEM? Is there AV, change management, and other security solutions involved?

You've now looked at the individual solution and the risks involved. But, from an architectural point of view, there's one more thing to look at. What happens if the solution fails, from the point of view from other solutions? Or, what happens to this solution if a different solution fails? In other words, there should be the following questions?:

- **Will this solution work without other systems?**: You are now asking if the solution will work without other solutions or, if those other solutions disappeared right now, whether the solution will continue working. An example might be a virtual server farm. If the ESX was to fail, would your solution still work? If you are built on virtual servers, probably not. But if you are on physical servers, it'll probably still work. Or is there a different application that your application is receiving feeds from? If the different application is no longer receivable, will your application still run?

- **Are there systems dependent on your solution?**: With this question, you need to factor in the criticality of the other system. A high criticality system dependency will impact the requirements on your solution to perform; otherwise, you may end up with a cascading risk level.

Okay, you've figured out the likelihood of the threat to occur by adding up the values from all your questions to this point. Most people use a RIA scale associated with low/medium/high, so try to put the range your scores can be into some range system associated with low/medium/high, and make sure your scores adequately reflect the risks associated with those individual areas. Once you have your scores, move on to the impact measurement.

Likelihood and Impact are two different things and, when combined, will give you your risk levels. So keep your impact scores separate from your likelihood scores so that you can properly measure your risk:

(RISK = Likelihood X Impact).

In the preceding diagram, impact is shown as a "consequence of threat".

If you were to talk to a chief risk officer, they will typically tell you that there are five different consequence areas. Break them down into ranges, just like with your likelihood questions, so that you can measure what the actual impact will be. There will be times where the threats will create numerous impacts (for example, if a utility has a power outage, there will be a risk to safety as well as a reputational loss). Take the highest impact and use that as your consequence measurement.

The five areas that will provide a consequence if a threat was to actually occur are as follows:

- **Risk to safety**: If your system was to fail, will someone be in danger or at risk of injury? For some industries, this is definitely the case.
- **Risk to the environment**: If your system fails, will there be an impact to the environment? How long will the impact last? To what extent will the damage harm the environment?
- **Risk of financial loss**: If your system fails, will there be money lost? A lot of businesses have applications critical to the financial health of the business. What will that impact be?
- **Risk of reputational loss**: If you were the **Democratic National Committee (DNC)**, don't you think their reputation took a hit as a result of the Russian hack of their systems? They didn't lose money but, boy, did their reputation take a hit.

- **Risk of availability**: In some industries, not having a system available will result in a huge impact. For example, if an airline's systems are shut down, they may not lose money, but they definitely won't make money. The same goes with the network associated with banks' ATMs. People expect those systems to be available all the time.

Give each one of these consequence types a range of possible results and then score them. The end result is a way to measure consequences. Talk to your chief risk officer to see if they have a risk matrix (assuming you have a chief risk officer). Then, give your scores based on that.

Final measurement of risk

Once you have the consolidated measurements of the likelihood of threat and of the impact of the threat, you are at the point where you can assign an actual risk level. Most organizations use low, medium, and high for measuring risk levels, although you can have measurements in between, such as low-medium or a larger range of measurements, such as extreme or negligible.

Take the ranges that you have from the lowest possible all the way to the highest possible and determine where the cut-off points are for each level. Then, again, using your decision tree logic, just create a table that should look something like this:

		Likelihood of Threat		
		Low	Medium	High
Impact of Threat	Low	Low	Low-Medium	Medium
	Medium	Low-Medium	Medium	Medium-High
	High	Medium	Medium-High	High

You then take the individual risk measurements (shown in grey in the table) and create your mitigation priorities around them, including when you put these risks in your risk register, which drives your strategies and program initiatives.

Now you have a way of measuring your risk that is both automated (if you put the logic into a spreadsheet or a SharePoint site or some other tool) and has the personal biases removed. Work the scoring system as well as the logic through with your major shareholders so that they understand how it works and then, once you have agreement from everyone, you only have to show the user interface to people and they can all understand how your organization views the risks that they want to identify.

Whitepapers

Whitepapers are a device that enterprise security architects use to communicate thoughts and ideas. They aren't really structured, but they are a useful means of communication and, remember, an architect's role is all about communication. Some of the things that you'll want to create whitepapers on might be the following:

- **Research on a technology**: I've written a number of whitepapers on various topics that helped clarify my thoughts on the various topics that I wanted to communicate. When cloud started to become of interest, I wanted to provide some guidance as to what I thought so I did research and wrote a position paper that I provided to my clients. I did the same for IPv6 when I was doing work for the utilities because, with the sheer volume of devices that were involved in utilities (utilities that deal with smart meter/smart grid technologies literally have millions of devices that they have to connect to), it pointed to IPv6. But IPv6 hasn't really been a standard that many people have worked with, so there needed to be a way of communicating the security issues and ways to deal with those issues.

- **Review of a vendor's products**: There are times when you want to provide a security review of a product, but your organization isn't at the stage that they want to do a vendor selection. For example, maybe there's a new product out on the market that someone on the business side is interested in but want a quick review prior to a more in-depth look at it. A whitepaper is a very useful way to document your thoughts. In this case, you are looking at the pros and cons of a specific product without looking at the requirements or comparing the product to a different vendor's product. You could almost think of this the way you would read an article in your favorite security magazine that is reviewing a product, just without being provided by the vendor itself.

- **Integration of security into a solution**: When there's a project that is being considered at the initiation stage of your PMO processes, often, you will be asked for your initial thoughts on the project and how security should be integrated into the entire process. This isn't with respect to doing a **risk impact assessment (RIA)** but, rather, an architectural comment on security technologies and how they should be put into a solution.

- **Vendor suite commentary**: Different companies have different approaches to selecting a solution for their organization. Most of the time, organizations will take a best of breed approach to selecting a product, but there are times when organizations will want to take a best suite approach. This is useful from a business perspective because you can lower your total cost of ownership by buying in bulk, minimize the amount of internal bureaucracy involved in licensing and managing products, and the integration of products should be much smoother than trying to get products from different vendors to work together, so a whitepaper with a review of a vendor's entire suite can be useful for communicating thoughts.

Whitepapers themselves typically have different structures and formats, depending on what you are writing on. When you write them, try to take the approach of looking at the different areas of a solution (people, process, technology, and governance) and commenting on each one of them.

Evaluation of the current state

There's an entire section on determining the current state of your organization's security architecture in `Chapter 4`, *Cybersecurity Architecture Strategy*, because it's a base activity when you are looking at your security architecture strategy. So if you want more details, go to that chapter.

That said, there will be times when you need to get a handle on the current state and it's not associated with your strategy creation. Sometimes, you'll get a new CISO that comes onboard and they want to understand exactly what the current state security posture is so that *they* can create their strategies. In that case, having a current state assessment in a standalone state is useful.

Summary

There are a number of activities that an enterprise security architect has to get involved in at the strategy and program levels. These activities drive the direction that the organization is going to move in from a security perspective, so it's really important to have a handle on them. Remember that the role of the security architect is to communicate and each of these deliverables is a way of communicating some specific area within your strategy or program. This is especially important when you move to the next level, the security architecture activities associated with project delivery, as discussed in the next chapter.

Questions

1. What is the best way to approach creating a key decision document (KDD)?
2. What are the different types of risk?
3. Why would you want to have a fixed score decision tree for RIAs?
4. What is the purpose of a whitepaper?

6
Security Architecture in Waterfall Projects

So far, this book has covered the security architect's activities in the governance layer and in the strategic (or program) layer. However, the vast majority of work that a security architect does is performed in the project delivery layer.

The project delivery layer is where all of the projects are delivered, regardless of whether they are security projects. They might be technology-based, or they might just be changes in processes and roles. The project delivery layer is where security architects mainly get involved.

This is where your security architecture gets put into place, one tactical effort at a time. This is where the actual security posture of your organization is directly impacted with an immediacy that is not found in strategies or governance. The other two layers can take years to impact the organization. The project delivery layer will impact your organization the moment it is moved into production (and, in some cases, even earlier than that).

This chapter will be all about the delivery of IT projects and how important the different phases, are from a security architect's perspective. The following chapter will look at how to deliver specific artifacts, but this chapter will also look at the project delivery process as a whole, as well as the security architect's involvement in the different phases.

Overview of waterfall project delivery

The vast majority of projects are delivered by using the traditional waterfall methodology. This methodology was originally introduced in the manufacturing and construction industries where there are **Bills of Materials** (**BoMs**) and a need to move in a linear path. For example, when you are building a home, you can't really pour concrete foundations, construct the wall frames, and install roofing, all at the same time.

You need to move in a linear progression. This is actually one of the reasons that I believe the IT industry is following in the footsteps of the building industry which might indicate the future of security architects (more on this in the last chapter of this book).

There are a number of pros and cons associated with the waterfall methodology. On the pro side, the waterfall methodology is very logical and provides a step-by-step approach to delivering a project. With this methodology, you are able to separate tasks logically and build on each phase, while at the same time ensure that phases are properly executed by using approval gates.

The downside, however, is that the waterfall methodology can provide an opportunity for numerous groups to put in their own requirements to get past gates and; as a result, it can take quite a long time to go through, relatively speaking. Something that is long and provides an obvious governance approach is a magnet for people to put in their own controls. That's why the Agile methodology has taken off: it provides a much quicker approach to delivering a project, and you can see results very quickly. There are a lot of downsides to Agile, as well; they will be dealt with at the end of the chapter.

The waterfall methodology is so well understood that it's a natural progression for anyone delivering projects. The Agile methodology will be commented on at the end of this chapter, but the current focus here will be the waterfall methodology.

Depending on the organization or website you are looking at, there are typically six phases in a project. Those phases are shown in the following diagram:

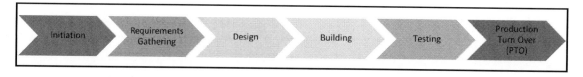

- **Initiation phase**: This is where the projects are initiated and get approval to move forward
- **Requirement gathering phase**: As the name suggests, this is where requirements are gathered
- **Design phase**: Here, the design is put together for the end solution
- **Building phase**: The building phase is where you start to put the various components of the solution together
- **Testing phase**: Here you can test the solution that you built, and look for any issues that need to be dealt with
- **Production Turnover (PTO)**: Don't forget that your solution needs to be put into the hands of people that will have to maintain and sustain it

In the typical waterfall methodology, each phase is separated by a gating process. This is where the primary stakeholders and governance bodies look at how a project is going and indicate whether the project can move to the next phase. This is a great way to keep an eye on a project, control costs, and enforce governance requirements. But the act of gating a project can also insert unnecessary delays allowing for the addition of bureaucratic requirements into each phase. One of the reasons why so many people avoid the waterfall methodology is that it can take a long time and, in this day and age, patience is not everyone's virtue. Time is money, after all, and the longer it takes to deliver a project, the higher the cost to actually deliver it (and the higher the likelihood that the business unit that is sponsoring the IT project will find some form of shadow IT solution that bypasses the IT department, creating all sorts of security issues.)

Here's the thing: from a security architecture perspective, we have a vested interest in making sure things are done right. Business may want to move quickly but they may not understand the costs of doing quickly. There have been a number of research papers written on when defects and issues are often created (that is, during *which* phase of the waterfall methodology) and what the cost is to fix them. What they found the later that the defects are found, the higher the cost to fix them is.

First, let's look at what phase the issues or defects are introduced into the waterfall process. The following diagram focuses on software development but works just as well for infrastructure. It breaks down where the issues are and what the costs are to fix those issues:

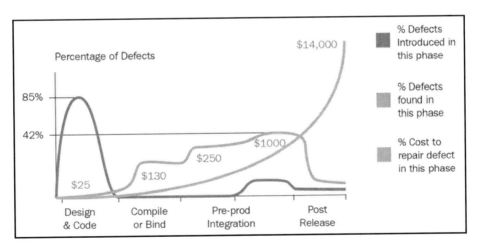

If you look at the purple line, you will see that most issues are introduced at the design stage but that most defects are found way later at the pre-production stage, just before the solution is put into production. The result: the longer it takes to find an issue, the higher the cost.

The following table breaks down the cost to fix a defect versus the cost that was spent in creating it in the first place (the ratio of fixing versus creating the defect). What you see is that the costs keep going up, the later you find the issue:

Phase in which defects are found	Cost Ratio
Requirements	1
Design	4
Coding	10
System/Integration Testing	15-40
User Acceptance Testing	30-70
Operation	40-1000

Most issues arise because the requirement gathering phase was not done properly. I can't tell you how many times I've seen projects where the requirements are five or six points. This book detailed the collection of requirements in the strategy chapter and will go into greater depth in the next chapter when it comes to gathering requirements for projects.

In short, if you are going to do anything well, make sure that it's the gathering of requirements. The better you perform that task, the more successful your project will be.

In all of the phases in the waterfall methodology, iterative approach that needs to occur. Most people think that each phase is isolated by the gates at the end of each phase and, to some degree, they are. But an architecture is never stable until the solution is turned over to the production team. Also, notice that we are talking about architecture and not design. That is because design is only one component of an architecture.

An architecture is made up of all of the phases, design being only one of them:

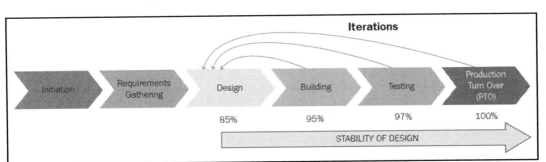

When you initially create your design (in the design stage), it is typically around 85% stable. That is because, no matter how hard you try to find all the information that you can, you won't find everything. When you do your build, you will find issues that will change your design. The changes may not be very large, but you will still find them. This will bring your design to 95% stability.

The same will occur when you get to testing your solution. You'll have your test scripts and plans, but something will be discovered. Not much will be found, but still there will be something. That will, yet again, result in a change to your design, and it will bring the solution to, let's say, 97% stability.

Finally, when hand the solution over to production and the operations teams, those teams may ask about some aspect of the solution. This will result in one last change to the design. Maybe it will just be a role name change, or maybe the inclusion of a device. Regardless of the change, once the solution is handed over to production, you will see the end result of a 100% stable solution.

Now, notice where the iterations always go back to? They go back to the design stage. You should never be changing your requirements. If a new requirement comes along, then put it into a new phase. Once you are past the requirement gathering phase, you need to put a stake in the ground and say that those are the requirements that you are designing for. If you have missed requirements, or if new requirements come along, that means you didn't do a good enough job gathering your requirements. Successful requirement gathering will result in a successful project.

One other thing: the Enterprise Security Architect in me cringes every time a Project Manager de-scopes requirements because of costs associated with the project or because timelines are running long. This was commented on in the strategy chapter but it bears repeating here. Ignoring requirements on a specific project will impact strategies moving forward. It will cause a cascade effect in the ability to deliver other projects and may impact the ability to support business goals (assuming that you have created strategies that support the direction of the business). So, really push back when a Project Manager wants to de-scope requirements. They are focused on one thing, and one thing only: completing a project. They are not focused on the overarching strategy.

I highly recommend that you work with the project management office to get security built into their processes, so that for passing any gate. Don't let it wait for the individual projects, because you'll then have to fight the same battle every time a project gets initiated, and that can get risky.

The difference between the Solution Architect and Supporting Architect

Now that you have an understanding of the waterfall methodology and how it works holistically, you need to understand that the security architect will be involved in projects in two fundamentally different ways.

The first is the obvious way, and that's as the Solution Architect. When the project that is being put together is focused on a security solution, typically, the solution architect is a security architect. This doesn't just mean that the security architect has to look at risk. This also means that the security architect has to be able to go through the waterfall methodology and deliver the various artifacts associated with delivering a solution, and some of those will have nothing to do with security.

For example, suppose that the project is about putting a **Security Incident and Event Monitoring (SIEM)** solution. While the solution itself is focused on delivering reports on security events that are occurring within your organization, that solution still needs to sit on a network and that means understanding VLANs, IP addressing, and the impacts on firewalls and network traffic. Your solution will typically be put onto a server of some sort. That means you'll have to understand the underlying operating systems, as well as how your organization will support and maintain the OS, and there may be a desire to integrate your solution with some other solution. That means there will be a need to understand XML or APIs and how they work with.

Remember that implementing a solution is not just about security. The end goal may be to support a security strategy, but the activities associated with a security project are not just about risk management.

That brings us to the other way that security architects get involved in project delivery, and that is when the security architect is supporting the solution architect. If you look at all the things that the solution architect has to deal with, it's important to understand that there's no way that a solution architect can be an expert in all areas. They get very familiar with the different architecture towers but they aren't the SMEs in those areas. As the security architect that is supporting the solution architect, you can expect the solution architect to view you as the SME.

At this point, the security architect is expected to provide guidance to the solution architect, as well as to the entire project, from a security perspective. Some organizations may have security analysts providing support, but those types of roles are coming to a project from a risk management perspective rather than an architecture point of view. This can be a limitation because the tendency is to then tell the solution architect what they CANNOT do rather than providing them guidance on the best way of doing something. The security architect that is supporting a project should be looking at things from a holistic point of view, which includes but is not limited to risk mitigation.

Typically, you will have a **Project Manager** (**PM**) that is assigned to the project to own the delivery of the project. This typically results in a person with limited solutioning capability making decisions on all aspects of a project. Most of the projects that have success tend to have build a partnership between the PM and the solution architect. In those situations, the PM owns the business processes (including the administration activities) associated with a project and the Solution Architect owns the solution. Together, those two roles can create a really dynamic team that can get a lot of things done. But, there will often be a PM that views themselves as the manager and top dog in a project. The two roles can actually end up reporting to different areas in an organization: the PM reporting to the PMO group, and the solution architect reporting to the enterprise architecture group. My recommendation is to make sure that you clearly define the roles, and make sure that the PM knows that you are their partner and not their underling. That said, it all depends on how your organization has set up the roles.

There are two different approaches to delivering a project: one as a solution security architect and one as a supporting security architect. If you want a diagram that lays out the different things that a security architect does in each phase, make use of the following. The artifacts in each phase will be dealt with in the following sections:

	Project Delivery					
	Initiation	**Requirements**	**Design**	**Build**	**Test**	**PTO**
Support Role:	- Current Risk Project is mitigating - Alignment w/ Strategy	- Security Architecture Requirements (Policy/Std/Infra based)	- Recommended Sec. Infra. to use - SDA - Security Principles (to Soln. Arch) - Applicable Security Policies/Stds (to Soln. Arch) - Security Test Plan (to PM)	- Integration support - Validation of build against Sec. Arch.	- Validation of Vulnerability Scan, Whitebox/Blackbox testing - interpreting for Project	- Validation of Build documentation going to Security Operations
Solution Architect	- Project Arch. Risk Register	- Requirements Documentation - RTM	- Vendor Selection - Solution Architecture - KDD - mapping to RTM - Test Plan	- Build Documentation - Implementation in Test/Dev	- Test - Validate against Arch. - Correct Arch./Build Based on findings	-Build Documentation - Test Results - Architecture component of PTO docs.

Initiation phase

The initiation phase is when a project is approved to move forward and is provided the appropriate level of funding to move to the next gate. Most waterfall methodologies tie the funds for the project to the gates that are passed. But at the initiation phase of a project, the governance associated with the project will define what the scope of the project is, defining the budgets and providing a very high-level thought process on design.

That last part can be really troublesome because there is a tendency to pick a solution or a product, then initiate a project to implement that solution. While a project initiated this way can have some success, defining a solution BEFORE a project has even begun is often a template for trouble.

Most of the activities in the initiation phase will belong to the Project Manager. They will have to put together budgets, find the appropriate resources, and create project documents such as project charters. You, as the Security Architect, need to influence those activities in order to ensure that security is baked into the entire project process. If you can get ties into any initiation phase meetings, that will allow you to create a relationship with the Project Managers. Just like Architects, the vast majority of Project Managers are brought in as contractors and, as a result, they are trying to get things done as quickly as possible. If you don't set up a relationship right at the beginning, you will have a very high risk of a project being delivered without security architecture involvement.

In terms of the security architect's activities in the initiation phase, there are typically three things that you need to deal with:

- **Defining the project risk mitigation**: Regardless of what role you are playing in a project (solution architect or supporting architect), you need to identify the risks that the project is going to have to deal with from an architecture point of view. Don't get pulled into the project risk conversation because that is owned by the PM. Look at the project charter and you'll get a handle on what the potential architecture risks are. Document those risks and provide them to the PM and Solution Architect so that they understand the things that you want them to keep an eye on. Some organizations have predefined **Risk Impact Assessments (RIAs)** that are started at this stage. The best RIAs are not completed until the project is completed simply because, like a design, risks can change as the project goes along.

- **Alignment of project architecture with strategy**: Remember, no project is implemented in a vacuum. If the enterprise architecture group is doing their job, all projects should be used to move the organization in the direction of the overarching architecture strategy. And you, as the security architect, need to ensure that your project is supporting the enterprise security architecture strategy. Make sure that the scope and direction of the project align, even if the project itself is not a security project. This can be a great way of moving the strategy along, without getting dedicated funds. If you are the supporting security architect, provide the solution architect with the appropriate security architecture strategy information. And if you are the Solution Security Architect, you are responsible for ensuring that the direction of the project supports the strategy.

- **Project architecture risk register**: Remember that RIA from two bullets ago? Well, you will want to make sure that the individual risks are documented in the project risk register, as well as the requirements that are needed to mitigate those risks. For example, if the project is associated with connecting with a cloud vendor, you know that there will be data in flight risks. Document them and make sure the solution architect knows what is expected. The risk register itself is a great way to start gathering security architecture requirements for the next phase.

One last thing about the initiation phase. This is the one phase of a project where architecture is typically left out of the conversation, regardless of which tower. A good Chief Architect will make sure they are part of the governance body that reviews and approves projects moving forward so that they can influence the direction for ALL architecture strategies.

But the PMO will view the delivery of projects as their area of expertise and, as a result, won't include architecture in the initiation of a project. That can be a mistake and can cause trouble down the road. As the security architect, you need to make sure you are involved in a project as early as possible, and your organization should know that you want to be involved even before projects get approval to move forward.

Requirement gathering phase

The requirement gathering phase is the most important phase of a project. Bar none. Don't question this statement. If you don't do the requirement gathering properly, your solution isn't going to meet the needs of ALL the stakeholders and there is a very high risk that the project won't be successful. Success should be defined as a solution that fully meets the needs of the stakeholders and 80% of the capabilities of the solution are being used.

Many projects implement a solution, and then the end users don't use the solution, or only a small percentage of the capabilities are leveraged. We have all seen organizations that have a solution that has been implemented but no one uses it. I had a client that wanted to implement a **Data Loss Prevention** (**DLP**) solution because they were concerned about documents making their way out of the organization. I reached out to similar companies to find out whether they had implemented DLP solutions, and what lessons they learned so that we could figure out the best way to move forward.

It turned out that the companies that tried to implement DLP either couldn't get it implemented, took far longer than expected to get it implemented, or once it was implemented, never made use of it. This was a situation where the concept was great but the majority of stakeholders didn't want it. Sure, the CISO wanted the technology. But remember that security supports the business and if the business doesn't want it, it won't be used. It's kind of like when you decide to buy a hot tub for your backyard. Sure, you use the hot tub a few times at the beginning but, by the end, it's not used and becomes an eyesore. You've spent your money on something that is never used. Maybe you could have used the money better elsewhere.

The example of DLP is a clear case where someone fell in love with a trendy technology without looking at the requirements. In simplistic terms, they wanted to make sure that sensitive documents didn't leave the organization. They didn't want a DLP solution, they wanted control over documents. When you look at the requirements properly, you end up finding the proper solution.

This story also is something that you really have to be aware of when it comes to projects, especially ones that are back at the initiation phase. There are too many projects that have been initiated because someone fell in love with a shiny new toy. We all do it. Just look at your cell phone. Why do you have the most recent version, when an older version would probably meet your needs just fine? It's because we get hooked by the marketing, or a sales person does a really good job.

Remember back in the governance chapter when we discussed the **Security Architecture Guidance** (**SAG**) document? Well, this is where it comes in. When you are talking with a solution architect or the PM of a non-security project, you'll want to give them the SAG so that they have some understanding of the things that you'll be looking for in your requirements.

For the requirement gathering phase, there are two different types of activity that the security architect has to perform, depending on whether they are the supporting security architect or the solution security architect. Those three activities are as follows:

- **Provide security architecture requirements**: If you are the supporting security architect, the solution architect should be asking you want to have as the security requirements. You should be able to review the charter and then provide the appropriate security policies and standards, as well as the appropriate infrastructure that needs to be put into place in support of those policies and standards. For example, if they want to use a cloud solution, then you may want them to make use of your federation infrastructure rather than let accounts be set up as standalone roles in the solution. This will allow you to make sure that the deletion of accounts is done in the time frames laid out in your policies. You'll probably have a requirement that the security logs of the solution are forwarded to the SIEM. These are costs that are part of the project and they have to pay for them. You'll have the infrastructure already in place but the incremental costs will have to be handled by the projects themselves.

- **Requirements documentation**: If you are the solution security architect, you will need to collect the requirements for the project and those requirements will be larger in scope than security requirements. Using the implementation of an SIEM as an example, your organization may have a standard operating system they want to use for support reasons. Or, they may want to ensure that system management software is installed on all infrastructure. Or, support personnel may be located at a third party, so those roles will need to have administrative rights for the underlying infrastructure. If you gather your requirements and you only have five or six requirements, then you haven't done your job right. Oh, and make sure that you talk with the people that are going to be maintaining and supporting the solution. Too many operations groups aren't talked to when it comes to a project and, as a result, the cost to support a solution is much higher than it needs to be.

- **Requirement traceability matrix**: Requirements are not something that you do once and then put away and forget. Requirements should flow through your entire project and be something that you can ensure is being met with every artifact that you create. To do that, you create what is called a **Requirement Traceability Matrix (RTM)**. The RTM is basically just the individual name of the requirement and a checklist for each following project phase deliverable. You use the RTM to make sure that the design document has met all the requirements. You use the RTM to make sure that the build meets the requirements. Testing is measured against the requirements. And, at the end of the project, you should be able to point to the implemented solution and say, without a doubt, how the requirements were met. While the **Architecture Design Document (ADD)** is the most important artifact that a security architect will create, the RTM is the document most used by the person in the role of security architect.

We will go into more detail on the process of gathering requirements in the next chapter. Make sure to really follow that section because it's the most important thing you can do as a security architect. Just remember that all requirements are driven by business requirements, including the security requirements.

Design phase

The design phase is where most smaller organizations automatically jump to. The inexperienced architect will bypass the requirements phase and then implement a solution on the fly. And, quite honestly, there's a tendency in the industry to ask what the value of the architect is because of how much longer it takes to implement solutions. But there's doing things quickly and doing things properly. Sure, it may feel like things are done quickly but how much time was spent going back to change designs, or backing out of solutions that had unintended consequences or had costs that weren't thought of?

The design phase is probably where the most effort is put in by the architect. If you look at the following diagram, you'll see that the effort of the architect peaks in the design phase and then tails off over the rest of the project:

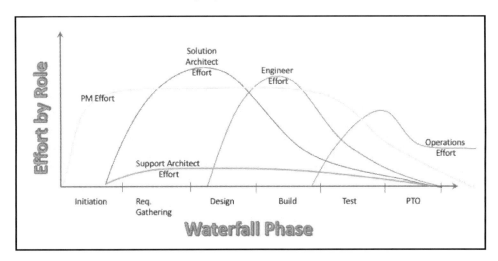

This is because the architect role will shift to one of oversight and you'll want to make sure that the design you've put together is implemented as expected. You'll also have to adjust the design as you go along as different issues come up to drive the design to one that is more stable.

For the design phase, it's really important that you are involved in the design early if you are the supporting security architect. You want to provide your input as the Solution Architect puts together their design because it's a lot more conducive to teamwork if you adjust the design as it's created, rather than waiting until it's completed and then telling the solution architect to change something.

An appropriate metaphor for this would be for the solution architect to fire an arrow at a target and for you to run along beside it, continuously nudging it until it strikes the target dead center. The end result is exactly as you like, rather than letting the solution architect shoot the arrow without the benefit of knowing where the target is in the first place.

In this phase, the security architect can expect to deal with the following deliverables, depending on what type of role you are performing.

For the supporting security architect, Because the supporting security architect is focused more on the security technologies and components of the solution, the following are components that should be made ready for the Solution Architect:

- **Recommended security infrastructure**: As with the requirement gathering phase, you want to make sure that the solution architect has all the information that they need associated with the security infrastructure that you want that person to use. If you said in the requirement gathering stage that they have to use the federation solution for authentication to the cloud, in the design phase you want to give the solution architect the exact information that you have associated with the federation solution. Then it will get included, in detail, in the design.

- **Security Design Assessment (SDA)**: Unfortunately, you will have quite a few instances where you won't get pulled into the design process early. This happens especially often for projects initiated by a business unit that wants to do things quickly, without understanding what might occur as a result. The SDA is the supporting security architect's way of reviewing the design, after it's been created, and providing recommended changes. This will add time to project delivery if done after the design is completed, whereas working with the Solution Architect from the beginning will actually speed the process up. See the difference? The next chapter will go into the SDA process and templates in more depth.

- **Security principles**: Not to be confused with security policies and standards, principles are the way you view a solution. The governance section talked about security architecture principles in depth, but in the design phase you want to give them to the Solution Architect so that they understand the approach that you would like them to take.

- **Applicable security policies and standards**: You already gave the security policies and standards in the requirement gathering phase. In the design phase, you'll want to make sure that the policies and standards are actually being designed into the solution.

For the solution security architect: These are probably artifacts that are included in your PMO process. But, in case you aren't aware of them, these are typically what the solution security architect has to deliver. Remember that this is for the entire solution, not just the security aspects:

- **Vendor selection**: If the project has been initiated properly, you have gathered requirements and then will look for a vendor or product that meets those requirements. Unfortunately, projects are often initiated to implement a solution that has already been decided on. The vendor selection process will be reviewed in depth in the next chapter but, in short, you want to take the requirements that you have gathered and then put them out to a group of vendors for response (often referred to as responding to a **Requirement For Purchase** (RFP)). Once you have the vendor's responses to the requirements, you can filter the vendors to those that most closely match your requirements and invite them to do a bake-off (actually implement a proof of concept in your QA environment) or a presentation if you don't have the appropriate QA environment. The end result will be a solution that should, in theory, be close to matching your requirements. The intent is to get past a sales person's presentation and get to the meat of the solution.

- **Architecture Design Document (ADD)**: The solution architecture document will be reviewed in depth with its own chapter, but the ADD is the most important artifact that the security architect, acting as a solution architect, can create. It communicates the solution that you are proposing to all parties involved, whether the stakeholders, the governance body, the operations teams, or the actual engineers that put the components into place. It has all the detail that will be needed to actually put the solution in place and, at the end of the day, should be able to stand on its own without you being around. It is to the Solution Architect what a set of blueprints is to the Building Architect.

- **Key Decision Document (KDD)**: The KDD was described in the strategy chapter. In the case of project delivery, you make use of the KDD for major decisions in the project itself. Where the KDD is covered in the strategy chapter for dealing with strategic decisions, the KDD in project delivery activities is used for more tactical activities. For example, once you've selected your vendor, you'll want to write a KDD describing the options that were available and then why you chose that particular vendor. The KDD for project delivery will be covered in more depth in the next chapter.

- **Mapping to requirements**: Whatever phase you are in, you need to pull out your **Requirements Traceability Matrix (RTM)** and make sure the design is mapped back to the requirements. This ensures that you are continuously keeping in mind what it is that you have to meet. Think of the requirements as the report card you are measured against, and the RTM the way you track each one of your test marks on the way to a perfect grade.
- **Test plan**: The next phase after the design phase is the build phase, followed by the test phase. So, you'd think that the test plan would be created in the build phase. And in many organizations, that is when it is created. The test plan is in the design phase with this approach, simply because the design will start to indicate what exactly should be tested in order to ensure a successful implementation of the design. It will be expanded as you go through the build phase with tests specific to the infrastructure put into place, but you should start creating your test plan in the design phase.

Build phase

Different organizations have different definitions and views of the security architect. Some view the security architect as a role that is all about tracking risk through a project, regardless of which phase the project is in. Some organizations view the security architect as the person that will design a solution, and then provide oversight of the implementation of the solution. And some organizations view the security architect as the role that will design as well as build the solution.

There are pros and cons for each role definition. The skill level that is associated with the tracking of risk through a project probably isn't nearly as high as the role that needs to actually design something. It's easier to criticize something than it is to design and build something. Often, organizations will have Security Analysts performing the **Risk Impact Assessments (RIAs)** on projects for each phase, whereas they will have security architects in place to deal with actual design needs.

Having the security architect design and build a solution can ensure that the design is understood by the person that is implementing it. After all, if the security architect doesn't understand their own design, they are going to be in trouble. But there's a separation of duties that you want to maintain, even in the building of a solution—not to mention that the operations groups typically don't like someone not of their own group actually putting hands on their equipment.

In the build phase, the security architect is primarily focused on making sure that the design is implemented as intended, regardless of whether they are the solution security architect or the supporting security architect. So, based on that, the following are the activities or artifacts that the security architect will be involved in during the build phase.

For the supporting security architect: In the build phase, the supporting security architect is focused on ensuring that the security components in the design phase are actually implemented as approved. As a result, the following are the focus for the Supporting Security Architect:

- **Integration support**: This is the type of activity in which the security architect is helping actually integrate the solution with the recommended security infrastructure. While the security infrastructure is already in place, there is always going to be some sort of gotcha that needs to be worked out.
- **Security architecture validation**: Every solution should have security built in. In the build phase, the supporting security architect should be checking to ensure that the security architecture components are actually being put into place, regardless of whether it's security infrastructure or some other architecture tower that has security built in (for example, network security zones are network architecture, not security infrastructure).

For the solution security architect: The solution security architect, on the other hand, has to make sure that all components, not just the security components, are implemented properly. The following activities are performed as a result:

- **Build documentation**: When the solution is actually built out, there needs to be build documentation that specifically details what is in place and where. While the **Architecture Design Document** (**ADD**) will often have all this detail, there are times where the ADD will be a little higher level and the build documentation is something that will detail every IP address, VLAN, and account that is used in the solution. It's provided to the operations groups so that they know exactly what has been put into place and where.
- **Test/dev implementation**: While you'll want to have the actual solution put into place by the engineers for the appropriate operations groups, you'll first want to test out the design in your test/dev environment. This will allow you to learn about the implementation, and what things you may have forgotten in your actual design. This will be done by the solution security architect for a full understanding of the solution.

- **Production implementation oversight**: When you are ready to have your solution implemented in production, you'll want to be working closely with the operations teams as they implement your design. They will have questions and there will be coordination that needs to occur. The PM isn't the appropriate person to coordinate these activities, because they typically won't have the technical expertise to understand what order things should occur in. That's your job. So, make sure that you are working closely with each operations team to ensure that they have the information that they need to implement your design.

Testing phase

In the testing phase, your solution should be 95% stable and you are now testing it to see if it's actually meeting all the requirements gathered back in the requirement gathering phase. Back in the design phase, one of the artifacts that you created as the solution security architect should have been the test plan (which was driven by the requirements gathered). That test plan will have been adjusted as the solution was being built, based on changes to the design. At this phase, you are now making use of the test plan itself.

In security, we typically think of testing from a security point of view, and that's a correct way of thinking—if you're the supporting security architect. But if you are the solution security architect, you want to make sure that the solution will support the demand that is placed on it. You don't want to just put something in place that doesn't scale and that after one year, you have to start changing. So, keep in mind that there are different types of testing that you need to deal with.

From the supporting security architect point of view, you may not be the person that is running a vulnerability scanner such as Nessus or Qualys on the end solution. But there have been too many security organizations that run the scans and then don't provide the support associated with the report. I guarantee that non-security people will look at a report with red, orange, and yellow colors and wonder what the hell the report is saying. Your job is to interpret the results for them.

And for the solution security architect, you have a responsibility to ensure that the solution works, not just at the point you hand it over to production, but also for the lifespan of the solution itself. If you expect the solution to support the organization for 5 years, then you'd better make sure your tests show that it can last that long. So, the following activities are those that the security architect gets involved in.

For the supporting security architect: The supporting security architect is, in the test phase, meant to support the security testing that goes on with the solution. They may not do the actual testing itself (that's usually done by a security analyst that specializes in that sort of thing) but the supporting security architect is meant to interpret the results of the tests. The activities the supporting security architect performs are as follows:

- **Validation of vulnerability scans**: Typically, vulnerability scans are all about the configuration of the underlying infrastructure that a solution is making use of. Are there any open ports showing up? Are there any known vulnerabilities that haven't been patched? Are there any default accounts being used? Your job as the supporting security architect is to look at the results of the vulnerability scans and indicate what the project team needs to mitigate. What I've found is that often one issue (for example, a missed patch) will show up in a multitude of different scan results. But if you fix that one issue, then most of the scan results are mitigated. The project team doesn't necessarily have to deal with each individual one, but your job as the supporting security architect is to work with them through the issues so that they can implement a solid solution into production.

- **Validation of white box/black box testing**: White box testing and black box testing are about testing an application and not the underlying infrastructure. Your vulnerability scan may come back clean, but if the application has a vulnerability built into it, then you can bypass even the most hardened and protected solution at the infrastructure layer. Firewalls will only protect a solution at the infrastructure layer. But if there's something in the Java code that allows someone to jump into the application, they are just bypassing the firewall. So, for application development purposes, you definitely want to make sure that white box and black box testing occurs. Again, you as the security architect may not be the person doing that particular testing. But your job is to interpret the results for the project team and guide them to fixing it.

- **Security functionality testing**: Normally, I would group this into the solution security architect's role under performance testing, but it's important that the supporting security architect gets involved in making sure that the security infrastructure that is involved in the solution is working. So, is the SIEM receiving logs from the solution? Is the AV solution integrated and working? Are the appropriate firewall rules in place and functioning properly? Check to make sure the security architecture components are working as expected.

If you are working on an application development project, make sure the scanning is done on each unit being tested in QA, as well as the integration testing for the unit as a whole. There's nothing worse that finding a result at the end that could have been adjusted in the individual unit. There's a cascade effect you have to consider.

For the solution security architect: Again, the solution security architect has to make sure the entire solution is working. That means testing the functionality of the solution, the capabilities of the solution, and making sure the solution meets the requirements of the stakeholders. That leads to the following types of test being performed:

- **Performance testing**: Test your solution against the expected benchmarks associated with the resources the solution will use. How much memory is being used? How much network bandwidth? How much CPU? Your infrastructure team can guide you through what to test for. Is your application throwing errors?

- **User acceptance testing**: Has a sample group of end users that represent the various roles you are designing for actually used the solution? What do they think? Did the solution meet their needs as laid out in the requirements?

- **Functionality testing**: Does the solution deliver on the functions that you planned for? While performance testing is checking the underlying infrastructure or application results, functionality testing is all about making sure that the functions required are working. So, is the solution working as expected? Are all the functions usable? What about the underlying management systems that you have integrated? Are you about to use SCCM with the solution? SNMP? Is your infrastructure team able to remotely connect and support the solution? Don't just think in terms of the specific technology you are implementing; also think about the various systems that are connecting to your solution in order to maintain and sustain it moving forward.

Always validate your tests against what was originally put together in the requirements. If your tests can show that the requirements are being met, then you are just about there in terms of having a successful project. Remember, it's all about the requirements. Don't look at your solution in isolation.

Production Turnover phase

The **Production Turnover Phase** (**PTO**) is the last phase in the project for the Security Architect. There may be some additional work after the solution is turned over to production, such as looking at lessons learned or logging residual risks in your corporate risk registry, but the PTO is the last major phase in any project.

Everything that you have done so far should have been done in isolation. There should not have been any impact to your live production systems or network. You've gone through all your gates and your solution is at the point that you believe it's ready for prime time. So, you will now want to flip the switch and let things move ahead.

Well, there's a few more things you need to do before that proverbial switch is thrown. What was the one group that I made special mention of back in the requirements gathering phase, the one group that very few people bother to gather requirements from? That's right: operations. These are the people that need to actually provide care and feeding for your solution. From the security organization, your SOC are the people that you need to consider. But, there are similar groups in the other IT areas as well that need to be aware of what you are doing. After all, if something happens, either to your solution or to someone else's solution, they need to troubleshoot and deal with the issue, and they will need to understand how exactly your solution works.

Before we look at the different tasks for the supporting or solution security architects, let's make sure that we actually understand these groups. The groups you need to interact with (and should have interacted with back in the requirement gathering stage) are:

- **Security Operations Center (SOC)**: This is the security group that needs to understand the solution. This isn't just about the security infrastructure, but also about non-security components. Remember, they will have to do periodic vulnerability or compliance scanning on infrastructure components, so they need to know the non-security components as well.
- **Network Operations Center (NOC)**: These are the people that provide the care and feeding for the network. Network people like to always say that their layer is working fine, and it often is. But, they need to know what impact your solution will have on it's traffic. If you are dealing with a new SIEM, there's going to be a large increase in network traffic with raw logs going across it (hopefully, you have designed your solution thinking about this, but it happens). Same goes with vulnerability scanning; those vulnerability scans will impact firewalls and network traffic depending on how hard you are scanning.

- **Wintel and UNIX teams**: These folks are managing your servers. Your solution is typically broken down into the application, infrastructure, network, and security layers and the server teams will be managing anything to do with the underlying operating systems. Different organizations may have different breakdowns where things like the application server (which will sit on top of a standard server) may be managed by the application group. Regardless, they need to know what the expected norms are for your solution and when alarms need to be triggered when resources reach a certain limit.

- **Application teams**: Most of the time, your security technology's application layer is managed by the security team. But there are organizations that have the application layer managed by the applications team and the security team is considered just the end users of the solution. That's fine, as long as everyone has clear distinctions as to who is responsible for what.

- **Help desk**: Ah yes—the help desk. The first line of response when end users are impacted. The first thing people do when they have an issue is call the help desk. Does the help desk know who to contact about an issue? Make sure you have a list of possible issues that may occur and how the help desk should be responding to calls. They are first-level support but do they know when to escalate an issue to the second level?

- **Change Advisory Board (CAB)**: The CAB is your last checkpoint with all the groups in IT. It's typically a weekly or biweekly meeting with the heads of each group to say, *Does anyone have any last questions or issues?* If you've dealt with each one of the previous groups, then this meeting should be a *fait accompli*, and no one should be surprised.

As for the things that the security architect needs to deal with, think about the following:

For the supporting security architect: The supporting security architect is there to represent the security organization as a whole. They need to make sure that the Project team is providing a solution that the security group can support moving forward. This means the following items need to be considered:

- **Build documentation provided to the SOC**: Your role as the supporting security architect is about representing the security organization. So, at this point, you need to ensure that the build documentation is adequate, and that it has been provided to the SOC.

- **SOC adjustments**: Make sure that the SOC has adjusted the various systems that they need to worry about. For example, they will need to include the new devices in their vulnerability scans. They will need to be aware that the alerts from the solution showing up in the SIEM are now real, live, and need to be responded to.

For the solution security architect: If you are the solution security architect, there are operations teams in all the various towers that need to be communicated with and supported. If you haven't actually had conversations with these people before you get to this point, it is guaranteed that you have missed requirements. For production turnover, you'll need to provide or perform the following things:

- **Build documentation**: Each team is going to need a copy of the build documentation so that they understand what has been put into place and how the solution works as a whole.
- **Test results**: Provide each team with the test results so that they can see that the solution works and what the baseline test responses should look like. If they are troubleshooting your solution while in production, it's useful to understand what good looks like.
- **Architecture Design Document (ADD)**: While the various teams may not need the actual ADD, sometimes it's useful for them to see how the whole solution work holistically. Your ADD should include things like the processes that have changed and the RACI chart associated with who is responsible for what.
- **Changes to ticketing system**: Make sure that your ticketing system has been changed so that the help desk (and the other teams) know how to deal with issues that arise.

There are other things that occur at this phase, such as the training of the end users or the support teams, and the security architect may get involved in those activities if they are the solution security architect. But, by and large, that is out of scope of the security architect and the responsibility of the PM to arrange.

Comments on the Agile methodology

One thing I get asked continuously is how to integrate security into the Agile methodology. Before I comment on the agile methodology and how security architecture gets involved, let's look at what Agile is in the first place.

The Agile methodology was originally created for developing software but has since drifted into being used for the delivery of other non-application-based solutions. Software itself is an applicable area for using Agile because of how you create individual units and then integrate the units into a whole application.

The Agile methodology is used where the solution evolves so that you aren't doing a Big Bang approach, but rather providing functionality little by little. Where the waterfall methodology is a, linear progression in delivering solutions, the Agile methodology takes a repetitive, spiral-type approach to delivering solutions. Think in terms of having multiple small phases for delivering projects rather than a monolithic approach that delivers a whole complete solution.

There are a lot of good aspects to the Agile methodology. You start to see results much faster than you would in with a waterfall methodology. While you may not get the entire solution, you get components of the solution that allow for ROI and cost recovery a lot sooner.

Here's the thing that I've found, though. Most people that say they follow the Agile methodology, aren't. They are using Agile as an excuse to not document and not do things properly. Agile gathers requirements a little at a time and then develops to meet those requirements. But if you don't keep an eye on the entire end solution, then you end up with solutions that just weren't done properly. Don't get me wrong, in the hands of a scrum master, Agile will work like a charm. But, very few people get the appropriate training in Agile and, as a result, you end up with a project with a ton of issues.

Integrating security architecture into Agile? Remember that the entire point of Agile is to speed things up and keep things simple. The goal of the security architect should be to do the same. Work with the Agile team in each micro-phase (my term used just to describe each iteration in the Agile approach) and remember to keep the scope of what you do to the exact same scope area that the Agile team is working on. You'll have your requirements for those phases, so make sure that you include them there. But don't over-complicate what needs to be done. Keep an eye on the strategic endpoint but work on the small, micro-tactical impacts.

Summary

This chapter included a lot of overviews. The intent was to give you a pretty good idea of what the security architect needs to be aware of and do in each phase of delivering a project; this factors can change, depending on whether you are supporting a project or are the solution security architect yourself. You'll probably have noticed that each progressive phase builds on previous phases, and that's the way it should be. But, like when you build a house, make sure you have a REALLY solid foundation to build on and that foundation is your requirements. If you don't gather your requirements properly, then your project will fail, no matter how effective a designer you are.

The next chapter will go into depth in a number of the artifacts that the security architect delivers. The artifacts that will be dealt with are the requirement documentation (and the security requirements that should be commented on), vendor selection, the **Security Design Assessment** (**SDA**), the test plan, and the build document. The architecture design document will be covered by itself in the chapter following the next one.

Questions

1. What is the most important phase of ANY project delivery methodology?
2. What is the main risk of using the Agile methodology?
3. What is the downside of using the waterfall methodology?
4. What is the difference between a Solution Security Architect and a Supporting Security Architect?
5. What stakeholder group is very commonly not interviewed for their requirements and, if you have gotten to the **Production Turn Over** (**PTO**) phase without talking to, will lead to issues?

7
Security Architecture Project Delivery Artifacts

The last chapter was all about the different artifacts that are delivered by the security architect during the waterfall project-delivery process. It's very difficult to deliver a proper project if you do not understand the importance of each phase in a project-delivery process and how your security architecture artifacts fit into that process.

This chapter goes into the details of the most important of those artifacts. The approach that is taken with these artifacts is from the point of view of an architect that specializes in security rather than a security person that dabbles in architecture. Each artifact is important and will have a security slant but, as with all things security-related, security needs to be baked into the artifact (or micro-solution) rather than appended onto something. Any time you add security onto something rather than integrate security into it from inception, you weaken the overall security posture.

Look at each artifact and remember that there's a way of looking at it from the security point of view.

Requirements Gathering Documentation

At the end of the day, our job as architects is dependent on how well we gather the requirements for whatever job we are working on. Remember, the very first step in the waterfall project-delivery method is the gathering of requirements and, if you don't do that correctly, you're damaging your ability to have a successfully delivered project. The first aspect to the Requirements Gathering documentation is the actual process. The documentation itself will come together if you follow the process properly.

With regards to the requirements documentation, you are looking to gather the business requirements from stakeholders and develop the functional and nonfunctional requirements that are to be used in measuring the project in each successive stage in the project-development process. These requirements become your stake in the ground and should not change after they have been formalized and accepted by the project-management governance process.

It's important to understand what functional and nonfunctional requirements are defined as. There have been too many architects that use those terms but do not fully understand what they mean or their importance:

- **Functional requirements**: Functional requirements are descriptors of how a solution should actually function. They are more qualitative descriptions (for example, easy to use) than quantitative descriptions (for example, requires 4 GB of memory). You can't measure functional requirements using empirical methods.
- **Nonfunctional requirements**: Nonfunctional requirements are the easiest form of requirements because they can be measured and you can either say they have or have not been met. Some examples of nonfunctional requirements include 99.9% uptime, specific amounts of memory (for example, 4 GB of RAM), and 4 cores of CPU. There is typically a number attached to the requirement.

Your job as the security architect is to translate the business requirements that you will gather into requirements that the project can use. It's the translation activity that is what an Architect (no matter what the architecture tower) does—we translate business language into technical language for use by the technical people and technical language into business language for the business people to use.

The requirements-gathering process is about gathering business requirements. The creation of the formal requirements documentation is then the process of translating the business requirements into those functional and nonfunctional requirements.

One last thing about gathering requirements. Most project managers will assign the collection of requirements to a business analyst, and a good business analyst is worth their weight in gold. But, ultimately, it is your responsibility to understand the complete set of requirements and that means you have to be heavily involved in collecting the requirements. If the requirements haven't been collected properly, it's your head that's on the chopping block, not the business analyst's, simply because it will impact your solution and the delivery of a solid solution. Don't abrogate your responsibility to someone else. Own the requirements-gathering process.

Requirement-gathering process

Requirements-gathering is actually an art rather than a science. It's meant to create a relationship with your stakeholders so that they believe that you understand what they are looking for and not just telling them what you are going to give them. All solutions are always meant to support your stakeholders–you just need to ensure that there is the proper quality control to those solutions in the form of integrated security.

Remember that, in virtually all cases, your stakeholders will not have actually given any thought to what their full set of requirements are. If you were to ask a simple question, such as, "What are your requirements?", they will probably come back with a simple answer along the lines of, "Well, it needs to be secure, naturally." That tells you nothing and that's simply because your stakeholders haven't actually given any thought into what their requirements are. Your job, as the security architect, is to lead them through the process of understanding what they actually want.

Donald Rumsfeld, former US Secretary of Defense, was famously quoted as saying that there are four different stages of understanding:

- **Unconscious incompetent**: The stage where you don't know what you don't know. How can you start to try to understand what you need to understand if you don't know what you don't know? This is where your stakeholders are before you get to them.
- **Conscious incompetent**: This is the stage where you become aware of all the things you haven't thought about and don't know. Think of the first time that you hear of the concept of cloud computing. Before you had heard of cloud computing, you were an unconscious incompetent. But once you had heard of it, you probably realized that you had to learn more about it. That made you into a conscious incompetent.
- **Conscious competent**: You've now gone out, learned, and become competent at a subject. You are aware of what you have learned but you haven't internalized it. It's sort of like learning the theory but not having done it enough in practice to truly understand the subject. This is the stage where you are a conscious competent.
- **Unconscious competent**: The last stage of awareness, the unconscious competent has learned an area extremely well to the point that they have internalized all the information they have and aren't even aware that they understand the information. They don't think about how to do something, they just do it. This makes them an unconscious competent.

You, as the architect, are typically the unconscious competent and it's for this reason that you need to make use of things such as templates so that you make sure you don't forget something. Your stakeholders, on the other hand, are at the first stage where they are unconscious incompetents and don't really know what they don't know. Your job is to guide them to become conscious incompetents at a minimum.

You do this through the interview process. Gathering requirements is fairly easy–you ask open-ended questions in specific areas and then let your stakeholders talk. You don't comment on what they say because you don't want to influence them. If they say something you don't agree with, hold your tongue and don't say anything. If they say something that is the polar-opposite from what another stakeholder has as a requirement (and this happens quite a bit), again, don't say anything. Your job at this stage is to document the requirements from the various stakeholders. Ask open-ended questions (that is, questions such as, "What are your availability requirements?") and then shut up and listen.

A lot of architects will have group sessions when gathering requirements and that's an approach I'm not fond of. While it's more time-efficient and specific to the actual requirements-gathering, in the long term, it can actually work against you for the simple reason that you won't get all the requirements. There is inevitably the "wallflower" that sits in the back and doesn't participate. That person often has very valid requirements but, because of social pressures, doesn't speak up. If you interview your stakeholders individually, you will talk with the wallflower in a one-on-one situation and get their requirements, thereby making sure you have a more complete set of requirements. So don't interview stakeholders in a group–interview them individually.

If you use a template, do not send it to your stakeholders before you meet with them. You want the conversation to be organic and allow the stakeholder to take the conversation in any direction they want. If you give them your template beforehand, you will end up with questions coming back about the different areas and it just makes the process more labor-intensive. If your stakeholder asks for something to prepare with, tell them one simple thing:

 You don't want to add additional work to their plate.

They will actually appreciate you for this. People are being asked to do more and more and, if you take the approach that you are helping them rather than asking them to do something, you will actually get more buy-in into the entire process and end solution.

Once you start your interview, tell your stakeholder that this is all about them. Explain that you will ask very open-ended questions and, as they answer, they may want to go off on a tangent. And that's okay because it's all relevant. They will go off on a tangent, so let them talk because you will get additional information just from that tangent. Just be prepared to loop them back to where you want to keep them if they go too far afield.

Describe what your scope is. If you don't describe your scope, there is a chance they will start talking about areas that are outside the scope of your project. Scoping was done with the initiation of the project but shouldn't be done at the requirements stage. The scoping statement gives a framework for your stakeholder to provide requirements. Once in a while, you will have someone who wants to do things their way and talk about things other than your scope. But you have to control the interview and keep them on track. That will allow you to stay on time.

One of two things will happen once you've asked your open-ended question. Either they will start talking and you will make notes. LOTS of notes. Or they will ask you to clarify what you mean. At this point, you have to be very careful not to influence them with a follow up question. Here's an example:

- **Architect**: What are your availability requirements?
- **Stakeholder**: What do you mean?
- **Architect**: Think along the lines of when the application has to be available to users. Can it be unavailable for any length of time? When can that be? What would happen if it wasn't available?

Don't give specific examples because your stakeholders will just parrot or repeat back what you just said. You want to solicit information from them and not plant your own thoughts into their heads.

Create a template that covers all the areas that are a component of a solution and then use that template to guide your questions or, even better, allows your entire architecture group to be consistent in their approach to gathering requirements. But using a template will allow you to make sure you don't miss an area. The template itself is covered in the next section.

The typical interview, if performed properly, should take around 45 minutes. Schedule an hour because it's an average of 45 minutes and, if it finishes early, you are giving them time back in their day. Just be aware that you have specific areas that you are going into and if they start talking about things that are out of scope (and it's really important to keep them on track), you need to bring them back on track.

The very last question you are going to ask your stakeholder is simply, "Is there anyone else that I should be talking to?" Your original project sponsor will tell you specific stakeholders but they won't know who all the stakeholders are. By asking this last question, you can make sure you have talked to all stakeholders. A Business Sponsor will naturally only talk about their own business unit, but they won't think about groups such as the help desk or the operations team that has to support the solution. They won't think about the HR group or the Legal team. So ask each stakeholder if there's anyone else you should talk to.

Once you've finished gathering the requirements from your stakeholders, show them that you have been listening. This will instill confidence in your stakeholder that you are actually thinking about what they need, and it will instill a level of trust between the two of you. This is done simply by repeating back the notes that you took to your stakeholders. They may correct you as you repeat what you heard and allow you to correct your understanding, a very important point. If you don't repeat it back to them because of time, just send them your RAW notes for them to review. Tell them that they are raw notes, filled with grammar and spelling mistakes, and are only intended to make sure you captured what they said. Then ask them to send back any corrections or (and this is important) anything that they think of after the fact.

That's how you interview a stakeholder for requirements. Now, the question is, what areas should you be asking about? That is covered by the next section, requirements-gathering spreadsheet.

Requirements-gathering spreadsheet

The requirements-gathering spreadsheet is your template for guiding you through the various requirements areas and for collecting your interview notes. It structures the entire process and ends up driving the more formal requirements documents.

Make use of an Excel spreadsheet for gathering your requirements. By using a spreadsheet, you are able to be flexible in your note-taking while making use of a structure for the requirements-gathering process. One good practice is to make a copy of this template for each stakeholder interviewed rather than putting all your stakeholder interview notes into the same document simply because it allows you to go back at a later date to remember which stakeholder provided a specific business requirement.

There should be three columns in your spreadsheet for very specific purposes:

Business requirement area	Requirement description	Comments provided
Is the intended scope of project understood?	Ensure that the interviewee understands the scope of the project that requirements are being gathered for	Column for notes to be taken during interview

The three columns are covered as follows:

- **Business requirement area**: This is simply the title of the requirement. Nothing more is required. Remember, though, that you are documenting business requirements and then it's your job as the security architect to translate those business requirements into the appropriate functional and nonfunctional requirements.
- **Requirement description**: This is a description of the actual requirement and will typically include sample open-ended questions. This column is used for the architect to understand what exactly they are collecting in terms of the requirements. If this is just for yourself, just include the sample questions. But if this template is used for your architecture team, make sure you have a descriptor for your business requirement area as well as sample open-ended questions.
- **Comments provided**: This is where you put your raw notes from the interview. Don't worry about being neat and tidy with this column or organizing your notes as the interview goes on. You'll do that for later artifacts. In the interview itself, just use this column for documenting what your stakeholders are saying.

Now for the important aspect of this spreadsheet and what will drive the structure of your follow-up requirements documents–the specific business requirements areas. Make sure you have covered all the different areas that requirements can be logically grouped into. My requirements-gathering spreadsheet has 22 business requirements areas. Yours may have more or it may have less. But by segmenting them appropriately, it helps organize everything else in your solution.

Some of the business requirements areas, and their sample questions that could be used during the interview process, are as follows:

Architecture restrictions	These requirements would capture any known restrictions to the architecture. For example, you may have to make use of alliance partners or take a Cloud-First approach. A parallel to these types of requirements may be in alignment with architectural principles.
Availability	These requirements define when the solution is available. For example, required up-times and maintenance windows.
Business continuity	The Architect needs to ensure business requirements for business continuity are documented so that a generic business-continuity plan/disaster-recovery plan can be defined and considered in creating a preliminary architecture and summarized in the business case/plan for the offering. The generic business-continuity plan must also be considered in the cost model for both development and ongoing support according to the needs of the client. Business requirements should address specific down-time requirements, back-up storage, data archival, disaster recovery requirements, and so on.
Client standards/audit	The architect needs to ensure anticipated standards and any associated audit requirements that the solution will need to adhere to are described in the business requirements. This will be used for estimating anticipated development and operating costs in the business case/plan. Requirements identify the following: • **Industry technical standards and/or best practice standards** to which the offering must comply. These are standards that would be: ○ Visible to the client either for interoperability and replacement of components or in the certification of service provided. ○ Required for integration of the solution's shared components or vendor products. Requirements should also specify when the solution should pursue development of industry standards in order to achieve long-term improvement of business value in the offering. • **Probable client expectations for third-party reviews/audits**: The requirements should indicate whether it would be necessary to provide an audit or review to meet regulatory-compliance requirements. Business requirements should indicate whether there may also be expenses involved in adhering to specific industry regulatory and/or standards compliance. The requirements should describe the anticipated cost model to reflect this expense or indicate that the contract must specifically place the expense on the project. If the contract is silent, the solution will have a compliance cost expectation on the part of the Project and therefore be included in the financial plan for the Project
Consistency	Consistency requirements go into any repeatability requirements (that is, how consistent a solution should be in providing the same answers). This may be along the lines of meeting things such as CMMI standards. Question: Describe the repeatability requirements.
Country-specific regulations	The Architect needs to ensure anticipated country-specific regulations are described in the business requirements and used for estimating anticipated development and operating costs in the business case/plan. The requirements should clarify for the Project team which country-specific regulations must be followed for any business inside or outside of Canada. For example: • Use of off-shore staff in some countries is prohibited by Canadian Privacy Laws • NERC is a US-based set of regulations • Ratios of on-shore versus off-shore staff Regulatory and/or compliance laws can have a big impact on staffing. Use of off-shore staff in certain countries may be prohibited by these laws. These types of regulations are not always obvious. Requirements should think about both current and planned country deployments for the offering and be described separately.
Documentation	List the user documentation components (such as user manuals, online help, and tutorials) that will be delivered. Question: Are there requirements associated with storage of documentation? Question: Are there requirements on what documents need to be created for the Project?
Features	Features can be quite extensive, so realize that some of the features that attract the stakeholders to specific tools/products will show up here. Question: What are some of the features you expect?

Finance	Financial requirements are, for some reason, one of the areas that very few people think about. They want a solution but haven't put any dollars to the solution. So really try to drill down into this area. Question: What are the financial requirements for this project? Question: What is the capital budget? Question: What is the operating budget? Question: What is the sustainment budget? Question: What type of ROI were you looking for?
Interface	Interface requirements are tied to human-to-machine interfaces and machine-to-machine interfaces. Find out about required links to other architectures, systems, or applications. Question: How do you see people interfacing with the solution? (Think business process interface–requesting for service) Question: Think technical–how does the solution interface technically with other systems, or how does the end user interface with the solution?
Leveraged assets	Leveraged-asset requirements specify the solution resources and components that are expected to be shared with other solutions in order to reduce cost and complexity. This may include components to be developed or adapted for sharing with other solutions (for example, ESBs, Federation/SAML solutions, or Cloud solutions) Question: What other Project should this Project be tied to? Question: What other solution assets/organizations should this solution be tied to?
Maintainability	These requirements address the ease with which the product/solution accepts repairs, patches, or adapts to new functionality, and they address the process by which problems are reported and resolved. Question: How often should updates be obtained? Question: How often should the solution's technical components be reviewed? Question: Who should be maintaining the solution?
Operational environment	These requirements address special considerations for the operation and ongoing support of the delivered product, if known. This is typically a question that is asked of operations teams. Question: Are there specific OSes that must be supported?
Performance	These requirements address system performance expectations, if known. For example, some of the performance requirements may address capacity, response time, or data throughput. You also may discover latency requirements if this is for a real-time system. Typically, performance requirements will end up being nonfunctional in nature. Question: What is the response time required? This could be for both technical and process responses. Question: What is the expected work load? Think both load on systems as well as load on employees (for example, increased number of help desk tickets may mean additional work for help desk personnel).
Portability	These requirements address the ease with which the product is implemented on or migrated to other platforms or operating systems. You may be porting a solution from a Linux platform to a Windows platform or you may be making a solution as a mobile application. Question: Is there a need for mobility? Question: Is there a requirement to change to a different platform?
Privacy	The Privacy Officer must be consulted during the requirements definition, design, and rollout to make sure all information privacy issues for the platform, network, and business processes are dealt with according to client policy, regulatory requirements, and potential generic client policies. Provision for privacy implementation and ongoing support must be included in the cost model. Also, specific countries may have different privacy laws that must be researched and adhered to, therefore included in the business requirements. Question: Are there any privacy considerations that you can think of?
Reliability	These requirements address the acceptable defect rate or failure rate of the delivered product. This is appropriate for more OEM-type products. Question: What type of accuracy of the results do you expect and require?

Reporting	These requirements address known desired or required reports and their types. For example, metrics, detailed versus summary, paper, electronic, and web. This is different from documentation requirements where reporting is for ongoing information, whereas documentation requirements are for one-time information. Question: Describe the reporting required. Question: Is a separated executive summary required? Question: What type of metrics are required? Question: Do you want Console access/self-service for stakeholders?
Scalability	These requirements address the ability of the project to adapt to new technologies and to changes in post-implementation metrics, including the ability of the product to accommodate product upgrades and new functionality. The future size of a solution is very often overlooked when being designed (novice architects tend to design for the here and now, not for the future). Question: How many users will use this system in 3 - 5 years? Question: How big will the database grow?
Security	Security Policies must be consulted during the requirements definition, design, and rollout to make sure all security issues for the platform, network, business processes and human safety are dealt with according to the Client policy and regulations. Provision for security implementation and ongoing support must be included in the cost model. Both physical and logical security must be considered. While every other requirement area can be looked at for security adjustments, this is the one area specific to security. Question: Are there any specific Security Policies that need to be adhered to? Question: Are there security technologies that need to be integrated? There will be a further breakdown of security requirements here, if you are a Supporting Security Architect.
Staffing/Labor mix	Determine the business requirements for the anticipated labor mix needed to support the offering once deployed for consideration in the technical design of the offering. The business requirements should define the appropriate breakdown of staff necessary to provide services for the capabilities of the offering. An incorrect labor mix can severely impact the delivery unit's ability to operate within the allowable costs, and in some circumstances may prohibit the client from being able to do business as noted in the earlier regulatory section. Consider the following when documenting the labor mix: • Ratios of full-time versus part-time versus contractors. 　○ Some business have peak times of operation that could be best handled by increasing staff at those peak times with part-time staff. • Union versus non-union labor mix • Best-shore considerations Question: Are there limitations to where Work can occur? Question: Can Work occur on-site? Question: Can Work occur at a centralized site? Question: Are there limitations on WHO can perform work? (for example, union staff, employees versus contractors, and service providers)
Usability	Gather usability requirements to address how easy it needs to be for the intended users of the offering to operate it. The usability requirements should cover things such as ease of use, ease of learning, accessibility, personalization, and internationalization (different cultures will have different understanding of symbolism, verbiage, and so on.). These requirements guide the architect in costing and building a product that will meet the expectations of the eventual end users. These requirements should be captured from the perspective of all the different types of users. Question: Are there requirements that the end user would have? Question: Are there requirements that admin/Ops people would have? Question: Are there requirements that client business people would have? Question: Are there any cultural or language issues that need to be considered?

If you are the supporting security architect, the solution architect will likely be approaching you to discuss to your security requirements. From the supporting security architect's perspective, you should be thinking in terms of the following requirements:

- **Security architecture strategy**: What direction does your strategy drive them in? Are there approaches you want them to take or technologies they need to use that will help your strategy move forward?
- **Security technologies:** Are there security technologies that need to be implemented in the solution? For example, is there a need for AV or some sort of change-management solution that needs to be implemented?
- **Logging**: Do you want to get the security logs to your SIEM? If so, how?
- **Data in flight**: Do you have encryption requirements for the solution as data flows from one system to another or from the system to the users?
- **Data at rest**: How about when the data is at rest? Do you have requirements associated with securing the data when being stored or residing in memory?
- **Identity and Access Management (IAM)**: What roles do you want to see in the solution? Do you have a RBAC strategy you are trying to implement? How about authentication and authorization requirements? Provisioning?

Use your RSA to get a good sense of what requirements that you want to see associated with the solution. This will go a long way to assisting the solution architect. One example might come from your border-protection section. Maybe you have specific security zones you want to see the solution. The same goes for encryption. Maybe you have specific algorithms or certificate/key lengths that you want to follow.

One last thing with regards to providing security requirements to a Solution Architect: remember that you have to be driven by approved policies and standards as well as an approved strategy. If you don't, then why would expect a solution architect to have to meet them?

Requirements document

The last section was quite lengthy and that is because requirements-gathering is the MOST important activity that a security architect can do. The rest of the requirements documentation is just that–documentation. It allows you to communicate the originating business requirements as well as deconstructed functional and nonfunctional requirements. Those requirements will drive your design, your build, your test plans, and how you implement the solution. In short, they drive what direction you need to take with your project, and are what you measure in each and every individual phase of your project for success.

Your requirements document should break down your raw notes into a usable form. From a structure perspective, the easiest way to create it is to just follow the business requirements areas in your requirements-gathering template so that you can translate your raw notes into the same order that you received the requirements.

Once you've consolidated all those requirements, break the business requirements down into functional and nonfunctional requirements tied specifically to the individual business requirements. Don't get lazy and think that there will be a one-to-one functional/nonfunctional mapped to a business requirement. Often, your business requirements may derive multiple functional and nonfunctional requirements. And, sometimes, those functional/nonfunctional requirements will show up in multiple different business requirements.

Finally, indicate how important those requirements are. There are typically different priority requirements, listed as the following:

- **Must-Have requirements**: Must-Haves are just that–the solution Must meet those requirements. They are the most important requirements and, if you were to give them a weight, they would have the highest weight. We will look more at the weighting of requirements in the *Vendor selection* section.
- **Should-Have requirements**: Should-Haves are those requirements that your solution should have. If the solution doesn't meet those requirements, you're going to have some explaining to do, but you may be able to justify not meeting these requirements.
- **Nice-to-Have requirements**: Nice-to-Haves are requirements that, if you are able to include them in your solution, they will be appreciated, but they aren't necessary and typically don't have to be justified in not being met. They would be the lowest-weighted requirements.

You may want to have something called use cases in your requirements document as well. This is where you use a narrative to show how the solution may be used and how the narrative will drive the actual functional requirements. For example, the following might be something you would see as a use case:

Mike comes into the office in the morning and logs into his computer. He opens his browser and clicks on the link to the ERP application in order to begin work. He connects without having to log in, making Mike not take an additional step in accessing the ERP. Once in the ERP home page, Mike navigates to the HR section and proceeds to review and approve the HR tickets.

The use case gives the architect a real-world understanding of how the stakeholders may want to make use of the solution once it's implemented. If you want to gather use cases, during your interview process, just ask for examples of how you see a day in the life of different types of users interacting with the solution.

Your requirements document can take many forms, depending on the organization you are working with. They can be in word form, in a presentation (which makes writing them very easy), or you can put them into an Excel spreadsheet. But, in each case, make use of a table of the following format (with two example business requirements):

Req. #	Bus. req. area	Business requirement	Functional/nonfunctional requirement	Weight
AV1	Availability	Must be available to End users during business hours.	Available from 8:00am to 6:00pm Eastern Standard time.	Must
AV2			Uptime of 98%.	Must
SC1	Scalability	Able growth of 10 GB of data a year.	Database size of 60 GB capability required.	Must
SC2		Plan to support Asia Pacific region in two years.	Be able to make use of duplicate databases in Singapore.	Should

As you can see in this example, it is possible to have more than one business requirement in a business requirement area, and it is possible to have more than one functional/nonfunctional requirement per business requirement.

One other nice thing about this format is the requirement # column. By identifying each individual functional/nonfunctional requirement with its own requirement number, it becomes easy to communicate with others and to port the requirements to other documentation. If you start each requirement # with a pair of letters to represent the Business Requirement area, it becomes apparent that AV1 can be talking about Availability and not Architecture Restriction. This numbering system becomes really useful when you are creating your **Requirements Traceability Matrix (RTM)**.

Finish off developing your requirements documentation by presenting it to your Stakeholders, both in the drafting process as well as once you have the finished product. You want to show the stakeholders that you heard what they said and want to get them to sign off on the requirements. Once they've signed off on the requirements, you are cleared to move forward, and the stakeholders can't say later that the solution didn't meet their requirements. The requirements document can also be used to hold the stakeholders to account for what they wanted in the first place.

One more thing about requirements and it's been talked about multiple times in this book–once you get the sign-off on requirements, don't add more requirements. That will lead to scope creep and will add costs or require you to go back and change design (which will have a cascade effect through the rest of the project). If a new requirement comes up, add it to a phase 2 of the project.

Requirements Traceability Matrix (RTM)

When you create your requirements document, you don't just walk away from it. It becomes the measuring stick to determine how well your project is meeting requirements as you go through the project-delivery process. Each phase should be checked against those requirements each time you finish a phase. If you don't, you run the risk of finishing a project without actually knowing whether your project is meeting the requirements of the stakeholders. Can you imagine implementing a project in production and then the primary stakeholder says, "But where's capability XXX?" You'd have to go back to redesign your solution, build it, test it to make sure it's working appropriately, and then go back to the stakeholder (who now doesn't really trust you) and say that you have met that requirement.

A better case would be to sit down with the stakeholders after each phase and show them how you are meeting the requirements. You do that using the RTM. The RTM is a simplified version of your requirements document and is how you track whether a functional or nonfunctional requirement is being met. You can do a simple cut and paste of the functional/nonfunctional into your RTM and then track your progress as you go along.

A good form of the RTM is as a spreadsheet, as shown in the following image, and would have the following column headings:

- **BR#**: This is the business requirement # that you used in your requirements document. This allows you go tie two different documents to each other.
- **Category/functional activity**: This is your general business requirement area.
- **Requirement description**: This is the actual functional/nonfunctional requirement you are trying to meet.
- **Use-case reference**: If you have a specific use case that you want to show making use of the solution, tie to it here.

From this point forward, you are using the RTM to document how the requirements are being met. The columns you should consider in your RTM are as follows:

- **Design document reference**: Show how your **Architecture Design Document (ADD)** is meeting the requirement. Use a page number if you want or a reference to a section. You don't have to rewrite the ADD here.
- **Code module/reference**: In the build phase, point to the code that was written or the Reference component that was implemented to show that the requirements have been met.
- **Test-case reference**: In the test phase, you want to show the test case that is being used to test whether the requirement is being met. This could be through **User Acceptance Testing (UAT)** to meet a use case, a QA test to see whether a nonfunctional requirement has been met, or it might be a peer review showing that the functional requirement is being met, but point to your Test documentation rather than rewriting the entire document here. The RTM is all about tracking, not re-documenting.
- **User acceptance validation**: This is where you have end users signing off that the requirement has been met. Your End User will be the representatives of all the various stakeholders, including operations. If you are handing the solution over to Operations and they aren't willing to sign off on their requirements being met, then you haven't been looking at their requirements appropriately.

The RTM is probably the most-used document by an Architect throughout the project-delivery process. It allows you to make sure that you are meeting all the requirements that you have gathered and can trace those activities back to the original business requirements. Make use of it so that you have a successful solution implemented.

Vendor selection

The requirements that you have gathered should drive your solution forward, and a big component of that solution will be the product that will be at the core of your solution. Don't get fooled into thinking that technology will fix all your problems and meet all your requirements. It won't. Often, the best solution to a set of requirements may be a change in process or the use of a different set of people resources.

To give you an example of this, back in 2004, we were looking at dealing with a project for a large automaker that wanted to consolidate more than 100 web portals into 4 or 5 web portals. The problem was that each web portal was tied to a specific domain. When we looked at the requirements for the project, we came up with two different possible solutions. We could either move a lot of the process to a Best-Shore location (a location that had the lowest employee costs, which at that time was Indonesia) or we could implement SAML for authentication across domains. We ended up choosing the SAML solution but it was, in theory, only cheaper by 0.5% compared to the Best-Shore solution. In this case, after implementation, it turned out that the theoretical cost of the Best-Shore solution was cheaper than the actual implementation costs of the SAML solution.

The point is, don't assume that a technical solution will be the better solution. Take your requirements and compare all possible solutions, including changes in processes and the changes in the use of personnel. That way, you can find the best solution possible.

But this section talks about Vendor selection. Once you've determined that a technical solution is probably the best route to go, it's time to pick the appropriate product. Unfortunately, a very large percentage of projects initiated by the **Project Management Office (PMO)** are driven by the business saying that they want to put in a specific product. The business unit has been sold on the shiny new toy by a good salesperson, so it's now the solution architect's job to implement it. The entire process of looking at requirements and then choosing the correct solution has been bypassed and there are all sorts of companies that have duplicate solutions in place simply because one business unit wanted a specific solution rather than making use of something else that was already in place.

If you are in a situation where the business has chosen a solution, you still have to gather the requirements associated with the solution and then focus on the process changes and people changes that need to wrap around the technology that has been chosen. You also need to have a conversation with the architecture tower whose strategy will be impacted by this solution. Who knows, maybe the appropriate Enterprise Architect has enough clout to change the decision to align with the strategy that is being followed.

Let's assume that the process is going the way it should and you are now looking for a product to fit the technological requirements. There's a very well-defined process that you should go through to ensure that you select the proper product. As with all things, you don't do this by yourself but, rather, include representatives from your stakeholders to ensure that they have buy-in with the product that you select. If you were to select the product without including your stakeholders, then later on they can say that they don't like the product you selected. But if you involve them, everyone has a stake in the ground.

The process for selecting a vendor is shown in the following diagram and has the following stages:

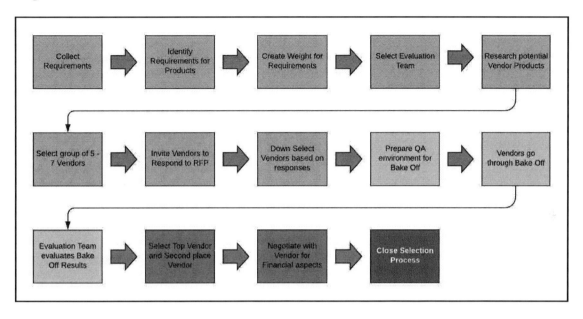

1. **Collect requirements**: This was discussed in the last couple of sections and won't be reviewed here.

2. **Identify requirements for products**: Once you've identified the requirements, you want to select those requirements that are appropriate for the products and for the vendors. Those requirements are not just technical in nature–remember that you are getting support for those products from the Vendor and, if the Vendor isn't financially viable or going to be around in a year, do you really want to purchase a product from them? Make sure that you have both technical requirements for the product and business requirements for the vendor themselves. A sample spreadsheet will be dealt with later.

3. **Create weights for requirements**: Not all requirements are created equal. Pull the importance of those requirements from your requirements document so that you know what weight to give to the responses. If a vendor has a great story around one particular requirement but it's not an important requirement to you, the weighting will make sure that you and your team focus on what is important.

4. **Select the evaluation team**: As indicated earlier, make sure you have an evaluation team that represents your stakeholders. These are the individuals that you are going to have evaluate both the written responses from the Vendors as well as review the actual presentation or bake-off from the down-selected vendors. By having an Evaluation team, you are able to ensure that the solution is bought into by the stakeholders and, if something happens later on, you can ensure that all possible opinions are included in the selection process.

5. **Research potential vendor products**: Do your research first. There's plenty of research organizations around such as Gartner, Forrester, or IDC, that provide research into the various vendors that are in your area. They cost money but they are worth the expense of purchasing their research reports. But if cost is an issue (and smaller companies may not have the funds available for these types of research reports), you can probably get a free copy of their reports if they are made available through the Vendors themselves. Often, the vendors will make the reports available as long as you give them your name so that a salesperson can contact you. They like to brag if they make the Magic Quadrant or are viewed as a Tier 1 vendor. But understand who the various vendors are and what their potential value is to your solution.

6. **Select a group of vendors**: At the initial stage, you want to select a larger group of vendors than you actually are going to evaluate. Your evaluation group may have specific vendors that they want to review, and your research may come up with other vendors. By having 5 - 7 vendors to review, you are giving yourself the chance to see multiple options for the technical component of your solution.

7. **Invite vendors to respond to an RFP**: RFPs are just for big businesses and governments. Remember when you identified your requirements and weighted them? Well, take your requirements and then send them to the Vendors for them to provide written responses. This will allow you and your evaluation team to understand their capabilities based on their responses. How quickly they respond (or if they even respond at all) will also tell you what their corporate culture is with regards to serving their customers.

8. **Down-select vendors based on responses**: Review their responses and, using your weighted scale, select the top three responses. Those are the Vendors that you want to invite into your house to actually review the product. Make the Vendors work for you rather than just respond to a sales call. Most of the time, Vendors will say either that they are the best at a specific requirement or that they can't do a requirement. That's fine–just remember that they are responding with sales language. Also, remember to weigh the business requirements, not just the technical requirements. You want to make sure that the company you are going to partner with is going to be around for a while.

9. **Prepare QA Environment for Bake-Off**: For those of you that aren't aware, a Bake-Off is a simulation of the implementation and operation of a solution. You want the Vendor to implement a solution into a lab environment so that you can see all the gotchas associated with their product. They may have great features but if it's a pain in the butt to implement, how can you make use of the features? So prepare your QA (or a lab environment, if that's all you have) to see how they implement the solution. If you don't have either a QA environment or a lab, have them present in a manner of their choosing how to implement the solution and then show the actual features that you want to see. Many vendors will have a lab environment of their own so they can VPN into that from your site and you can watch as they implement in that environment. Not as good as in your environment, but good enough.

10. **Vendors go through the bake-off**: Schedule your bake-off so that your evaluation team can be there to see the product in action. They may not have to be there for all of it (for example, the End User representatives don't need to see the actual implementation, only the actual operational tool), but you want them to see the solution in action so they can evaluate it. Use your requirements spreadsheet that you created when you identified the product requirements so that they can make notes as the evaluation goes along.

11. **Evaluate bake-off results**: Once each vendor has completed their bake-off component, you want to bring your evaluation team to sit down and go through what they thought of the results. Use the requirements spreadsheet and have each evaluator provide a score on a scale. A numerical score is best so that you can take the average of each and multiply the weight against it. At the end of the evaluation, you can aggregate the average weighted score and this should give you a good understanding of which solution best meets your company's requirements.

12. **Select top vendor and second place vendor**: Your evaluation has now selected the top vendor. But don't ignore the second-place vendor because the next step will be negotiation with the Top Vendor. If those negotiations don't go well, you want to go to the second-place vendor and negotiate with them. Reach out to the Top Vendor and indicated that they won the bake-off and that you want to move forward with them. Also, let the losing vendors know what the results are and be prepared for them to ask questions as to how they could have done better. There will be the occasional vendor that will argue and want to escalate this to someone higher (if the revenue deal to them is big enough). By going through this evaluation process, you are able to justify your selection if an escalation occurs.

13. **Negotiate with the vendor**: Negotiations fall into either your Project Manager's domain or your Purchasing department's area. Let them deal with the actual negotiation. But by giving them a second-place vendor, you are giving them additional power in negotiation because it's no longer an all-or-nothing proposition.

14. **Close the Selection Process**: At this point, the selection of a Vendor or product is complete. Sometimes, the best thing at this point is to create a **Key Decision Document (KDD)** that talks about the various requirements, how the different Vendors met them, and why the Vendor was selected. This is a great way to document the entire process for future reference and is the exact reason why you have a KDD in the first place. The KDD was talked about at length in the Strategy chapter earlier in this book.

The most important artifact that you are going to use throughout this entire process is your product-evaluation matrix. This is where you will list the product requirements, provide the weighting, and then provide this to your evaluation team so that they can score in the appropriate manner.

The following table gives you an example of one possible product-evaluation matrix:

Based on paper evaluation: 100% = Requirements met or does not apply. 75% = Requirement partially met, but good. 25% = Requirement partially met, but poor. 0% = Requirement not met. Requirement	Weight	Solution name goes here	Solution name goes here
Overall Score (out of 100%)			
-Unix	5	0%	0%
-Windows	7	0%	0%
-Combined for all platforms	12	0%	0%
Cost			
-License			
-Maintenance			
-Mgmt infrastructure per 100 target servers			
Availability Date			
Detailed Evaluations			
Unix			
Requirement category name goes here			
-State requirement here.	1		
Requirement category goes here			
-State requirement here.	1		
-State requirement here.	1		
Platform Support			
-AIX	1		
-Solaris	1		
Weighted Score (out of 100%)	5	0%	0%
Windows			
Requirement category name goes here			
-State requirement here.	1		
-State requirement here.	1		
Requirement category name goes here			
-State requirement here.	1		
-State requirement here.	1		
Platforms			
-Windows 2000	1		
-Windows Me	1		
Weighted Score (out of 100%)	7	0%	0%

Notice how the scores are weighed and then combined? By taking this approach, you are better able to keep the emotion of a salesperson out of the conversation.

Again, don't forget about the business criteria you are evaluating the Vendors on. Some of the things that are going to be important to you are:

- **Frequency of patches**: The more frequent the patches, the more effort required to support the solution once in production.

- **Reference documentation**: When you are trying to work with the solution, the vendor documentation is going to be important. How clean and clear is that documentation?
- **Age of the vendor**: How old is the vendor? A young company may not have processes in place or the products may have issues that won't come up in evaluation because the bugs haven't been worked out.
- **Financial viability of vendor**: Are they going broke? Seriously, are they? Because, if they are, you'll be buying a product that can't be supported by the company.
- **Track record of the vendor**: Have there been many implementations of the vendor's product that didn't go well? If you do a search in Google, you'll get comments from past customers. Read them to see what the opinions are.
- **Market share**: A company with a big market share will have a lot of people that have experience with the product. This makes it easier to find external support if you need it. It also tells you whether other companies like this vendor (it doesn't take long for a vendor to get a bad reputation and that will show in the market share).
- **Location of support**: If you need to get support from the Vendor, where is their support desk? Is it available during YOUR business hours? Or do you only get partial support because their support area isn't in your time zone?
- **Roadmap for improvements**: This last one is actually important for your security architecture strategy. If you can get information about their roadmap (and not all vendors will provide this), it will allow you to evaluate whether the product can take on different areas in your strategy in the future.

Business requirements are just as important at technical requirements. Don't forget to evaluate them.

Security-design assessments

If you are a supporting security architect, you are eventually going to be asked to evaluate a project's solution just before it gets to its design gate. This means that you weren't involved in the early stages of the design and, as a result, didn't have the ability to influence the design early, and the design team is now going to have to take your evaluation and update their design prior to moving forward.

This is unfortunate because there will now be much more additional work that they need to do. They will be defensive with their design and will push back at any evaluation that you provide. It's for this reason that you have to evaluate against company security policies and standards because, if you use your own opinions, you won't have any authority to push back. Again, try to get involved in the design process early so that the extra work and the defensiveness doesn't come into play.

But you will still have to do an evaluation of a design after it's been worked on. As a result, you will have to provide a **Security-Design Assessment (SDA)**. This is different from a **Risk-Impact Assessment (RIA)** or **Threat-Risk Assessment (TRA)** in that you are looking at the design rather than the risk. Remember that a Security Architect focuses on the architecture first but with a security slant.

There are a number of ways to perform an SDA, but you will typically will want to have four template artifacts that you work with moving forward.

SDA project plan

The Project Plan sounds like it's going to make a big production on the evaluation, but all it does is lays out for the Project Manager the solution that you are evaluating and what the process is for that evaluation. Trust me, the PM is going to appreciate knowing what your steps are so that they can plan accordingly. They'll probably be pushing for a very quick evaluation because they want to get through their design gate and, if they bring you in at the end of the design phase, they haven't thought about how long it will take or the impact to changes in their design. Plus, it allows the two of you to ensure you are on the same page with regards to what you are evaluating and what will be done as a result of the evaluation.

The project plan should contain the following:

- **Scope statement**: Describe what is inside and outside the scope of what you are evaluating. This way, the statement is very clear about what you will be evaluating. The out-of-scope area is just as important, if not more so, as the in-scope area. Try not to evaluate areas that are not part of the actual project itself. Only focus on the infrastructure/environment that is being changed.
- **High-level requirements**: These are very simply statements of what is being required of the Supporting Security Architect by the Project team.
- **Deliverables**: Indicate what you are going to be delivering to the Project team and when it will be provided. Make sure your timelines are realistic and, while you may be pushed by the PM to get it done quickly, make sure you have time to do the job properly. It's better to do it properly than quickly.

- **Satisfaction criteria**: In what state should the PM be expecting your evaluation? What does complete look like?
- **Assumptions/Constraints/Risks**: Make sure all the things that may impact the actual delivery of your artifacts are documented. This way, the PM can understand what may impact your delivery dates. These items are delivery-based issues, not architectural, which you would normally see in Architectural documents.

SDA checklist

Once you've provided a project plan to the PM, you need to provide them with a list of the information you're going to be looking for. Trust me, seldom will you get all of this information (or even a majority of it), but it's better to ask for documentation and not receive it than to not ask for it but it's available. The SDA Checklist is a standard document that you don't make adjustments to. You create it once and give the same document to every PM and Solution Architect that you talk to. It's just a checklist of documentation that you would like to see.

Your checklist allows the Project Team to pull together the documentation that will allow you to evaluate the design properly. Remember that the solution hasn't been implemented properly, so you can only evaluate what they plan and not what they've built. Here are some of the things you should ask for:

- **Administrative documentation**: This goes more to the project documentation than the architecture documentation. You can learn a lot about the direction and scope of the project simply by looking at the Initiation phase documentation. Also ask for the contact list of stakeholders.
- **Architecture documentation**: This is what the Project team will be expecting you to ask for. Obtain the architecture documentation, diagrams, and network information. Remember that you are looking for all the architecture-layer information, so start from the physical layer and work your way up (network layer, infrastructure, application, information, processes, people). Also, get the requirements documentation that drove the design, and don't be shocked by how limited it will be. If the project team is coming to you late in the design phase, then they obviously didn't come to you for the security architecture requirements, which is an indication they probably didn't do a good job gathering requirements.

- **Design documentation:** Design is different from architecture in that you are looking for the actual physical build information. Get information such as the product design guides, the **bill of materials (BOM)** that should be purchased, and the Test Plan that will be used for testing the actual builds.
- **Product literature**: This is specific to the product itself. Get the User Guide as well as any Vendor documentation.
- **Operational support**: Once the solution is in production, what will the DR plan and backup plans look like? How about the RACI chart, has that been put together yet? Also, make sure you have the appropriate process documentation they are leveraging as well.
- **Compliance documentation:** Are there any deviations that have been applied for? How about compliance reports–is the solution dealing with any compliance issues? If so, what caused the original compliance issue?
- **Information documentation**: Everything that we do as security architects should be focused on the information that we are trying to secure. Get as complete a list of the information types as possible. What are the information flows? What is the criticality of the information? And don't just focus on the information flowing through the system. Also be aware of other types of information, such as authentication information for getting into the system, system maintenance information, and logs.

The checklist allows the project team to communicate all the appropriate information at one time rather than having a continual back-and-forth for getting information. You won't get it all, and the information that you do get will be incomplete, so be prepared to interview the Solution Architect and others for additional information as part of your SDA.

SDA workbook

The SDA Workbook is where the bulk of your work as the supporting security architect will occur. You use this to collect the information relevant to the assessment and to consolidate it into one place. Then, as an output of your workbook, you want to be creating your recommendations (again, tied to specific requirements such as Policies and Standard or Compliance requirements).

How you do your assessment is dependent on how you think things through in terms of security architecture as a whole as well as the framework that you make use of. But remember that this process should be focused on communicating to the project team and not making yourself feel more comfortable. If you were the Solution Architect, how would you create your solutions? Answer that question and you will get a better handle on how to create your SDA.

The following is just one way that you can create your SDA. It is meant to look at a solution from the various architectural towers and then determine what the applicable security components are for that tower. A useful way of doing this is to start from the Network layer and work your way up to the Information Layer. Follow a logical process when you collect your information and you should be okay.

To create your workbook, make use of Excel and use one tab for each architecture tower plus one for a few other areas, such as references and deviations from policy. Remember that this is for collecting your findings rather than creating something that is primary documentation. The output of the workbook is provided to the Project Team but the workbook is just for you, as the supporting security architect, to organize your thoughts.

Oh, and pull pictures from the Project team documentation rather than creating your own. That way, you are saving yourself effort and speeding up the process. Just make sure that you understand the pictures. This is not a make-work project but, rather, an effort for you to understand what is being proposed so that you can recommend improvements.

This book would recommend that you have the following tabs in your Excel workbook and collect the following information:

- **Information**: Document the information that is core to the solution. You don't have to document the information flow in this tab (that shows up in your **Network** tab), but you do want to document the information assets and the associated Confidentiality, Integrity, and Availability aspects of the information.

Create a table on this table with the following headings:

Info ID	Data groupings	Confidentiality	Integrity	Availability
IA001	\<simple description\>	Low/Medium/High	Low/Medium/High	Low/Medium/High

Note that you are documenting how important the Confidentiality, Integrity, and Availability of the information asset is. By doing this, you are able to identify the important information and then recommend the appropriate protections for that classification.

- **Network**: Use a Visio diagram to show how the network layer of the solution fits together. You want to document the paths that correspond to the various information flows. For example, show how an End User will connect to the solution. Show how the different components will connect to each other. Show where the components reside in the overarching enterprise network model (including the security zones). And keep an eye on how the information flows to and through the solution. You can tie the Information Asset Identification from the Information tab into your Network tab so that you can see what the flow will look like and whether the information protections are in place regarding that flow.

- **Application**: Use a logical diagram of the application architecture so that you can understand how the different components interact. The diagrams should show the components and/or products that comprise the solution and how they are related to each other. Annotations, such as shading, can be used by the security architect to illustrate the portions of the solution that were actually evaluated/assessed (within the scope of the assessment). Where possible, the diagram(s) should be provided by the project team. Sources of such documents may include project architecture and design guides. In certain situations, the security architect may need to draw their own diagrams.

- **Infrastructure**: This worksheet is used to identify and record the non-data assets that are within the scope of the SDA. By itself, a piece of hardware (for example, DNS Server) may not have any logical security implications, but the combination of OS, middleware, and application services will typically result in a number of security risks that should be eliminated or mitigated. Tie each infrastructure component to the Information Asset that you identified in the Information tab so that you can understand how the confidentiality, integrity, and availability is applied. of the information asset needs to be protected. A system or network diagram is often useful in identifying the infrastructure components. As each infrastructure component is identified, create a meaningful name and record it in a table and, if possible, tie it to the other tabs.

A useful table for this tab would look something like this:

Infra. ID	Component name	Component purpose	Subcomponents	Info. asset supported
INF2	<Web Server>	<tie to Application tab>	OS? Software? Resources (Mem, CPU, HD)?	IA001 (from Information tab)

- **Compliance**: Compliance is concerned with the compliance requirements of the project. Identify the Compliance areas that need to be checked. The security architect should ask the stakeholder whether they have already been in contact with their Compliance Officer (if there is one). If so, make sure you have actually seen the communication. Some of the compliance areas could be PCI, Freedom of Information (if a government entity), Privacy, NERC (if you are dealing with a Utility), or contractual. Contractual compliance is a big one that is often overlooked by Project teams. Make sure that all contractual obligations have been looked at.

- **Risks**: This is a tab that may or may not be useful to you as the Security Architect. It may overlap with a **Risk Impact Assessment** (**RIA**) that the Security group is doing on the solution and, if so, don't include it in your workbook. No need to duplicate efforts and double-charge your Project team. But, if you do include risks, remember to document them as appropriate for the project. Look at both intentional risks as well as the unintentional risks that the project needs to anticipate. Intentional risks may be a disgruntled employee, credit card number theft, or dangers to critical infrastructure from nation states. Unintentional risks may be accidental use by an employee, an earthquake causing damage to a datacenter, or an unknown bug in the software triggering a failure due to a specific set of circumstances.

- **References**: This is a non-essential tab that is useful for listing the various sources of information that you used to create the assessment. You should separate the information sources into Project documentation, Vendor documentation, People Interviewed, and Other sources. This is a useful tab for going back at a later date to see whether you actually reviewed all available documentation.

- **Deviations**: There will be times when a solution has asked to deviate from an existing Security Policy or Standard for a business reason. If there are deviations that have been applied for, document them on this tab. That way, if at a later date someone looks over your assessment, they understand why you may have let a specific finding pass.

Once you have collected all this information, you can now understand what the appropriate security requirements are in association with the proposed design and then what your recommendations are going to be. You document them in the following two tabs, the most important tabs in your workbook:

- **Requirements**: Document the security architecture requirements that the solution needs to meet. As stated earlier, if the project hasn't talked to you before you have done your SDA, in all likelihood they haven't done their requirements-gathering correctly and, as a result, they are going to be set back. You could legitimately push back on previous gates (specifically the Requirements Gate) in the Project-Delivery process since the project passed through the gate without having done the appropriate work.

  Document the requirements and tie them very specifically to the Business Requirements, your Security Policies and Standards, or a Compliance requirement. If you can't do that, you don't have the authority to impose specific requirements (and this goes back to the Governance chapter and the importance of creating security architecture policies and standards). The documented requirements are tied to the Recommendations tab and allow you to provide guidance to the project team.

  A good table for this tab might be as follows:

Req. #	Requirement name	Requirement description	Security control	Recommendation ID	Notes
REQ001	<Simple and Short>	<1 or 2 sentences in length>	<Specific Security Control ID>	<tie back to Recommendation tab>	

- **Recommendations**: This is the most important tab in the workbook simply because it is what you will be communicating to the Project team. It should indicate the criticality of the recommendation and the justification for the recommendation. If you cannot justify your recommendation based on approved security controls, don't make it. And remember, there has never been a book written titled Industry Standard, so don't use that as a justification for a recommendation.

A useful table for this tab might look something like as follows:

Rec. #	Rec. criticality	Recommendation	Justification
Rec001	Low/Medium/High	\<be very specific and measurable with your recommendation>	\<tie back to Requirements tab>

You have now collected all the information you need in your assessment and should be able to provide justifiable recommendations to the Project team. Now, you just have to present it to the Project team, which leads us to the last SDA artifact–the executive summary.

SDA executive summary

The executive summary is a short templatized report that you use to provide your recommendation to the project team, and typically to the project sponsor so that they understand what is being asked from a security architecture point of view.

Basically, your executive summary has one key section, which is the results of the SDA. You can restate some of the information in the other SDA artifacts, such as the process that was followed, the scope statements, and the person that put the SDA together but, at the end of the day, the core aspect of the SDA executive summary is the findings.

In your Executive Summary template, create a section titled Results and use the following verbiage for that section:

The architect provided a total of \<number> recommendations to address the collective residual risk:

- **\<number>** of the recommendations had a criticality that the architect judged to be *high*.
- **\<number>** of the recommendations had a criticality that the architect judged to be *medium*.
- **\<number>** of the recommendations had a criticality that the architect judged to be *low*.

The following is a list of the major findings from the security-design assessment along with the recommendations required to reduce the risk of these findings:

- <finding text> <**HIGH/MEDIUM/LOW**> [RECxxx]
- <finding text> <**HIGH/MEDIUM/LOW**> [RECxxx]
- <finding text> <**HIGH/MEDIUM/LOW**> [RECxxx]
- <finding text> <**HIGH/MEDIUM/LOW**> [RECxxx]
- <finding text> <**HIGH/MEDIUM/LOW**> [RECxxx]

Those recommendations with a criticality of *high* **must** be addressed immediately.

Those recommendations with a criticality of *medium* **must** be addressed <**prior to xxx**>.

Those recommendations with a criticality of *low* **should** be addressed <**prior to xxx**>.

Note: Detailed information for each recommendation (those items denoted with a REC*nnn*identifier) can be found on the recommendations worksheet of the Security Design Assessment Workbook.

A few things to note about this verbiage. First, you want to just pull your recommendations directly out of your workbook so that you don't have to retype everything. This is just being efficient with your time.

Second, it's important to include the criticality of the recommendations because the criticality of the recommendation will drive how quickly a change has to be made. If you are dealing with a project that has already built the solution and want to put it into production but have just come to you for an assessment, your high recommendations should be addressed before the solution goes live. Medium recommendations are mandatory changes that need to be made but can be lived with after the project goes live. Low recommendations are those things that should be done but aren't overly critical.

If you follow this process in doing an SDA, you'll be able to justify any recommendation that you provide and you shouldn't slow down the project. Just remember that it is always easier to adjust a design as it's being made rather than ask a project team to go back after the fact and make changes. That approach is a lot more expensive to your company.

Test plans

One of the more counter-intuitive artifacts that you will have to create is the Test plan, typically made in the Design phase of your project delivery. The Test Plan is made at this time because, as you are creating your design, you also have to figure out how to test your solution to make sure that it is actually usable and workable. You also have to provide the Project Manager a synopsis of what tests have to be run so that the PM can arrange for the resources. The sooner they know what resources they have to arrange for, the better, and the project team won't have to run around at the last minute. Everyone's stress levels will go down.

The Test plan actually has a number of different test areas, all related to the solution itself. If you are the supporting security architect, you have to provide the solution architect with the tests that need to be run from a security perspective. If you are the solution security architect, you have to work with the different operations teams to get the appropriate test scripts and consolidate them all into one test plan. Remember, you are not a SME in all areas, but you are expected to understand what has to be done for testing. Reach out to the appropriate areas to understand what needs to be tested.

There are typically two different times associated with testing and you have to have Test plans for both timeframes:

- **Test-Readiness Review (TRR)**: At the end of the build phase will be the Test Readiness Review. The TRR is meant to test the actual build of the solution to make sure everything is working as expected. These types of tests evaluate the build progress and test plan, and determine whether the solution is ready to enter the test phase.
- **System-Evaluation Review (SER)**: The SER evaluates test results associated with the deployment and cut-over plans, and looks at any outstanding architectural issues/risks. The SER is meant to determine the readiness of the solution for product launch.

Typically, your test-planning is meant to provide a number of specific deliverables:

- **Test plan**: This is how you are going to actually perform your tests and the specific tests that are part of the plan. Remember, the tests should align with the requirements you have in your Requirements Traceability Matrix (RTM) so that you can show that the requirements you gathered at the beginning of the project are flowing through everything that you are architecting.

- **Test schedule**: The test schedule will document when you are going to be doing the tests, in what order, and who will be assisting/evaluating the results.
- **Test criteria**: The test criteria is the pass/fail metrics that are used to determine whether a test is actually passed. You can easily add the criteria directly after the test plan so that there isn't any searching for how to measure results.
- **Test results**: The test results are where you actually log the results of your tests and then compare the results against the Test Criteria. In your test plan, you'll want to have a table where you record the results.
- **Defect log**: The defect log is where you document the failures from your testing. Part of the defect log will be the mitigations or corrections that you will be taking to make sure the solution meets requirements. You can have an entire separate document or put this into your Architecture Issues Log, or you can have a standalone section in your Test Plan for where you identify the failures.
- **Test Sign-off**: The Test Sign-off is something that you want to make sure you have ready for passing your Test phase gate. This sign-off should be from your primary stakeholder(s) to indicate that the test results show that the solution is working as planned.

Types of testing

Okay, now let's talk about the testing, both from a supporting security architect's point of view as well as from the solution security architect point of view.

From the supporting security architect point of view, your primary focus is on ensuring that the project you are supporting will provide a solution that has had the risks reduced to an appropriate level that is acceptable and in support of the business requirements. As the supporting security architect, you are going to be needed to interpret the results of the scan reports because often, one specific issue will result in multiple different alerts. You will also need to review the test results prior to submitting them to the project team to clean out false positives. Never give the raw reports from one of these tests to a project team because you will inevitably have arguments about whether something is actually a vulnerability.

So, to that end, there are going to be five possible security tests you may want to think about, depending on the project, and ensure that the solution architect has included in their test plan:

- **Vulnerability testing**: Vulnerability testing is a series of automated tests that look at the actual infrastructure level of the solution, as it would look on production machines. It looks for things such as open ports and services, default passwords, and known vulnerabilities that are found in the Common Vulnerabilities and Exposures (CVE) database that are managed and monitored by NIST. This is the most basic of cybersecurity testing and can be done with any number of tools, such as Tenable's NESSUS or Qualys' scanning solution.

- **Penetration testing**: Penetration testing should be a must for any solution that is externally exposed (for example, A Web Portal, a Externally-exposed ESB, or an API Management solution). It is a much more rigorous set of tests and will include manual probing to look for unknown vulnerabilities (vulnerabilities that haven't been found yet but exist because of poorly written code). If you want to make sure that you are using products that have a higher level of cybersecurity assurance, look to have the Vendor provide a report from an authorized ISA99 (https://www.isa.org/isa99/) test lab. Very few vendors actually have their products tested by an independent third party, but if enough customers start demanding it, maybe the cybersecurity quality of the products will improve.

- **Static (Whitebox) testing**: Static testing is the testing of code prior to being compiled. By checking code before it's been compiled, you will find vulnerabilities that are the result of poorly written code or code that hasn't been peer-reviewed. This should be a standard test for any unit of code in a custom application project. Be aware, though, most Automated Static testing tools do not uncover all vulnerabilities. When the tools first came out, they found only around 10% of vulnerabilities. They're much better now, typically in the 60% range, but this still leaves a number of vulnerabilities undiscovered. So a combination of automated and manual static testing is best for custom or customized COTS applications.

- **Dynamic (Blackbox) testing**: Dynamic testing is the testing of code after it's been compiled. This means that you can't actually see the individual lines of code and are only able to test how the application behaves. You'll have the application you are testing on a test computer and focus on the application itself. This is not meant to find things such as unhardened servers but to see whether there are vulnerabilities that exist as a result of poor coding practices.

OWASP is a great resource for looking into application-security vulnerabilities. But don't settle for the Top 10 list–these are only the most common vulnerabilities. There will be all sorts of other vulnerabilities that will exist beyond the Top 10. Do you really want to ignore them?

- **Fuzzing**: No, fuzzing is not about cuddling with your Teddy Bear! Fuzzing is testing an application by putting in unexpected input into the various fields of an application and seeing what the result is. What happens if you put a SQL command in a name field? Does it get rejected or accepted? Again, there are fuzzing tools out there, but it's often best to reach out to an application security company to do a combination of automated and manual testing of applications.

That takes you through the tests that a Supporting Security Architect should be looking at. Now, if you are the Solution Security Architect, you need to be looking at a number of other types of tests. Those would be:

- **Performance testing**: Performance testing looks at how the solution is working and whether the underlying resources (for example, memory, CPU, and I/O) are behaving as expected when the solution is working.
- **Unit testing:** Most solutions will have multiple components. If you are looking at a custom application, unit testing will test whether each standalone unit of code is functioning as expected. For an infrastructure project, you'd be looking at the individual components of the solution, such as the web server, the authentication components, and the database. These are components of the overarching solution and you want to make sure they are functioning as expected. Some people term this type of testing as Functional Testing.
- **Integration testing**: Once you know that your individual components are working as expected, how do they work when they are integrated together? If you were to test the entire solution all at once and something fails, how do you know which component is the cause of the failure? Test the individual components first to make sure they are functioning and then slowly integrate the components to make sure they work as expected.
- **High-Availability (HA) testing**: HA Testing is meant to ensure that the solution keeps on working if you take some redundant component out of the solution. There's a reason why projects are deemed as needing to be Highly Available, so test to see whether the solution stays functional if you take individual components out of the solution.

- **Disaster-Recovery (DR) testing**: Too often, architects forget to check whether there's a requirement for a solution to have a disaster-recovery component. If there is, you need to test the ability of the solution to recover in your DR site. If the production solution goes down, how long does it take to get the DR components up and running? Is that within your **Recovery Time Objectives (RTO**–how long it takes to recover) and **Recovery Point Objectives (RPO**–how much of the production data is the DR site working with) requirements?

- **User-Acceptance Testing (UAT)**: UAT is all about whether the stakeholders are getting what the requirements said they wanted. You want to put a sample group of stakeholders in front of the solution and have the users test the consolidated functionality of the solution. Do they accept the result? If so, you know your solution has met the requirements. You should have this test as the last one in your Test Plan since the other tests may result in changes to the architecture.

These are a lot of different tests that you need to think about as a solution security architect. Many of these tests may not be applicable to you simply because solution security architects tend to focus on security technologies and not have to go into things such as code testing, or your solution may not be deemed important enough to have a DR component. But you should be aware of the different types of tests in case you need to manage those areas.

Build documentation

The build documentation is the final major piece of documentation that the architect needs to put together in a project. There will be other documentation that you need to provide but the build document is the last major piece. It is meant to provide the nuts and bolts, the physical architecture to the operations teams that are supporting the solution. They don't care about things such as requirements (other than their own) or the various other higher-level components in an ADD. If they have to support a solution, they want the information at their fingertips. And that's where the Build document comes in.

In short, the build document is a listing of the physical components, how they are connected, and the authentication information needed for getting into the solution. It contains the specific physical details about the solution that would be needed to support the solution if something were to happen. Often, there will be actual screen shots of the installation of the solution so that things such as the paths and configuration information is captured appropriately.

When you create your build document, focus only on the actual information about the installation and think about having the following tables in your document:

Installation table

The installation table will contain the host names of the components in the solution, which environment the components reside in, and the installation path for where to find the application that is the primary purpose of that server. An example table would be:

Environment	Server host name	Primary installation path
<DEV/QA/PROD>	<Server Name>	<Installation path of the solution>

Database table

Very few solutions don't have a database. Include a table that has the information about your database and try to include the following information:

Group	DB User ID	Password	Database home	Database name	Encryption
<DB group name>	<Username>	<password>	<home path>	<DB name>	<if encryption is included, information on encryption>

Note: Do not include production password information in the Build document. Provide that in a separate document for operations.

Administrator table

The operations team is going to need to know the administrative information for accessing the various components of the solution. Again, provide that information for accessing the components:

Environment	Administrator ID	Password	Suffix	Hostname
<DEV/QA/Prod>	<ldap path to Admin ID>	<password>	<FQDN path for component>	<hostname>

Note: Do not include production password information in the build document. Provide that in a separate document for Operations.

Username tables

There are going to be non-administrative usernames that are going to access the various components. Again, provide that information as follows:

Environment	Username	Password
<DEV/QA/Prod>	<username>	<password>

Note: Do not include production password information in the build document. Provide that in a separate document for operations.

URL tables

The vast majority of solutions are now being made available through web access rather than a Java console. Include the URLs for all appropriate connections, including the web administrative console and end user connections:

Environment	Solution URLs
<DEV/QA/Prod>	<Server Administration Console URL>
	<User URL>
	<Database admin URL>
	<ldap admin URL>
	<Web server administration console URL>

Additional information

There's quite a bit of other information that is going to be needed in your Build document. Include the following information in the appropriate sections:

- **SSL certificate**: Document information about the SSL certificates that you are using in the solution. Include the path to the certificate locations, the age of the certificates, the source of the certificates (even if they are self-signed), and the encryption information about the certificates. Often there are multiple certificates used in a solution, for both the Production environment as well as the other non-production environments, so make sure you document all of that information.
- **CLI Commands**: If you are using a non-standard application that has **Command-Line Interface (CLI)** commands, you want to document those commands and when you use them. Some of the different types of commands you may want to document are:
    - Application start/stop
    - SSL configuration commands
    - Launch of consoles
    - Configuration-check commands
    - Password-change commands
- **Log information**: Many solutions will have their logs in specific locations that aren't necessarily normal or easy to find. This includes your security logs, error logs, and application logs. Include the locations of those logs in your build documentation.
- **Support systems**: There are going to be systems that are connected to your solution in order to support it. From a security perspective, you'll probably have to record the information relevant to the SIEM, Anti-Virus solutions, and change-management solutions (among others). From the infrastructure-support point of view, you'll have server-management systems and database-management solutions. Make sure you document the support systems that are connected and what information is going to be needed for those systems.

Remember that Operations teams don't tend to be overly technical, and are made up of more junior personnel. They will have a tendency to want to use GUIs or web interfaces and won't as comfortable using the CLI. Document as much as you can that is going to be needed from an operational point of view so that they can access the areas they need to be for support and maintenance purposes.

Summary

There are a lot of different artifacts that a security architect needs to be involved in throughout the project-delivery process. The most important of them all is the requirements documentation because the requirements will flow through all the remaining phases of the project. And remember that the primary role of the architect is to communicate, so your documentation is a primary purpose of your role, used to communicate about the solution that the project team is providing. In the next chapter, we will look at the most important document in the architecture—the **Architecture Design Document (ADD)**. It needs a chapter of its own.

Questions

1. Have you done your requirements-gathering yet? Why not?
2. If you have new requirements come up after a project has moved past that phase, what should you do?
3. What is the purpose of the SDA workbook?
4. What is the difference between functional and nonfunctional requirements?
5. Once you create your requirements, how are they used?

8
Architecture Design Document

The **Architecture Design Document (ADD)** is probably the most important artifact that a security architect will create. While the gathering of requirements is the most important activity, the ADD is the most important artifact. It is meant to be a standalone document to indicate how a solution should reside in the environment, and it should be contain all of the information required to actually implement the solution.

The ADD is different from the build document in that the ADD is what should be created, whereas the build document is what has been created. Remember, the ADD will be 85% stable, whereas the build document should be 100% stable. But the fact that the ADD is 85% stable is huge. It's been created to meet the requirements that you have gathered and should contain the people, processes, and technology components that make up that solution.

This particular chapter is all about what the ADD contains and what you should be thinking about when creating it. The ADD is typically created by the solution security architect, but, when a supporting security architect is involved in the design phase of a project, they should provide input to the security components of the various layers in the solution. Remember, the solution security architect has to deal with the entire solution (the security components, as well as everything else), whereas the supporting security architect only has to focus on the security aspects of the solution.

Approaches to the ADD

The first thing to understand about the ADD is that there are different approaches to what you want it to contain, and that all depends on the framework that you are using for your architecture practice. If you are making use of TOGAF, then you are breaking down the architecture based on conceptual, logical, and physical elements. If you are using Zachman, then you are breaking it down based on a different set of elements. There are more than 60 different architecture frameworks, and each has its own elements. Make sure that your ADD is aligned with the framework methodology that your organization is focused on.

Next, you need to be aware of any architectural tools that your organization uses. One of the most common tools out there is ArchiMate. ArchiMate provides a very good image that allows a reader of your ADD to visualize how the architecture flows. But, again, you have to be aware of the architecture framework that ArchiMate makes use of and, in this case, ArchiMate is aligned with TOGAF.

The TOGAF approach is solid, because it allows you to drill down, with regards to big-picture concepts, to a more practical physical architecture. But that can create quite a bit of verbiage in your ADD, and it takes time to compile that type of architecture. So really, think about and the framework that your organization is using, and make sure that it is applicable to your organization. Every framework has its good points and bad points, and is just the starting point for what your architecture should look like.

A good way to view the ADD is to think of it as more of a strategic document than a tactical document. If you think of architecture as moving from a current state to a future state, leveraging the assets that you have at your disposal, you will end up with an ADD that works and can act as a roadmap to the final solution. Thinking this way can really help you understand what you put into your document.

Remember, making changes to an environment means that you have to understand what is there in the first place. Understanding that will also allow you to understand what changes have to be made to the current state. Following that line of thinking will then indicate that a portion of your ADD should be documenting the current state that is going to change. That doesn't mean that you have to document the entire environment-just the components that are going to change.

One example is your **Active Directory (AD)** structure. Maybe your AD has a particular user structure in place. If that's the case, the roles that you are going to need for authenticating into the solution can align with the AD structure, or you can make changes to the AD structure that support your solution.

These are two different approaches to creating a solution, but understanding what is there in the first place will allow you to make the appropriate decisions. Creating an architecture is all about making the best decisions for a solution, and making the solutions is most easily done if you have a good understanding of what the environment currently looks like.

Keep in mind that you don't necessarily have to document the current state in your ADD; rather, document the changes that have to occur. There are organizations out there that use the ADD to document the current state, simply because previous implementations were done organically, as a result, there is a lack of understanding of what is currently in place. This adds additional time to the creation of your architecture, and it is all dependent on how your architecture practice is moving forward. Keep in mind that time–and effort are money, and can lead to questions about why it costs so much to put together simple architectures. You need to do things properly, but there are those who don't understand the need for documenting future purposes. So, prepare for those points of view.

I'm a big fan of breaking solutions down based on the architecture towers. The rest of this chapter will focus on the real-world, practical approach to delivering architectures and it all starts with documenting the business architecture because we always need to support the business. If you can't clearly show how you are supporting the business and the changes that need to be made, you aren't focused on the business requirements.

From the business architecture, you should shift to the next level down, which is the information architecture. Business is typically adjusting or dealing with information, so it's important to document the information the solution is manipulating. That manipulation is done using applications, so the Application Architecture is a natural next step. Applications reside on infrastructure so document the infrastructure architecture. And the infrastructure is connected to the network so finish off with the network architecture (though some people view the infrastructure as containing the network components, so you may end up with the network architecture components as part of the infrastructure architecture).

What missing from this discussion? Well, this book is all about cyber security for architects, so where's the security architecture?

It's really important for the solution architect to remember that security is built into all layers in the architecture. Each layer has security components and to pull them out into a separate section runs the risk of allowing the quality of the security architecture to be ignored. Each architecture layer should have its own security slant right from the start and, at worst, a subsection on the security components. For example, information architecture should keep in mind the criticality of the information itself. Application architecture should be thinking about application security or security configurations. And so on and so on. This will be reviewed in detail a little later in this chapter. Just keep in mind that each architecture layer has its own security slant so make sure you tie security into each layer.

Keep in mind that the ADD is all about communicating a solution, including the security components in that solution. The ADD is then focused on only communicating solution-based information. Don't get caught up in providing project information in a solution document–that's for the PM to do in their documentation. Your job, as the solution Architect, is to make sure all aspects of the solution are understood and that goes beyond just the actual physical changes to the environment, it includes things such as the reasons for your design decisions. If the decision is big enough, that will go into a separate **Key Decision Document (KDD)** but not everything needs a KDD. You can just document the decision in the KDD.

Finally, remember one thing about the ADD (and it's something that too many architects forget): the ADD is a set of instructions for implementation. It's not meant to be wishy-washy. It's not meant to document what could happen but what will happen. You are making a statement and telling the people who are reading the document what will be done. If you leave decisions in the could realm, you risk that the people implementing the solution might misinterpret the design and make erroneous decisions during implementation.

The more detailed information you can put into your ADD, the more you are assured of having actually thought of all issues and the smoother the implementation will be. There will be issues and changes to the architecture simply because you won't think of everything, but the more you understand, the more solid your architecture, and the better your business sponsor can make decisions. Think of it this way–if your design says that a design will cost $XXX and it gets approved based on that cost but then an unplanned factor causes the cost to be 50% higher, who do you think will get the blame?

Make sure your architecture has thought about as many things as possible so that you have accurate information to decide whether to move forward. One of the decisions as the result of an architecture may be that the business sponsor decides it's not worth the expense and effort and that's perfectly fine. Remember it's the business sponsor's decision to make because it's their money. But if you can't give them a thoroughly thought-out design, you are doing your stakeholders a disservice.

The rest of this chapter will go into the structure of the ADD and the reasons behind it. These sections, while they may seem unimportant to the overarching design, actually contain information about the solution that is as important as the design itself. Think of the non-solution sections as the metadata about the solution.

Header sections

The boilerplate information isn't something that we'll deal with in the ADD simply because that has no impact on the architecture itself. Add whatever information you want in relation to that. Some people will include the following information:

- Release histories
- A list of reviewers
- A list of documentation used in the creation of the architecture (which can be very useful information later)
- A glossary of terms
- A table of contents

Beyond that, though, is the actual information that impacts the ADD. The header information will provide a frame into which the actual architecture is presented. It's that information we'll talk about now.

Purpose, summary, and usage

The purpose, summary, and usage section of the ADD is meant to provide the background as to why the architecture was created in the first place and how the architecture is to be used moving forward. It will lay out the issues that required the creation of the architecture and, typically, the problem statement.

The summary of the ADD is different from the executive summary. In this context, the summary is meant to explain what is contained in the ADD itself, whereas the executive summary is a short summary of the architecture.

Executive summary

Whenever a report is provided to people to read, remember that very people will actually read it. You'll have the people that implement the solution looking for the sections specific to their area of expertise, but they won't read the entire document. If you send the document out for review, you will be lucky to get more than a small handful of reviews back (often only one or two people). When it comes to those people aren't actually going to make use of the ADD, it's the executive summary that they want.

It's called an executive summary, because it was typically written for the executives that have to see all sorts of documents and don't have time to read full documents. The executive summary in an ADD is a section that summarizes the main points of the solution. It's a page or two at most, and won't typically have a whole lot of technical jargon. It is meant to give an overview of the solution so that the reader, whatever role they may play in your organization, can decide whether they want to read further into the solution.

Be short, concise, and use broad strokes to describe the solution itself. If you have technical information in the executive summary, you probably putt too much detail into that section.

Scope

The scope is a very important section of the ADD, because it describes the limits of what the solution will deal with. Many people just put what's in the scope into the document, but it's just as important to include the out-of-scope areas, because it makes it very clear as to how far the solution is meant to go.

The scope statements are really the outlines of what the project is about. They're meant to provide an outline of where the solution can and cannot go. They should align with the architecture strategy for that solution area, and it's really important to keep in mind that the architecture strategy should be lay out the scope for each individual project. As a result, the scope statement for your ADD should align with the scope assigned by the strategy. There may be some other project that covers an area that your project is running beside, so you don't want two separate projects covering the same area.

Compliance

The compliance section of your ADD should list the specific policies or compliance areas that the project has to keep in mind. Similar to the requirements sections, compliance sections discuss the guidance that the architecture practice provides the project for moving forward. List the policies and/or standards that the project has to align with, but don't rewrite the entire policy. Just provide a pointer to it (for example, a URL link to the policy or standard, if it's located in a place that provides a URL).

References to requirements

As we talked about in the requirements gathering section, everything that we do has to be aligned with the requirements. The reference to requirements section provides a link to the requirements documentation, and, if there's a requirement that is especially important, calls it out in this section. Again, the point isn't to rewrite previous documents; the purpose is to link to the primary document.

Target architecture

The target architecture is meant to document what the end state architecture is going to look like and the changes that have to occur for the solution to be put into place. This area of the document is the meat of the ADD and is the primary reason for it.

The following sections cover what should be in the ADD from an architecture perspective, and break the architecture down into various layers, from the business layer down to the infrastructure layer. You may want to put the current state of the architecture into these sections, in order to identify exactly what is changing. The current state shouldn't really be necessary if the solution is brand new and is not making any changes to the current state architecture. But that doesn't happen very often, since there are typically VLAN changes or firewall rule changes that have to occur.

Business architecture

The business architecture section is focused on the business aspects of the solution and this area is always impacted by the solution. There may be people that need to be assigned responsibilities for maintaining a solution, there may be processes that need to be updated, and there is likely to be some governance function that needs to be adjusted.

Too many architects just focus on the technical components of a solution, and, as a result, don't think of the entire cost and impact of a solution. That's the primary reason that you need to include the business architecture as a standalone section in the ADD template-so that you always think about it.

In the business architecture, make sure that you include the following components:

- **Process flows**: If the solution involves a change to a process, document the change using an appropriate swimlane diagram. There are a lot of similarities to the RACI chart, but the purpose of this section is to document the order of multiple processes, and to make use of a decision tree, if there are different options. Your swimlane diagram might have different lanes for different groups or roles (depending on whether you are looking for a group to act on a specific action in the process).

  Process flows have a number of different icons for different actions in the process (for example, the decision, initiation of process, and process step), so become familiar with them in Visio.

- **RACI chart**: The RACI chart is a listing of the various processes associated with the solution, the roles involved in those processes (don't use peoples' names, because people change roles), and how those roles are involved, using the **Responsible, Accountable, Consulted, and Informed (RACI)** aspects. A typical RACI is put together in a chart that looks like the following:

Process	Role A	Role B	Role C	Role D
<Process #1>	R/A/C/I	R/A/C/I	R/A/C/I	R/A/C/I
<Process #2>	R/A/C/I	R/A/C/I	R/A/C/I	R/A/C/I

Most processes have multiple responsibilities assigned. For example, if there's a change to the firewall rules, one role might be responsible for approving the rule change, one role is responsible for approving the rule change, and one role may need to be informed about the rule change. That particular table might look like this:

Process	Firewall admin	CISO	Auditor	Mgr, Infra.
Implement firewall rule change	Responsible	Accountable	Informed	Consulted

Think about every process that needs to be involved, so that you can document the responsibilities appropriately. Also, make sure you inform the people that you are assigning responsibilities to; there's little more disturbing that discovering than that you have been made responsible for something without being told about it or asked beforehand.

- **Governance model**: The governance model is going to be there, even if you aren't aware of it. For example, your solution should have defined criticality and; as a result, will fall into your audit activities. An audit is a form of governance. There may be alignment with some union agreement, or a need for approvals associated with changes to the environment. All of these are changes to the governance model that you need to document.

From a security architecture point of view, there are different things that can be looked at in the business architecture. There are different security processes that will need to be documented or changed. There are security personnel that will need to be informed of changes or that will have to take responsibility for certain things.

For example, if you are implementing a solution that is not security-related, there are still things that need to be done from a security point of view. Some things that may have to occur (and this is dependent on the scope of your security team) include the following:

- Updating scheduled vulnerability scans
- Updating assets lists
- Changing business-continuity plans
- Approving process flows that may involve the security team

Remember and this goes for the following sections as well: every layer in an architecture has a security component. That includes the business architecture layer.

Data and information architecture

The data architecture layer is the architecture layer dedicated to the actual information that the solution is meant to manipulate and present. It's also the layer that is probably the most important to security architecture, because it's the layer that drives home the term information security. You are, at the end of the day, securing the information that the solution is making use of.

First, let's discuss the information that you will find in the solution, as well as what you will want to have in the data/information architecture section. There are be two primary types of information that you need to understand as a part of your solution:

- **Solution information**: The solution information is what your solution manages. You'll typically see this information stored in some manner within the solution, and the solution will access and adapt that information moving forward. The solution information can also include metadata about the solution information.

  - **Database structure**: While the database system information itself belongs to the infrastructure layer, the structure of the database including the tables, the data included in the tables, and the relations between the different tables are considered data architecture and should be included in the data/information architecture section.

  - **Data structure**: Your solution should also document the structure that the data should be in. For example, there may be a database with first names. You'll want to detail that the first names need to be no more than 20 characters, only alpha characters, and the first letter should always be capitalized. By documenting the data structure, you will be able to ensure that the solution doesn't crash because of malformed data. This is especially important when dealing with XML structures.

- **System information**: The system information is information that the system has to refer to, or that guides the solution in its actual actions. It's not the core solution information, but indirectly, it's just as important. Some examples of this type of information are as follows:

  - **Logs**: Most operations teams (as well as implementation teams) need to be able to access log information in order to ensure that the solution is working as expected. You'll want to list the log information that is made available, regardless of whether it is in the application layer or the infrastructure layer.

  - **Metadata**: Metadata is information that describes the data in the solution. For example, you may have a database that contains customer information. Anything that lists that type of information is considered metadata.

From a security architecture point of view, the data/information architecture is key. It's where you start to lay out a number of different security requirements and structures for the solution. Some of the security architecture information that you will want to include in your ADD is as follows:

- **Criticality classification**: Take the information that you have documented in the solution and identify exactly what the criticality of that information is. Keep in mind that the information itself can be critical to the solution, and that the solution is putting out information that other solutions will make use of. Therefore, the criticality of the information can flow through to the rest of the enterprise, in a worst-case situation.

- **CRUD matrix**: The CRUD matrix is a table that lists the information used by the solution, the roles that are used by the solution, and what rights/permissions those roles have. The term **CRUD** comes from **Change, Read, Update, and Delete**. This is along the same lines as the permissions you find associated with UNIX files where they have read/write/execute permissions. The CRUD rights/permissions are specifically tied to the information itself.

- **Data at rest**: Data at rest are protections that you put into place when data resides in one place prior to or during manipulation. This can be in the database or in a flat file. PCI actually expects data at rest capabilities when the data resides in the CPU. You can logically separate the infrastructure-level protections for data at rest with the protections dedicated to the information itself.

- **Data in flight**: Like data at rest, data in flight is about how you are going to protect the information as it traverses a network. Focus on the data itself, rather than on the medium that is transporting the information; the medium information will reside in the infrastructure section.

If you are dealing with a solution that is cloud-based, realize that you are now dealing with someone else's infrastructure and you don't have control of it. Make sure you are controlling the security of the information itself rather than the security of the infrastructure. This also goes for information that goes onto mobile devices. The mobile device can get lost or stolen so you will have limited control over the infrastructure (that is, the mobile device) but you can control what happens with the information with things such as encryption and tokenization.

A special note on tokenization

Tokenization is a technology that is starting to come to the foreground because of the growth of cloud solutions and the sensitivity around personal information. If you want to learn about tokenization, there are a number of different books out there that you can refer to, this is just a commentary on the technology.

Tokenization is a method of substituting information that you are concerned about with data that represents your information. For example, if you are making use of a cloud solution such as Salesforce, you may want to make sure that the personal information of your clients is protected appropriately. But you lack the controls over Salesforce that you may have in place internally. Rather than send something such as a name (for example, Neil) to the cloud application, you send a representation of that data (for example, X23r).

A database is located, typically in your DMZ, the tokenization solution will substitute your information with the representation, and then store the mapping in that database. Then, when the cloud application is sending information back to you through its presentation layer, the representation is substituted back to the original format. The cloud application is able to do its work but the actual information never leaves your environment.

There are some limitations with tokenization where some Vendors may only be able to work with certain cloud applications. Work with your tokenization vendor to determine whether they can work with your cloud application and keep in mind how you want to protect that information based on its criticality.

Application architecture

The application architecture section of the ADD deals with the actual interfaces and application associated with the solution. Remember that ALL solutions have an application architecture component, even a solution that has to do with networking or infrastructure. Every solution has an application that interfaces with it's technical components.

Keeping that in mind, there are basically three types of application situations:

- **COTS application**: A **Commercial off-the-shelf (CTOS)** solution is one where no customization is required, and you can start to use it the moment that it's installed. You don't care what language the application is written in because you are purchasing a compiled application and have no need to see the underlying code. This is the cheapest application solution you can find, but it may not fully meet your requirements. When looking at COTS applications, try to choose one that matches the most requirements possible. You'll also look at COTS applications if one of your architecture principles is to buy before build. This is also typically where you find the cloud-based solutions termed **Software as a Service (SaaS)**.

- **Custom application**: A custom application is completely unique and is written specifically to meet your requirements. This is the most expensive application solution but it's also the one solution that will fully meet requirements. There are any number of languages that can be used and this is dependent on the speed the application needs to work at. Real-time applications will need to be written in lower-level languages because the application needs to act in real or near-real-time on the data that is presented, with a minimum latency (which points to the question about what your latency requirements are). Custom applications will also have the highest level of security flaws simply because you aren't starting with an updated application and need to find the flaws as they are written.

- **Hybrid application**: A hybrid application is typically a COTS Application that can be customized to meet more of your requirements than a simple COTS application. It has a lower cost than a custom application because much of the code has already been written, but will more closely meet your requirements. From a security point of view, this application solution will balance the needs of the business (meeting as many requirements as possible) while increasing the security risk resulting from custom code.

When you deal with application architectures from a security point of view, you need to start to think about introducing a **Secure Development Life Cycle (SDLC)** into your environment. This isn't as much a security architecture as it is a security practice. The following table will give you some guidelines about the application-security activities that you should be looking at doing as part of the development process.

Notice that the COTS applications will have a lighter SDLC footprint than a full custom application:

Type of app	Risk impact assessment	Threat-modeling	Security-design assessment	Internal code review	Testing and review	Preproduction	Production protection
Custom code	Full	Full	Full	Full	Full	Full	Full
COTS	Full	Full	None	None	Partial	Full	Full
Hybrid	Full	Full	Partial	Partial	Partial	Full	Full

From a security architecture point of view, there are certain components that should be included as part of this section. They are as follows:

- **Application level roles**: Like with any layer, you need to determine the roles that the application itself will contain and their rights and permissions. This is all part of **Identity and Access Management** (**IAM**) and may be an opportunity to leverage your SSO or provisioning solutions.
- **Authentication source**: If possible, make sure that your application is leveraging your enterprise AD solution. Typically, you will have a security policy saying that a person needs to have their accesses removed within 24 hours of leaving the company. If you are tying your applications to AD, any changes to AD will automatically change the access associate with the person. The same goes for when people change jobs within a company. If you are making use of; an RBAC architecture, changing roles in AD will change permissions in your applications.
- **Security logging**: Very few applications actually have security logs, and this is typically left to the infrastructure level. If you are having customization done for an application, try to get the development team to include security logs. If they ask what should go into the security logs, have them look at how Windows machines log security events and then have the development team try to log in a similar manner.
- **Web Application Firewall (WAF)**: While a WAF is an infrastructure component, it is an external capability that allows the protection of applications from application-level threats. If you have an externally-facing application, definitely make use of a WAF. There are load-balancers (for example, F5) and other solutions that have WAF components that can be integrated for a lower cost, if that is a concern.

- **Application-security architecture checks**: The actual coding of any custom components also need to have security architecture components. When you review the actual application architecture, look for the following security architecture capabilities:
    - **Deployment and infrastructure considerations**: Make sure the design considered the environment that the solution will be rolled out into.
    - **Input validation**: Every input needs to be validated for appropriateness. This is how things such as cross-site scripting occur, when the input aren't what the application was expecting.
    - **Authentication/Authorization considerations**: The processes within the application should have the appropriate authentication activities. Make sure that there isn't any hardcoded passwords, that the solution doesn't run with administrative rights, and that the context for the application processes is appropriate (using the principle of least privilege).
    - **Configuration considerations**: How is the application going to be configured by administrators? Are there any issues there?
    - **Sensitive data considerations**: How does the application treat sensitive data? For example, PCI has specific requirements on how credit card data is stored so make sure you meet compliance requirements.
    - **Session considerations**: Don't let an application run a process with an unlimited timeframe. Typically, you'll want sessions to time out in 15 minutes, though that is highly dependent on the criticality of the data as well as the usability requirements of the business. There's a balancing act that needs to go on here.
    - **Cryptographic considerations**: When does the application need to leverage encryption? Do you encrypted the data for storing in a database or do you encrypt for transmitting across the network or internet? Make sure that the development team is using approved cryptographic code and the appropriate algorithms.
    - **Exception-handling**: Every application will run into issues at least once in production. There isn't a single application that has been written that is perfect from day one (it's the reason why there are so many versions for different applications). Make sure the way that applications handle exceptions is appropriate. How will the application fail?

One last thing, and it's something that has been stated before within this book: a lot of organizations claim to look at OWASP's top 10 issues. But there are so many more issues that can allow someone to hack an application. Make sure you have a proper SDLC and that, from a security architecture point of view, you are making use of a checklist that ensures you don't forget about an area within the application itself.

Infrastructure architecture

The infrastructure architecture is where the vast majority of security architects spend their time. As you can see from the previous architecture layers, there's so much more to security architecture than just looking at the packets that are going across the network or how a server is implemented. Because information security/cybersecurity/IT security (or whatever term you want to use) has been around since the late 1990s, it started off focusing on the network layer and then on the server level. As a result, your non-security architect will have had to deal with this layer quite a bit and this will typically be the most robust area of an ADD.

Regardless, the ADD should be broken down into the various layers within the infrastructure architecture. There should be the following components, starting from the lowest level and moving up:

- **Network components**: Include the network-level information about each component in the solution. This would be information such as the IP addresses, VLANs, MPLS network information, and VFRs. If there is new routing information needed for implementation, include that as well as any firewall rule-changes that have to be made. Remember, typical organizations will have the firewalls managed by the networking team rather than the security team and that is appropriate considering there needs to be a separation of duties involved.

    Include information such as the physical layer information (for example, WLAN, and LAN/MAN/WAN) here as well as any Layer 2 information (for example, switches, hubs, repeaters, and load balancers). Also include the network-protocol information that is going to be used if necessary.

- **Server components**: Each component within a solution will have a server. So include the operating system information, such as the ports and associated services that are needed on each server. Document what each Server name is going to be and what data each server will be handling (this will go to the criticality of the server since the criticality of the server is dependent on the criticality of the information contained within the server).

  The server components will also have information about the supporting server services, such as DNS, NTP, DHCP, LDAP/Active Directory, clustering, and virtualization. The virtualization information can be extremely important just from a redundancy point of view.

  Lastly, if you are making use of a middleware solution, such as an **Enterprise Services Bus** (**ESB**), talk about the services that are either going to be made available for the ESB or for the standardized interfaces that are going to be used. This information can be made available in the application architecture section instead of here since middleware overlaps between infrastructure and application architectures.

- **Database components**: The database information in this section is associated with the database server rather than the tables within the database (which is documented in the data/information architecture section). Document any controls that are to be in place for the databases and any configuration information needed. If the database is going to reside on a SAN, document which areas are associated with the SAN and make sure that the criticality of the information on the SAN aligns with the criticality of the information that is being put there by your solution. What are the connections to the database (ODBC, JDBC) and what are the credentials that are needed for that connection to occur?

- **Application server components**: The application server will sit on top of the underlying server, so document any configuration associated with application server. The same goes for any web application server. For example, IBM's WebSphere is a web application server, focused on hosting Java-based applications, that may reside on a Linux server. As a result, there will be information about the Linux server (documented under the server components section) and separate information about the WebSphere application server in this section. Again, talk about configurations that need to be made to the application server in support of the application itself.

- **Management/Monitoring tools**: Architects will focus on the documentation of the solution, itself but often forget about the management tools that are needed to support the solution. But the operations teams will need to monitor the solution once it's in production so there's a need to consider what tools will support the solution and how those tools will communicate back to their management consoles. And don't forget to talk about things such as how the operations teams will connect to the solution if a component fails. Will this be through an out-of-band connection? An ILO connection?
- **Backup component**: How will the configurations be backed up? How often? Where will the backups be stored? How often/how will the backups be checked to make sure they are actually functioning? Don't forget to include the actual backup information for your operations teams because they are the ones who will have to perform the backups.
- **Endpoint components**: Finally, is there any architecture information that is required for the endpoints? Remember, no solution is useful unless a workstation/laptop/mobile device can connect to it so you need to consider any changes that are necessary for the endpoints to be able to make use of the solution or for the endpoints themselves to be managed.

That's a lot of information that will be put into place in the infrastructure architecture. From a security point of view, there's a whole slew of things that can be done as well and this makes the use of your **Reference Security Architecture (RSA)** especially important. If you go back to the RSA chapter in this book, you will see different areas that would be put into this section of your ADD.

Break your security architecture into the sections of the RSA. When you deal with the network architecture, include comments associated with border protection. When you look at the infrastructure architecture, look at the detection services as well as the configuration services. If auditing is something that needs to be focused on because of compliance, include your audit services. Every layer in your architecture is going to make use of your IAM section of the RSA, so make sure you really focus on that.

Security architecture isn't just security tools but how security is applied throughout a solution and that includes making use of security tools within your solutions. Anti-Virus needs to be in place on servers and Endpoints unless there's a reason for it not to be there. Logging needs to go to a SIEM, so how are you going to get the logs from your infrastructure and application architecture components to the SIEM? Make use of your RSA so that you don't miss an area within the various architecture layers in your solution.

Concluding sections

The end of your architecture design document will have some sections that are important because they go into the areas that aren't included in the solution. Where the scope section at the beginning of the ADD talks about what is and is not in scope for the solution, these sections talk about requirements that haven't been put into the solution even though they may be included in the requirements. These two sections are called the Gap analysis and the Recommendation sections.

Gap analysis

The Gap analysis section is used to describe any gaps in the solution compared to what was documented in the requirements. In this section, indicate what requirements have not been met and why they haven't been met. There may be an issue associated with the current environment that doesn't allow for a requirement to be met, or there might be two requirements that impact the delivery of each other.

Talk to the impact that the gaps will have, in terms of meeting the original goal of the project, as well as how the gaps will impact the architecture strategy of the company. Document the business risk that is created by not dealing with the gaps, as well as the architecture risk and the security risk.

Like in other sections of the ADD, a table is a nice, clean way to document gaps. A sample table for gap documentation might be as follows:

Gap#	Gap name	Gap description	Gap impact and recommended mitigation
G1			
G2			
G3			

Often, project managers will de-scope requirements, citing cost or delivery-time issues, without taking into consideration that the requirements don't go away and will have to be met in some other manner, which will also have a cost and delivery impact. Ensure that the impacts outside of the project are documented here.

Recommendations

The final section of the ADD should cover recommendations. These deal with things that you, as the architect, have learned through the process of creating your solution, and have nothing to do with the solution itself. Maybe you learned about an issue within the environment that impacts multiple solutions, not just your own. Maybe you discovered an improved way to deliver on an architecture strategy that may change the approach for future projects. But, in all cases, recommendations deal with things that are outside the scope of your project.

Document your recommendations in a table, just as you document other items. A good sample table for recommendations might look as follows:

Rec. #	Recommendation name	Recommendation description
Rec1		
Rec2		
Rec3		

Summary

The architecture design document is the most important document that an architect can create. Regardless of whether you are a solution security architect or a supporting security architect, you need to make sure that the solution design has integrated security into each individual area, from a quality control point of view. Resist the temptation to create separate security sections or security architecture documents, because that can easily lead to missed security controls.

Chapter 7, *Security Architecture Project Delivery Artifacts*, covered the build document, which is documentation of how the solution is actually put into place. It's important to remember that the ADD is only going to be 85% stable once complete, but that the build document should be completely stable since it documents how the solution is finalized in production. This illustrates that architecture is an iterative process, so don't take changes to the ADD as it's being put into production as something that is a personal affront to how you think things should be. However, if there are a lot of changes, you haven't done a very good job of putting your design together in the first place.

That iterative process then goes to how the architect works with the operations teams. Remember, these are the people that actually have to work with the solutions that are put into place and they will have recommendations on how to improve the environment as a whole. In the next chapter, we'll look at how the architect should work with the operations teams.

Questions

1. How should you document security architecture components in the target architecture?
2. When would you document the current state of the architecture?
3. What two architectural artifacts are essential when putting together your target architecture?
4. Why is documenting the out-of-scope aspects of the architecture important?
5. Is an SDLC a security architecture activity or a security practice?

9
Security Architecture and Operations

Remember how you created your strategies in a previous chapter? Creating strategies requires first understanding what you have in place and then understanding what the requirements are of your stakeholders in order to ensure that your strategy is moving things towards where the business needs to be in the future. The same goes for creating a solution. You have to talk to your stakeholders to understand what their requirements are so that your solution can meet their needs.

And that is where operations come in. They are probably your most common stakeholder.

Most people think that stakeholders are only those people that are actually driving a project or that are paying for a solution to be put into place. But financial costs come in many forms and operational aspects of a solution are an ongoing expense of any solution. In order to ensure that you are minimizing the costs of any solution or any strategy, you need to take into consideration the needs of the operations group.

Operations groups are created to maintain solutions and ensure that things run smoothly. If an operations group is doing unique things on a regular basis, that means they can't be gaining efficiencies, which lowers costs. They are, by nature, looking for solutions that are repeatable and measurable so that they can keep getting better and faster at responding to operational needs.

If you are an architect and you don't have a strong relationship with your operations group, it means that you aren't helping your overarching business get as efficient as possible and, as a result, aren't helping them lower their costs or create as many benefits as possible. This chapter is all about how the architect will deal with security and how the security architect will work with all operations groups.

Strategy feedback loop

Basically, if you look at the process flow of strategies and solutions, you get the following diagram:

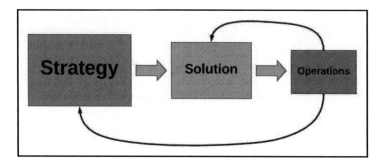

Strategies drive solutions. Solutions will then be handed over to operations to maintain and sustain. But operations will provide feedback to the strategies and the solutions. What ends up happening is that you have a feedback loop that is going on between operations and strategies/solutions.

So how do you deal with that feedback loop as an architect? Let's take a look.

Security operations strategies

Remember, strategies are meant to look at how to move the organization forward to some distant future vision. But when you deal with strategies, you have to think about the operationalization of those strategies. You can't just put a solution into place and hope someone takes care of it. And that has to be considered in the creation of your strategies. Maybe your operational groups don't have the capability to take on the solution that you have in your strategy. If that's the case, what do you do? You have to consider how to improve the capabilities of your operational teams.

Improvement in capabilities

The people that know the solutions that are in place the best are the operational teams. They are the ones that have to deal with the back-office needs of the solution and, if it's a security solution, they are typically the administrator of the solution itself. So why wouldn't you ask them what the current solution is capable of, what are its strengths and weaknesses, and what are the issues that need to be addressed?

Do those questions sound familiar? They should—they are the questions that are associated with the SWOT analysis that we discussed in the `Chapter 5`, *Program and Strategy Level Work Artifacts*. Talk to the operations group about the individual capabilities of the solutions they are currently supporting and find out what they think the current solution is good at and what it's not so good at.

But don't just talk to them about the technical capabilities. Every solution and every strategy have to consider the three components of a solution—people, process, and technology. Talk to your operations teams about the people that are needed to support the solutions currently in place. Is it easy to administer? Are the people using the solution properly trained? Do they have the capabilities? The components that you need to take into consideration from the operation's team's point of view are:

- **Number of staff**: The number of staff and the growth of that staff will indicate what the work load will be on each individual staff member. It will also indicated the number of potential roles that the staff will be composed of and those roles can/will make up any roles-based access controls that you will put into place.
- **Experience of staff**: The more experienced your staff is means they are more capable of taking on complex tasks. Just remember that operations groups will be made up of different levels of skill, so keep in mind what the average experience level is rather than what the top level is.
- **Expertise of staff**: This is different from the experience of the staff. Sure, maybe you have staff that have been around for 10 years but if they've been focused on audit or were originally trained on an older operating system, their expertise isn't necessarily appropriate for some of your projects.
- **Staff turnover**: The sign of a poorly run operations group or, worse, an overloaded staff, is a high turnover rate. There are two types of turnover that you have to be aware of. The first is the turnover of high performance staff, the people that are the core of the operations staff. That should be below five percent. Turnover for marginal performers should be around ten percent. But staff turnover will require constant training on the solutions that you are putting into place or may drive the use of certain technologies that are more automated than others.
- **Staff organization**: This is highly dependent on what the purpose of the operations group is. For security operations groups, the CISO may have a certain vision for what tasks they are going to perform and then farm out non-core tasks to other operations groups. For example, maybe the CISO views his operations group as focusing on **Identity and Access Management (IAM)** but does need to be involved in firewall management. Firewall management is then moved to network operations but IAM operations is then an area that the CISO endeavors for his operations group to be experts at.

From the process point of view, you want to be asking about what processes have been put into place to support the solution. Is the process smooth or could it be more efficient? How many check points are there? Who has to provide approvals, if approvals are needed? The process components that you need to think about will actually really impact the people side of things because manual processes need more people/staff than automated processes. And processes often have approval steps involved, which starts to bleed into governance. Some of the process components that you want to think about include the following:

- **Workflow**: Workflow is becoming more and more a capability of products. Originally, workflow was a product suite that stood alone but then, around 1998, workflow product vendors were being purchased by provisioning vendors and being integrated into their solution. The end result was an automated workflow solution that would trigger the automated provisioning of roles into various different solutions. But workflow doesn't just involve IAM. It also goes into purchasing of products, arranging for cubicle space for transitioned employees, and overall changes to the organization. Understand what the workflow is that will impact on your operations groups so that you can anticipate whether there is an ability to automate that capability.

- **Process improvement**: Many of your solutions or strategies will touch on existing processes that the operations teams have currently in place. But maybe there's a reason for those processes being in place, such as they are there to deal with weaknesses in the current solutions. Your strategies and your solutions may be a way of improving the processes that the operations team has to deal with and *that* may be a way of meeting the operation's goals. But remember what was talked about in the **Reference Security Architecture (RSA)** section when it comes to reference security processes: you want to determine the appropriate KPIs and metrics so that you can actually measure what is going on and how your strategies/solutions are improving the operations group's capabilities.

- **Crisis response/incident response**: Remember, one of the core things that a security operations group does is deal with crises and incidents. What you do has to be able to support that core capability. Can your strategy improve response times? Can it improve the way that the operations group tracks crises and incidents?

- **Personnel changes**: Every operations group will have changes in personnel, regardless of whether there is a shift turnover or whether there is a person changing roles within the organization. Your strategies and solutions need to take into consideration how the operations group has to deal with changes in personnel. Don't assume that personnel will remain stable. A normal staff turnover will be in the 5 – 10% range so you'll have to plan for how new staff learn your solutions.

- **Business engagement**: Finally, remember that all operations groups have to interact with both lines of business as well as the other IT groups within the organization. Your strategies and solutions can't impact those interactions negatively because, at the end of the day, it's not your reputation that you are affecting but the operation group's reputation.

Operations groups are all about process. They are the front line between people and processes and, as such, have to be as efficient as possible otherwise people start to go around them. Make sure you have the operations teams on your side and you can get things done even quicker than you expect. But if you damage your relationship with them, things can get worse right across the board.

One of the big things about operations teams is that they understand all about the people/process/technologies of the current situation simply because they handle them all the time. When you ask them about current solutions, you are guaranteed to be told about all the problems with a solution and what the operations teams would like to see put into place to replace it. Listen to these people; they are the ones that know the current solution the best. And they may even have ideas that your solution could use to improve the entire situation, ideas that may not require the expense of new technologies. They may think that there's a bureaucratic bottleneck that is causing issues, not just with this one current solution but with all sorts of other solutions. Maybe the answer isn't a new technology to replace the old technology, but a change in approach overall.

Now, one other thing about talking to operations teams. Regardless of what type of architect you are, there are going to be multiple types of operations teams, each of which may have requirements. Your Windows support team may have requirements for how the Windows servers are spun up and supported. Your desktop team may be looking for ways to improve deskside support that you can help with. The same with your application support teams. Maybe they have security requirements that you can make more efficient while maintaining security levels.

Inputs into security architecture strategy

Each of these areas become inputs into your security architecture strategy. Now, how to organize these inputs. You'll need a structure for organizing them just as you need a structure for your strategies and just as you need a structure for creating your solution design.

Maybe you should use your RSA! amazing how having a reference security architecture allows you to be consistent in everything you do!

Okay, let's take an example of your border protection area of your RSA. If you don't remember border protection, a good idea would be to refresh your memory by going back to the `chapter 3`, *Reference Security Architecture*.

Border protection is one of those areas that can reside in either the security operations group or in the network operations group. But in either case, these two operations groups will need to keep close relationships with each other because their work impacts each other. Take firewalls as an example.

Many organizations will have firewall management being done by the network operations group. That is because firewalls have a routing capability and have a dramatic impact on how network traffic flows. If your organization is structured along functional lines, then firewalls is a natural fit into network operations.

But network operations isn't a security group. So how do you put them into your security architecture strategy as an input? Simple—you talk to them. Maybe you have a plan to move the organization to a cloud data center posture. If that's the case, what changes will need to be made to the firewalls? What network routing changes will be necessary? See what I mean?

The same goes for security zones. Security zones are concepts that are security architecture in nature but managed by network operations groups. Maybe you are thinking of expanding the number of security zones. If that's the case, can your firewalls handle those changes? Maybe you have to move your firewalls to a virtual firewall situation. That means making sure that your network operations team actually has the expertise in managing virtual firewalls.

Let's take a look from the security operations side of things. Say you are looking to implement a new anti-virus solution and it works best on Red Hat Linux. Your security operations team will be administering the new anti-virus solution, but it will be residing on Linux, which your Unix team manages. Now, you have two operations teams that you have to discuss requirements with. What tools do the Unix team have to have on the Linux servers for monitoring performance and what configurations does your security operations team need to ensure that AV is properly implemented throughout your organization? Your network operations team will need to know about any new traffic as well so maybe you have to talk to them about the network load that AV communication will have between the central servers and the desktops/servers that the AV is protecting.

See what I mean? Each operations team will have their needs as an input into solutions and into strategies, so make sure you talk with them when you are creating your strategies and solutions.

Monitoring for architectural risk

A while back, we talked about the different types of risk. Business risk was discussed because, at the end of the day, we need to support the direction that the business is going and make sure that the business is able to operate. We talked about security risk because, well, we are talking about security in architecture in this book. Security risks have to be considered for any solution that is being put into place and how those solutions will change the security posture of the organization.

But, at the end of the day, we are architects that have to focus on security. As a result, there are architectural risks that have to be thought about and provided as an input into the strategy.

What are architecture risks? Well, architecture risks are those risks that arise as a result of the architecture components that are in your organization. You can have different types of solutions that provide the same security posture but have different architecture risks and those are things that have to be considered.

Take, for example, the ever-present legacy infrastructure. The infrastructure that everyone wishes would just go away but you can't get rid of because of the dependencies. Every organization has a legacy Windows NT Server still sitting around simply because there's an application that can only run on Windows NT and there is a business requirement to keep that application. Having the Windows NT server in your environment will create an architectural risk because of the lack of support from Microsoft.

Legacy systems are the biggest source of architecture risk that you have be considering. Let's use the anti-virus example from the last section as a way of talking about architecture risk. When you look at the current AV solution, you have to look at both the capabilities of the AV package as well as the infrastructure that it is residing on. Maybe, in your analysis, the AV package is able to support the needs of the business for another three years. But the operating system that it is residing on will go end of life in one year. Now you have to put into your security architecture strategy a change to the AV because the infrastructure supporting the AV has to be changed.

When you are working with your security architecture strategies, look at the different components and the dependencies of those components. Look at the age and capabilities of those components and then map the architecture risks associated with those components. Do this using a table of sort, such as the one shown in the following example:

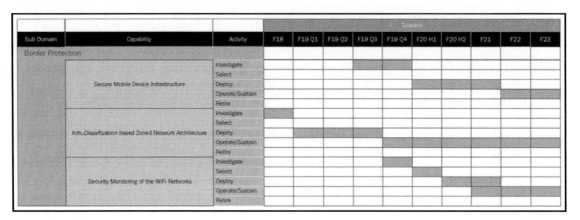

In this example, there are three sample projects but, more importantly, there are five options for laying out how to deal with your architecture risks by planning longer term. Those five options are:

- **Investigate**: The investigative option is all about looking into the current solution, the requirements that a solution is supposed to meet, and then determining if there are options out there that might be better than the current solution. In this option, you want to be looking into all the possible solutions, including just sticking with the current solution.
- **Select**: The selection option is about making a decision on which solution to use and how to use it. You'll be comparing the pros and cons of each possible solution and, if you do this properly, you'll make use of your **Key Decision Document (KDD)** for describing what your final decision is with regards to your longer-term strategy on reducing architecture risk. We talked about vendor selections and bake offs in the last chapter. This is where you are making your solution selection.

- **Deploy**: The deployment option is the timeframe that you need for rolling out a new option and it's never as easy as you expect. Remember that the preceding table is also describing the timeframes for the activities, so don't discount how long it will take to deploy a new solution. There will be all sorts of gotchas that come up and you need to plan for it. One of the mistakes that is commonly occurring with architects is that they assume that the amount of time to deploy a solution is similar to how long it would take them to deploy a solution. But there's a reason why architects are more senior to other roles—they've been through the trenches and learned the lessons to dealing with solutions. The people that will actually do the deployment will be more junior to you so really build in a buffer for time to deploy new solutions.

- **Operate/sustain**: Once a solution has been deployed, it will sit in production for a long time, likely several years. This will be the longest timeframe associated with the strategy timetables and it's easy to forget about solutions during this period. This is why your asset inventory is so important and what you use in your planning (so that you don't forget about solutions once they've been put into production). Keep an eye on the solution and touch-base with the operations group to determine how it's doing. Is it continuing to meet its original requirements? Are changes to other environmental component impacting the solution itself to the point where the solution may need to be upgraded? Remember, technologies change, and the direction of organizations change. This may impact the functionality of a perfectly good solution in a way that may require changing directions.

- **Retire**: Here's where you want to actually retire the older solutions. Many times, you'll want to maintain the old solution in parallel with the new solution, just in case something happens. But then you want to retire the old solution and that isn't as easy as just pulling the plug. There will be tools that have to removed, IP addresses released, VLANs changed, and so on. All these can impact an organization if not done correctly, and that also raises the architectural risk.

Align your retirement option with when your current solutions are going end of life. Ideally, you replace the current solution a year before it goes end of life so that you don't have to deal with a raised architectural risk.

One other thing to remember about retirement of solutions—you don't necessarily have to be bound to them when they go end of life. Sometimes, if you talk with the vendor, you may be able to pay a premium to continue getting support from them even after products go end of life. Vendors may be ending support simply because they have a new product that they want to be pushing. But they seldom will turn down money.

Another option for a solution that has gone end of life is to find support from unauthorized sources. Say, for example, that a piece of infrastructure has gone end of life and is no long supported by the vendor. You've talked to them and they don't want to continue providing support even after end of support. Maybe there's someone in the marketplace that has deep expertise of the product that would be willing to support the product. Support doesn't necessarily have to come from the vendor itself. And this will help your operations teams as they are trying to support the product inhouse.

Supporting operational strategies

Remember that strategies and future plans aren't just the purview of architecture, though this is where it primarily resides. Operations teams have their strategies as well, though those may be associated more with people and process than technology.

When you are creating your strategies, you always talk to your stakeholders to determine what their strategies are so that you can support them appropriately. Since operations teams are stakeholders that have a very big profile for the architect, you should be talking to them as well. There are three different types of operations teams that you need to consider:

- **Security operations team**: The security operations team will have their own strategies specific to supporting the business from a security point of view. Typically found under the **Chief Information Security Officer (CISO)**, you will find that their strategies are very focused on reducing security risk to the organization.
- **Non-security operations teams**: These are the teams where security is not the primary consideration for their activities. Typical IT organizations will have network, Windows, Unix, database, middleware, help desk, desktop, and application support teams. Each one will have their own requirements and future strategies which, when you break them down, will have security architecture support needs.
- **Outsourced operations teams**: IT operations are central to any outsourcing agreement because they are all about doing things consistently and efficiently. The outsourcing organization will negotiate an agreement for a fixed price per device supported (for example, support for a single Windows server will equal $XX.) and then look to be as efficient as possible in order to improve their profit margins. But they will also use the outsourced agreement as a leading edge in order to get projects, which is where the biggest profit will be.

Each operations team will have their requirements, some that are based on planning (as per the security operations and the non-security operations teams) and some that are driven by contractual agreements between the organization and the outsourcer. Your role as the architect is to understand each team's activities and plans and understand how to support them moving forward.

There will be times when the different operations teams will have conflicting goals and that will impact the architect's plans. For example, the Unix team may plan on moving from SUSE to Red Hat, supporting JBoss web servers, while the application team is planning on moving to applications supported by Apache. This is a conflict between two groups regarding direction and it is typically adjusted by either the enterprise architecture group (of which the security architect may be a part) or by the overarching IT management. But, in either case, the security architect will have to determine if their various solutions can support either of those web servers.

The conflicts caused by business unit plans will happen even more often, especially if you have a larger organization with overlapping responsibilities. What will often happen is that a business unit will decide that they like a specific application because of one specific functionality and then they commission a project to implement that application. If this happens often enough, you end up getting multiple applications that can do the same thing, which will require multiple instances of support infrastructure and security architecture.

If you have regular conversations with your business units to understand where they are going and what their plans are, you'll be able to anticipate potential duplications of functionality. From a security architecture perspective, it's better to have a simpler environment than to have multiple systems that have to be protected. Try to consolidate capabilities from your operations groups and your overall costs will go down as well as all potential support costs.

Summary

Architecture is all about strategies and solutions, so, as a result, very few people think about how the architect needs to interact with the operations groups. But you can view the operations groups as the canary in the mine that will be letting you know how the organization is doing. If you interact with them enough and appropriately, you'll be able to understand where the organization can improve, not just for security operations but for all areas of the organization.

Will that change? Possibly, but don't plan on it. The future path for the security architect is dictated by the trends and those trends are what we will talk about in the next chapter.

Questions

1. Why is it important to talk with the operations groups for input into security architecture strategy?
2. What tool can you use so that you don't forget about a solution that is in production?
3. What are some of the considerations you have to think about when it comes to the staff of the operations groups?
4. Do you just have to think about the security operations group or all operations groups? Why?

10
Practical Security Architecture Designs

Every organization needs to assume that it has been compromised. This is critical for all employees to understand, regardless of whether they are C-Level executives or employees working in the IT and Security departments. James Comey, former FBI Director, famously said that there are two types of organizations: those who know that they have been compromised and those who don't know. When delving more deeply into the threat landscape, you can identity four different threat actor groups, as in the following:

Nation-states

- The primary motivation for nation-sates is the protection of national security, global competition on for example trade deals and the execution of sanctions.
- Cyber attacks carried out by nation-states are often very targeted and long-term campaigns. In some cases these might be executed by insiders and/or 3rd-party advanced persistant threat groups.
- The impact can vary between the disruption of critical infrastructure, monetaery loss or also the loss of intelectual property.

Cyber criminals

- Often motification by identitiy theft or fraud campaigns to gain large amount of data.
- Campaigns can be very targeted for individual identity theft or larger scale data breaches. While majority of threat actors operate in isolaten there are some instances where certain aspects are outsourced to a 3rd-party APT group.
- Impact varies depending on the threat actor target. Many of the campaigns cause a monetary loss and raise privacy issues that might impact certain regularaties.

Cyber terrorists

- Mainly motiviated by ideological or political reasons.
- Leverage often opportunistic vulnerabilities that get executed by 3rd-party APT groups and/or Insiders.
- Focus of these campaigns are primary disruption of assets and fincial insitutions.

Hacktivists

- Primary motiviation is a political cause and not nessary profit. Its often driven by the ideology of the hacktivists.
- Targets organizations that are against the political and/or ideological motivation of the hacktivists.
- Impact varies between destablization of a organization, inject political messages into public relation channels of a organization and distruption of operations.

This is the reality, and thus, it is crucial for any successful security architect to have a strong understanding, not just of the theory, but also the threat landscape and how to build security controls in the security design that helps IT to protect, detect, and respond to today's threat landscape. The threat landscape has been changing due to the increase in computer processing power in the hands of attackers, the increased sophistication of attacks, and the introduction of new technologies. The last few years have seen the biggest types of attacks and increased financial loss, which is directly attributable to cyber threats. The five threat areas that attackers have focused on most are networks, endpoints, cloud platforms, **Internet of Things (IoT)** devices, and organizational implementations of **Bring Your Own Device (BYOD)** policies.

Endpoint security

Over the last few years, there has been a shift of focus by threat actors from network-based attacks to direct endpoint attacks. Looking at global outbreaks such as WannaCry or sophisticated cyber-attacks, they all share similar attack strategies. Therefore, it is important to understand the threat landscape and how to mitigate these threats. There are never-ending attacks targeted at this attack surface which is made up of workstations, servers, and personal computing devices. The common threats are covered in the following subsections.

Ransomware

Ransomware was among the key security fears of 2017 after a vicious malware called **WannaCry** claimed over 200,000 victims and caused several deaths after locking up critical systems in hospitals. Ransomware is a special category of malware that encrypts a device's hard disk, shared drives, and removable storage media connected to it. This causes the files to become inaccessible. As an extension to the attack, ransomware causes direct financial loss by requiring a user to pay up a certain amount to salvage the victim device that's issued with a decryption code. There is another type of ransomware that only causes an image to be displayed on a device's screen, thus causing it to be unusable.

Prior to WannaCry, there were isolated cases of hacking where users were being warned that authorities had detected piracy material or access to illegal websites from that device and that a fine had been imposed. To decrypt or regain access to their devices, users would have to pay up the required amount and get a decryption key. WannaCry pushed the attack a notch higher by attacking a large user base and not hiding behind the shadows of big names such as the FBI. Even though the attack lasted a few days before the weakness was identified, it served as a wake up call to many users about the existence and extensive damage of ransomware:

Mitigation

The best way to be sure of the availability of files on an endpoint is through backing up. If a hacker encrypts one's computer with malware, it will be easy for one to wipe out the whole system and install a new operating system, programs, and restore files from backups. However, it is rather optimistic to believe that all users will back up their files before a ransomware attack happens. There are other mitigations that can still help mitigate ransomware attacks. One of these is having an active and updated end host antivirus program. After the initial cases of WannaCry had been reported, antivirus programs updated their virus signature databases with the signature of the new threat:

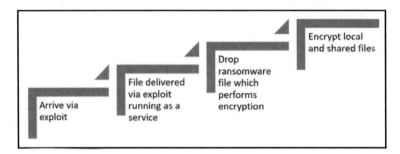

Antivirus programs such as Windows defender were able to prevent the execution of the malware on machines. However, those that did not have antivirus programs or had not been actively updating them were still under the threat of the ransomware. Another mitigation is taking the computer to reputable technicians. They will assess whether the computer can be repaired or if data can be restored. If indeed a walk around can be found, one will be able to access the encrypted files. The last solution, which is more of a compromise, is paying the ransom amount. Sometimes, the hackers use sophisticated mechanisms of hacking that not even technicians can find a walk around for. Therefore, one can weigh the perceived value of the data that will be lost due to the ransomware and the cost of paying to get a decryption key.

Spyware and adware

Spyware and adware are becoming of concern due to the increased motive of hackers to steal user data that they can sell on black markets. Spyware and adware collect personal information from one's computer without the user's knowledge. They mainly get downloaded and installed with other freeware that serves other functionalities. When these freeware are downloaded and installed, spyware will run in the background and steal one's information from the hard disk and from browsers. Spyware is hard to detect since it operates passively. A user will not naturally detect them through observable methods such as realizing that a computer is becoming slower or taking too long to boot up. Adware can be detected since they will start throwing ads on a device's screen. Although the adverts could be harmless, they cause quite a nuisance to the user:

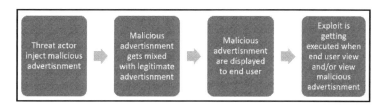

Adware also opens up unwanted sites and fills a screen with pop-ups. They also lead a browser to a number of e-commerce shops, hoping that a user will make a purchase since the hackers behind them rely on ad revenue. Spyware is mostly connected to hackers over the internet to enable remote control. Hackers use this to collect usernames, passwords, monitor browsing habits, check system settings, and read information about a system and installed applications. Some spyware is configured to execute commands that can change the way one's computer operates without the knowledge or consent of the user.

Mitigation

To prevent spyware and adware infections, users should follow some guidelines to minimize their chances of infection and to also ensure that they can be thwarted. One way is by ensuring that operating systems and programs are up to date. Updates, at times, fix bugs and vulnerabilities that are exploitable by spyware and adware. Another mitigation measure is safe storage of passwords. One should avoid saving passwords on a browser since adware, once it infects a browser, can potentially read the stored credentials. There are safer third-party options that give users the option to store all their passwords and access the passwords using a master password. One should also configure browser settings to add security. There are browsers that allow users to block all pop-up adverts, and these settings come in handy against adware. Lastly, one should install an antivirus program to help combat actions of spyware programs.

Trojan horses

These are programs that are downloaded as legitimate software that perform useful functionalities. However, the functionalities they offer only masquerade their true purposes as they do damage in the background. Trojan horses are quite dangerous since they can steal or delete files. The permissions they are given in a system to do their legitimate functions are the same permissions that they abuse to steal or delete files. Trojan horses can also use one's computer to hack into other computers. They can spread over the network where an infected machine is connected and get into other machines. They can also collect credentials as they are being entered into a browser or as they are saved on a computer.

An example of a Trojan horse execution is as follows:

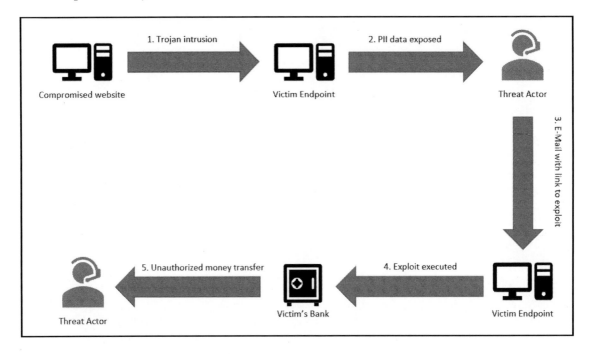

Mitigation

Users should also be cautious of the programs that they download and the sites they download them from. Trojan horses mostly come bundled with software that claim to do some functionalities such as converting videos to audio or even in the format of kid's games. Trojans can also be downloaded with other, more useful software that is downloaded from piracy sites such as The Pirate Bay. When a user installs these programs, the Trojan horses will run in the background doing other malicious functions. Therefore, it is best for users to ensure that they avoid downloading questionable software or software from questionable sites. As mentioned previously, it is also good for users to avoid storing passwords on browsers since these are the main targets when Trojans are installed into a system. Antivirus programs can help detect the activities of Trojan horses and thereby stop and eliminate them from systems.

Viruses

Viruses are out-rightly malicious and are used to steal, manipulate, or destroy data or perform malicious functions on a computing device. Viruses mostly enter into a computer through browsers. They can be automatically downloaded from malicious sites without a user's knowledge. Viruses use their victim's computational resources to reproduce copies of themselves and compromise other programs. They can also attach themselves into files that are sent as email attachments and compromise the recipient's computer. Viruses can use a compromised computer to send spam messages to one's contact lists, and they can also scan for private information stored on a computer. They are also used to hijack web browsers and lead it to malicious sites or sites running ads. Since they can perform functions on their own, they are also used to disable a computer's security settings.

Viruses spread over from a computer's hard disk to thumb drives and other removable storage media that are connected to an infected computer. They, however, are not passive like a few other malware and leave signs that can be interpreted to mean their presence in a computer. A user can determine that a computer is infected with viruses if it takes quite a long time to start up, if files seem to disappear or become corrupt, programs keep crashing, the computer keeps crashing, browsers open strange startup pages, and if other pages take a long time to load and programs run without being started.

Mitigations

Viruses are not only irritants, but they carry lethal force to take down a whole computer and those connected to it. It is, therefore, best to prevent them from entering a computer in the first place. To do this, users should avoid clicking on links sent to them by strangers via email. They should also be cautious when downloading email attachments sent by unknown people or emails from people in their contact lists that seem strange. It is also advisable for users to avoid connecting to public Wi-Fi hotspots since malware can easily traverse a network and infect computers connected to it if there is one infected computer in the network. Host-based firewalls can also come in handy to prevent browsers from opening known malicious sites. Users should also keep updated antivirus programs running on their computers to prevent viruses from taking over their machines if they manage to enter. In extreme cases where a computer has been overrun by a virus, the best option is to wipe out the entire hard disk through formatting and then installing a new OS.

In organizations, users can be best prepared to deal with viruses through training, especially on how to handle suspicious emails sent to the organization, how to handle emails requesting them to download attachments for more details, and also what to do when they have already downloaded and opened suspicious emails. Viruses can spread over an organization in a very short time due to the lack of knowledge of users. Enterprise antivirus programs are also a good option for securing organizational workstations since IT departments can easily control the client versions on each workstation. Organizations should also cease the use of Windows XP in all computers in their network. Even if such computers play trivial functions, they could be used by hackers as entry points into a network. There are programs that can scan whole networks and determine the operating systems that computers are running on. Therefore, Windows XP and other operating systems whose manufacturers have discontinued support should be avoided.

Summary

Endpoint security has become one of the most important aspects of modern security architecture. The primary reason for that is the fact that many organizations assume that the network perimeter is already lost. Besides **Advanced Persistent Threat (APT)**, ransomware has become one of the biggest threats for any organization, yet many recommendations have not changed in the endpoint security space. Backup remains a key aspect to be able to quickly recover from ransomware attacks, and strong password policies and modern authentication such as Windows Hello for Business further reduces the attack surface.

Mail security

Mail security involves a number of collective measures aimed at securing access to the contents of email communication or email accounts. These are mainly secured from compromised or unauthorized access. Emails are a common form of communication media. They support the transfer of other types of content such as documents, videos, and audio. However, they have also been extensively used to transfer malware and to conduct phishing attacks. They have been used to spread deceptive messages that encourage users to engage in risky behavior such as downloading malicious attachments, clicking on malicious links, or divulging personal information. Emails are also commonly exploited vectors to give attackers entry into an organization's network. Therefore, email security is of the essence for both individuals and enterprises.

The need for email security

Since emails have become popular attack vectors, it is important for measures to be taken to secure email accounts and communication from the threats that they face. There are two types of threats which can be broadly classified as malware and non-malware threats. Malware threats involve the use of malware on the email's contents while non-malware threats involve the use of social engineering attack techniques such as phishing. Malware threats are sent through emails as attachments or links and they are, at times, crafted and customized to look legitimate. They may be named to seem as though they are legitimate files or hyperlinks to legitimate websites, while in reality, they are all concealed deliveries for malware.

Malware can be downloaded in attachments and may infect one's computing device when the attachment is opened. There have been some security threats arising from Adobe PDF documents laced with malware that execute when a user downloads and opens such documents. Another trick to get a user's device infected by malware is to direct them to websites that serve malware. When a user clicks a link on an email, the link redirects to a website that begins the automatic download of malware. This malware will automatically infect the device that has visited the website. After the infection of devices, malware is used to steal data from a computing device. It may start by stealing the login credentials saved on browsers, and then may start logging activities on a user's browser and communicate this information back to threat actors.

Non-malware threats do not involve the use of malware. Rather, they rely on the deception and manipulation of users. Users could be manipulated into giving out sensitive information or obeying some commands. Social engineering techniques, particularly phishing, are used in these attacks. Phishing emails will mostly ask the recipients to confirm their login credentials or to try and login to a particular website to resolve an issue with their accounts. These types of emails will use cloned copies of legitimate websites. For example, a user could be told that their PayPal account has been limited and that they need to log into PayPal and resolve this issue. Such an email will have a link that either has a URL resembling that of PayPal or will have a shortened URL so that a user cannot directly tell if it is for the linked site. Upon clicking such a link, a site that is an exact replica may be opened and a user will be prompted to enter their login credentials. At this point, the malicious attackers will harvest their login credentials.

For organizations, there is another troubling email threat known as CEO fraud. This is where a malicious actor uses a compromised email of a senior executive in an organization to coerce other employees into doing some uncommon things. The email could be used to direct accountants to transfer a lump sum amount to an overseas account urgently. Unsurprisingly, humans tend to be obedient to authority and will, therefore, do that. Several organizations have already fallen victim and lost millions to such scams. Another non-malicious threat to emails is the unauthorized access and interception of emails in transit. Unencrypted email contents can be read if data packets transmitting them are captured by traffic analyzer tools. Unauthorized email access can be accomplished through the theft of login credentials from users. There is also the issue of the use of weak passwords. With many organizations using email addresses that have an employee's names plus the domain name, the main huddle for hackers is the password. If employees use easy to guess passwords for their business emails, they can easily be compromised.

Therefore, it is of importance for organizations and individuals to protect their email communication and email accounts. Sensitive information could be lost if emails are compromised. Users could be manipulated into giving out private details to attackers, while employees could be deceived into making huge money transfers to unknown bank accounts by thieves purporting to be executive employees. Malware could make its way into an organization's network if attachments with malware are downloaded or links to malicious sites are clicked. Emails are a significant threat vector that should not go unmonitored or uncontrolled. Fortunately, there are security practices that can improve email security, thus thwarting possible attacks.

Email security best practices

There are certain best practices that should be considered by any enterprise when it comes to email security. These should be carefully evaluated and then determined to see if they are adaptable for the enterprise:

Email security policies

Organizations should have strict email policies aimed at preventing users from performing actions that may threaten the security of email communication or that of the organizational network. Security policies should advise users on the types of attachments that they should or should not open. They should also guide users on the types of links that they are not allowed to click. The use of CC and BCC for outbound emails should also be guided by the security policies. Employees should be discouraged from using CC when listing a significant number of business email addresses as these addresses could be used by hackers for malicious purposes. The forwarding of emails from business to personal emails must also be guarded against. To ensure secure communication of sensitive details, these emails must only be received through business emails whose use can be monitored by IT personnel.

Another restriction that security policies should pass is the banning of sending plaintext login credentials through emails. Lastly, email security policies must touch on the use of complex passwords. This is because users are naturally lazy and, if unmonitored, will use the simplest but weakest passwords. For instance, in many annual security reports, the most commonly used passwords are either 123456 or password.

Use of secured exchange servers

A common choice for email servers by organizations that have a keen eye on security is Microsoft Exchange Server. There are reasons why big corporations choose it over other exchange servers. One of these reasons for this is that it has several security features to guard against multiple email threats. Microsoft Exchange Server has anti-spam and antivirus functionalities integrated within itself. It also can perform content filtering and scanning to protect against email content that could be malicious. The exchange server also boosts the confidentiality of emails with components that can encrypt both internal and external-bound emails to help protect them while in transit.

User education on security threats

One of the main threats against email users is phishing. Unlike malware attacks, it cannot be prevented from using security tools since it targets the manipulability of the human element in communication. The best protection against this is to educate users. Users should be taught on the common manipulation tactics that hackers pull in order to persuade them to take some actions. There should be an in-depth coverage on the issue of CEO fraud, thus cautioning them against blindly following strange orders given by executives, including emails that have content pressuring users to take certain actions with urgency. Being able to resolve some of these issues must also be highlighted in user education.

Users must also be educated on the issue of passwords. They must be made to understand the risk that they put the organization in when they use weak passwords. They might have the notion that they have nothing to lose when their accounts are hacked, but it must be laid to them that there is a lot at stake if their emails are compromised.

Host-based security tools

Security software such as ESET and Avast exist that can actively scan email attachments for viruses. These tools also ensure that one does not send attachments that may be infected with malware to other users. Organizations must put such tools in place that can prevent malware from getting into their networks by way of emails. These tools are also effective at preventing the auto-execution of malware. They also know many malware signatures and can stop their executions from either taking place or causing harm to a user's device.

Encryption

One of the sure ways of ensuring that emails are protected is through encryption. This prevents a common method of attack where emails are intercepted while in transit and their contents read. It also reduces the access to email contents by unauthorized people. This is because the email is encrypted from the sender's side and decrypted at the receiver's end. There is no way for a third party in-between the communication to decrypt the email. Organizations that have adopted business emails must, therefore, ensure that they implement an encrypting mechanism to protect their communication.

Securing webmail applications

Webmail applications are particularly at significant risk since they lay exposed on the internet. Hackers can subject them to multiple mechanisms of force access until they break. They can also be monitored so that if they are not secured, the credentials that users enter are stolen by hackers. It is, therefore, necessary for organizations or individuals using webmail to ensure that the web platforms they are using are secured against malicious codes that can perform SQL injection and XSS scripting alongside other types of attacks. Secured HTTP should be used instead of plain HTTP, which has been proven to be insecure when it comes to the transmission of information.

Email scanners

There are third-party tools that can be used to scan and block potentially harmful emails. These are emails that contain some type of known phishing content or have malicious files. These tools could be implemented in organizations to ensure that the malicious files do not even reach the end users. This reduces the risk of such emails being opened and malicious files from entering the network.

Email backup

There is also the risk of loss of emails that contain highly sensitive information due to other causes other than hackers. Environmental disasters could destroy servers and cause the data that they contain to also be lost. System crashes and hard disk crashes can also lead to loss of data. If an organization does not have a backup of such data, it could be lost permanently. It is, therefore, most advisable that organizations keep their email servers backed up so that they may be able to recover email data that may be lost due to unforeseeable future events. Cloud backups are highly encouraged since they are offsite and online. They are, therefore, secure and always available. Additionally, the cloud is highly scalable and could be made to accommodate more data without costing the organization too much.

End user security practices

Most of the practices we have just given are only applicable to organizations. However, there are users that still face security threats but do not have the resources that have been recommended or they cannot implement some of the discussed practices. Also, most end users have personal emails which already have the discussed safeguards such as encryptions, and it would be impossible for them to add their own layer of encryption. Therefore, a customized list of best practices for end users will be covered in the following subsections.

Avoid opening suspicious emails, attachments, or links

End users regularly get spam emails, which most email providers such as Gmail will identify and appropriately place in the spam folder. Users should not be curious and try opening such emails as they may contain malicious content that the email provider has marked as such. As for suspicious emails that make it into one's inbox, they should not be opened. These emails will generally tell one that they have won a prize or that they are required to donate a certain amount of money. They are written in a highly manipulative language and it may coerce users into doing inexplicable things. Lastly, users should avoid clicking links sent to them via email. If there are problems that require a resolution from the user's side, it is best if one uses the official URL instead of the one provided through email.

Changing passwords

End users should make regularly changing their passwords a habit. There are simply too many threat vectors that may have already stolen one's login credentials. It is, therefore, most advisable for users to change their passwords once in a while. If a malicious actor has stolen a password, it will be ineffective after a while.

Not sharing passwords

End users must avoid sharing their login credentials with other people, including their relatives and co-workers. They put their emails in so much risk while doing so. These credentials will be sent over unverifiable means in terms of security, and the commitment to the security of the party which the email has been shared is questionable.

Using spam filters

End users using common email services from companies such as Yahoo and Gmail do not have the luxury of putting in place some security tools to scan emails that they get. However, there are ways that users can implement spam filters using certain phrases. Also, if a user marks a certain email as spam, subsequent emails from the same sender or that contain similar content may also be forced into the spam folder by the email provider.

Avoid logging into emails on public Wi-Fi connections

Since end users may also have their own personal emails that do not enjoy the protection of encryption, it is highly advisable for one to avoid logging into such emails over public Wi-Fi hotspots. There are threats lurking in such connections and they may intercept login credentials being entered into unencrypted websites.

Avoid sending sensitive information via mail

It is not common for a user to be requested to send sensitive information to legitimate websites over email. Therefore, when one gets such requests from people purporting to be working with certain banks, institutions, and government agencies, it is best not to do so. A call to such institutions and organizations may be more prudent to avoid one's credentials from going to malicious people.

Email security resources

There are many email security resources being offered by third parties to help secure an organization's communication. In the following subsection, we will cover various resources.

Microsoft Exchange Server

This is a popular exchange server that many corporations have adopted. It easily links with other Microsoft products such as Outlook, thus making it a seamless experience from the exchange to the email client app. Something to note of importance is that Microsoft Exchange Server comes with a number of security features to protect emails. It has encryption to ensure that emails cannot be read by parties that are neither the sender nor the receiver. It also has an inbuilt antivirus and an anti-spam functionality to protect users from getting malware via emails or emails with spam contents.

Sophos PureMessage for Microsoft Exchange

This is a security addition to Microsoft Exchange that can scan inbound and outbound emails as part of its operation to secure organizational emails. It adds and data protection functionalities of Microsoft Exchange onto the email. It can block spam, attachments containing viruses, spyware, and even phishing emails from getting to a user.

Symantec mail security

Symantec offers an email security suite that is also meant for the Microsoft Exchange Server. This suite has tools to protect against viruses, spam, and other malware. In addition, this tool can enforce internal policies to offer customized security to each organization.

Websense email security

This is a tool that also offers email security, mostly by blocking potentially malicious emails from getting in or outside a network. It, therefore, sits at the network gateway. It is also highly effective at protecting confidential data contained in emails and attachments.

Summary

Email security is of importance today, particularly because there are many threats that are using emails as entry vectors into organizational emails. Hackers are also discovering new ways of targeting users and they are switching between hacking and social engineering techniques. End users must, therefore, be protected against the technical and non-technical threats that they face. The discussed best practices help to reduce the vulnerability of organizations or individuals in many email threat vectors. The outlined tools are some of the best on the market for providing email security. Emails are essential in today's business world, and so should their security.

Network security

Network security threats are on the rise and IT departments are having to deal with more sophisticated and resilient attacks than ever before. New technology in the possession of attackers has only made network threats more threating to an organization's network and systems. The following discussion explains the common threats facing networks.

DDOS attacks

This is a very effective network attack that has regularly been used on prime targets. DDoS attacks involve the use of a zombie army of infected computers to send a lot of illegitimate requests to a website or a server, thereby overloading its capabilities and causing it to cease operating or operate sluggishly. DDoS attacks are, at times, used as precursors or distractors of other attacks since they take away the attention of an organization from other security areas. DDoS attacks originate from many devices and these could be located all over the world since they are used without the knowledge of their owners. In 2016, Dyn DNS, a big networking company that is responsible for the resolution of domain names to websites, fell victim to DDoS attacks. It was reported that the company was attacked by approximately 100,000 machines which kept bombarding it with multiple rounds of illegitimate traffic. The outcome was that the crucial system services offered by Dyn were inaccessible for some time and this led to the inaccessibility of some websites since browsers could not resolve their domain names to the IP addresses of the sites. This is a common consequence for DDoS attacks where entire networks can be flooded with useless requests, thus causing it to shut down and deny legitimate requests from users:

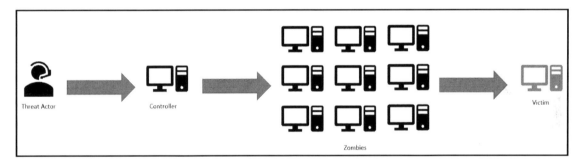

Mitigation

The best mitigation measure for DDoS attacks is the installation of an effective firewall on the network. Since traffic will have to pass through the firewall as it enters into the secured intranet, pools of illegitimate traffic will be identified and blocked from getting inside the network. Therefore, servers will not be tasked with the burden of processing illegitimate traffic at the cost of legitimate requests. Because attackers are growing in both tact and sophistication, they may be able to bypass normal signature-based firewalls. Therefore, it is most advisable that big organizations that cannot afford to go down due to DDoS attacks install intelligent firewalls and invest in cyber resilience. Intelligent firewalls are new types of firewalls that use machine learning to continually improve their performance. While some illegitimate traffic might pass through them at first, they will quickly learn of this kind of traffic and prevent it from further being allowed into a network. Cyber resilience, on the other hand, is a solution that organizations are taking to help them survive the unpredictable world of cyber threats. To protect against DDoS attacks, an organization can establish alternative sites that can take over the processing task once the main servers are downed.

At an individual level, one can guard against DDoS attacks through simple security practices. DDoS attacks facing individuals will mostly come in the form of emails. One can simply avoid giving out their emails carelessly to sites or on forms. Also, one can set up email filters to remove unwanted emails automatically when sent if they follow a similar pattern. Since individual users are the oblivious perpetrators of DDoS attacks when their computers are hijacked by attackers and recruited in zombie armies, users should install antivirus programs to help remove malware responsible for this. To protect one's device from being recruited into a zombie army in the first place, one should avoid visiting suspicious links or downloading attachments from strangers:

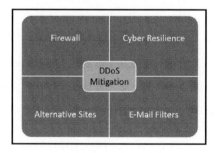

Eavesdropping

Eavesdropping is a technique used by attackers that want to gather sensitive data about an organization. An attacker intercepts communications in a network, either analog or digital. This can be done through direct listening or through the sniffing of data being exchanged between two parties. There are specialized programs that are used to sniff data inside a network. They work by capturing and reading packets that are in transit inside the network. These programs can also record packets over a long period of time, after which an attacker will subsequently listen to or read the packets to get the details that were communicated. Internal organizational networks are the most common targets since communication within parties in organizational networks tends to mostly take place unsecured. Therefore, when a hacker gains access to the network, he or she can listen to many of the communications taking place. Also, hackers can observe the network and get to know targets that can be attacked in future hacking expeditions.

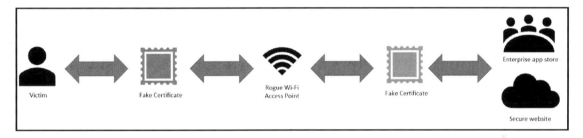

Eavesdropping is also used for more nefarious purposes than just reading the communication being exchanged by two parties. Where attackers target unencrypted emails, they could sniff the messages and alter them before they reach the recipient. The recipient will be easily tricked into thinking that the message has come directly from the sender. If the email requests some money to be sent to an overseas account, the recipient will most likely comply. In the case of e-commerce sites, sniffing is done mostly to read transaction details of shoppers such as their credit cards. A sniffer could leave the sniffing programs running for a long duration to record the details of various shoppers before reading the packets and getting highly sensitive information.

Since eavesdropping is mostly a passive attack, it can be done without detection. It can be done on both wired and wireless networks. For wired networks such as landlines, an attacker will directly meddle with the cables using hardware tools. In wireless networks, the attacker will use different types of packet capturing software. It is a constant worry for network admins who have not encrypted their networks.

Mitigation

Eavesdropping can be easily prevented in a network. Organizations can use SSL protocols to make their communication encrypted so that the data they sent cannot be read by anyone who intercepts it in transit. The only person that will be able to read the data is the intended recipient. Installation of firewalls could also help to detect unauthorized access to a network, allowing the network administrator to take some actions. Intrusion detection systems are also useful countermeasures against eavesdropping as they can identify sniffing-related behavior on a network and alert the network admins. Network segmentation can also help control and manage the impacts of eavesdropping. Even if a hacker is be able to break into a network and sniff, segmentation will help prevent a network-wide sniffing.

It is also the responsibility of the user to guard against eavesdropping. Since one cannot be sure whether a given website or online system that you are using is being sniffed, it is a good idea to create complex passwords and regularly change them. Also, one should not reuse the same password on many sites in case a sniffer will has read one out of an eavesdropping attack. Users should avoid typing passwords over insecure connections. Websites that do not have HTTPS should generally be handled with a great deal of caution since attackers might be waiting to steal credentials in the backend. One should be more concerned when doing online transactions since e-commerce and banking sites are expected to use secured HTTP.

Data breaches

Data breaches are occurrences where hackers are able to infiltrate a network and access sensitive and confidential data from computing devices or storage servers. It is common in instances where the motivation of the hacker is corporate espionage. The goal of performing corporate espionage is to get a company's trade secrets so that they can use them for competitive reasons. Companies have lost design blueprints, clientele data, supplier contacts, and valuable market information to hackers. Chinese hackers have been associated with corporate espionage with their trail of hacks going as high as hacking a US military contractor. The US indicted several hackers in 2017 with corporate espionage and identity theft:

Data breaches are carried out using other threat vectors. Mostly, hackers use social engineering methods such as phishing to get access credentials from oblivious users. Spear-phishing is a hacking method that is commonly used because it requires fewer resources and is quite easy to perfect. Hackers send users emails using compromised business emails, requesting them to either send sensitive files or give access credentials to files. In other cases, other hacking methods will be used if the hackers cannot get the required information through social engineering.

Mitigation

Data breaches are reportedly on the rise and therefore companies are being warned to put in place more security measures to protect themselves. One of these measures is by spreading user awareness of attack methods that can be used against them for the purposes of social engineering. Another mitigation is the installation of intrusion prevention systems on networks to detect and prevent malicious activity on their networks. Lastly, firewalls are a great addition for sniffing out malicious requests that comes into a network as a result of hacking attempts on organizational servers.

Summary

Even though many organizations consider the network perimeter to be lost territory, to the threat actors, it is still important to cover basic levels of network security. At the end of the day, the role of the security department is also to reduce the attack surface as much as possible while balancing between security and productivity. Across the security stack, more vendors focus on machine learning and artificial intelligence. The reason for this is that those technologies offer their customers intelligent services. Intelligent firewalls, as an example, use machine learning to continually improve their performance, which is tailored to your organization.

Cloud security

Cloud usage is rising and we're seeing major adoption by both individual users and enterprises. Therefore, a natural response from attackers is that they have also developed an interest in cloud platforms. Even at this point in their infancy, cloud platforms are seeing major threats coming their way:

The widespread use of cloud services by users who show risky behaviors and limited concerns for security have been met with cloud-based attacks. The following subsections cover threats that cloud users have been facing.

Data breaches

Even though cloud services vendors impose a number of security measures on their products, they are still facing this threat that has for long plagued traditional networks. Data breaches to cloud platforms have exposed customer information, trade secrets, and other sensitive content to hackers. With such kinds of data, breaches have resulted in massive lawsuits against the companies and extended lawsuits against the cloud vendors. It is always the responsibility of a company that stores user data to secure it from attacks, and thus data breaches on the cloud are almost certainly followed by costly lawsuits in terms of money and reputation.

Data breaches have occurred in the cloud due to human errors, vulnerabilities in apps that use cloud services, and the implementation of weak security policies by organizations concerning who has rights to access data in the cloud. The cloud has offered cheaper storage options for organizations, meaning that more data will be pushed to such platforms instead of local servers. Hackers are counting on these listed flaws to get access to this data. In 2017, it was said that over 1.4 billion records stored on cloud platforms were lost to hackers. A significant amount of these were as a result of a data breach on a company that provided sign-in functionalities to cloud platforms for an approximately 2,000 companies.

Mitigation

The most effective way to protect against data breaches on the cloud is by using two-factor authentication. This is because cloud data breaches are mainly the result of stolen access credentials from careless users. Two-factor authentication prevents direct access to cloud services by an unauthorized party that does not have the second factor of authentication other than the access passwords. Two-factor authentication uses something one knows, has, or is, as a second factor. An attacker will generally lack the ability to complete the second step of authentication. A common setup is sending of an authentication code to a phone number that has to be entered after login credentials are entered to complete the authentication procedure:

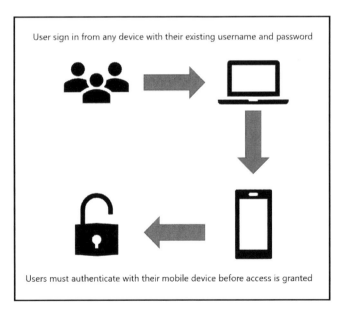

A user will have his or her phone at most times and an attacker will not, and this will save his or her account from being compromised if an attacker has managed to steal their login credentials. Another effective way of managing data breaches on cloud platforms is through the use of encryption. Encryption should be used to secure the transmission of data to and from the cloud. This way, attackers cannot sniff packets that are in transit and read them to find out the data that they were carrying. Most cloud vendors will have already put in place measures to ensure that their connection is encrypted and that **Software as a Service (SaaS)** products enjoy the security of encryption. However, users who buy cloud services that require them to set up their own encryption at times fail to do this, meaning that their data lies exposed to attackers when being transmitted to and from the cloud.

Compromised credentials

The laziness of users when it comes to passwords has been extended to the cloud. Unlike their local machines or host-based systems, the cloud is public and thus is accessible to many people, including hackers. These hackers can easily go around searching for cloud-based accounts that feature the common, weak credentials that users are accustomed to. There have been several studies on the most used passwords each year and the results are always disappointing. For four years in a row, the two most common passwords have been `123456` and the phrase password 4. Unsurprisingly, variations of these passwords are next in line of the famously easy to use passwords that most users have stuck to. It is estimated that 10% of internet users use or have used twenty-five of the yearly commonly used passwords:

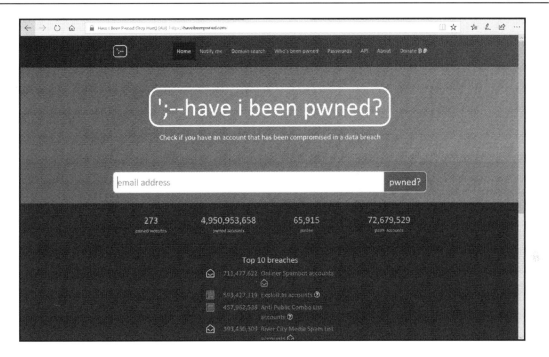

The habit of using weak passwords seemingly never dies, and in organizations, the IT department has to be rather strict with the implementation of the password policy or else most users will turn to these weak passwords. Other common passwords that users use are their birthdays, names of their pets or significant others, and their names with numerical combinations. On cloud platforms, hackers have an easy job when breaking into accounts if the users use these commonly weak passwords. It is almost not a challenge to hack into the cloud accounts of some users due to their laxity in setting up passwords. Cloud platforms are mostly logged into using an email and password combination, or a username password combination. It might be easy to tell one's email address since it might not be so secretive. The second portion of the login credential, the password, can be guessed quite a number of times by hackers that are dedicated to gaining access to one's cloud.

Perhaps the cloud puts users at a disadvantage since it exposes them to threats that they would not normally experience with their local systems. This is a threat that is completely avoidable, but will most likely continue to exist based on the types of users and user behavior that has been observed. If for four years internet users have not seen it as unsafe to keep on using 123456 as a password, there is a big challenge that people in charge of security in organizations have to meet to educating their users. Individual users also need some sort of intervention in order to let go of this dangerous practice of using weak passwords.

Mitigation

The only mitigation for this problem is forcing users to use strong passwords. Some vendors have password complexity requirements to help them weed out the use of weak passwords. Organizations that publish apps or install systems on cloud platforms should also ensure that users are made to use complex passwords to access them. This is because such systems are more exposed to hackers than systems hosted in an organizational server room. At an individual level, the reluctance to use complex passwords has to be avoided.

There are third-party alternatives that can be used to help those that feel that the burden of remembering passwords is too much. Third-party password managers can store user passwords and also generate secure ones. They can also protect user's passwords from prying eyes, as is the case when users write their passwords on sticky notes or on notepads. They are also safer alternatives to storing passwords on browsers since browsers lay exposed to malware designed to read credentials stored in them. Lastly, the use of two-factor authentication, as discussed in the *Mitigation* subsection, can help protect cloud-based systems from hackers. Even if a user chooses a weak password, there will be little chance that the hacker will have the second type of authentication to gain access of the target's cloud.

Denial of Service

Denial of Service attacks have been in the cybersecurity threat list for a long time, even before the cloud came was overwhelming adopted. Denial of Service attacks threaten the availability of the cloud to users. This is mainly because since a cloud user is not the owner of the cloud, when a DoS attack happens, the only thing they can do is sit down and helplessly wait for the attack to come to an end:

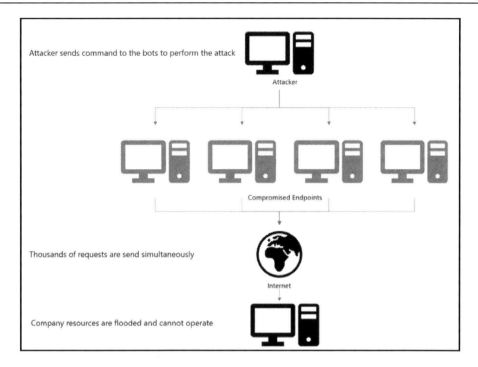

Attacker sends command to the bots to perform the attack

Attacker

Compromised Endpoints

Thousands of requests are send simultaneously

Internet

Company resources are flooded and cannot operate

Also, some cloud vendors who charge users per bandwidth used might charge more for increased loads, regardless of whether it was during a DoS attack or not. Other site users will be prevented from accessing data or applications that are hosted on the cloud since processing power, memory, and bandwidth will have been exhausted by illegitimate traffic. The threat of DoS and DDoS attacks is growing, and there are dark-web black markets that are offering to conduct such attacks against a chosen target for a fee. There was a listing in a dark web market that offered to carry out a DDoS attack against any target using 100,000 zombie computers for a given fee. The biggest fear is that competitors might turn to such types of attacks to bring down businesses or organizations that have adopted the cloud. DoS and DDoS attacks can be used to distract people from other attacks that attackers might carry out without being easily detected since all attention will have been diverted to another attack.

Mitigation

The best mitigation for DoS attacks for an organization that needs to be up and running continuously is to have an alternative site. The alternative site should be kept in a ready state to be activated when the main site has been overwhelmed by attackers. There is very little that an individual user can do to stop a DDoS attack against the cloud since that is the responsibility of the vendor. Therefore, when a user detects that such an attack is ongoing, it is best to contact the cloud vendor in time to see whether the attack has been detected and will be handled. This is the reason why an alternative site is always a wise idea for an organization that cannot afford to be offline, even for half an hour. The guarantee by most vendors is a 99% uptime, and the 1% might end up to be too costly if an organization does not have another plan for when an attack occurs.

Summary

Many enterprises have discovered the benefits of the cloud. When it comes to security, the cloud offers also many benefits. Data breaches are a pressing issue and through the cloud, vendors offer Multi-Factor Authentication, which any enterprise that takes security seriously should implement. Cloud Services such as Azure Active Directory or `www.haveibeenpwned.com` also offer the option to verify whether any of the organizational credentials have been compromised.

Bring Your Own Device

Bring Your Own Device (BYOD) is a workplace practice that has been received differently in organizations, some being highly in favor of it while others are openly opposed to it. It is an approach to lower the costs incurred by organizations in equipping users with devices that they can use to perform their job roles. It is also a practice that can increase the mobility and productivity of users by giving them tools to work using the devices they own. It came in as a trendy and employee-friendly practice, but since then has run into many security threats that are threatening its continuity. These threats are making organizations weigh the cost advantages of BYOD over the losses incurred when threats facing these user devices happen. The following is a discussion of these threats that are facing user-owned devices that are being put to use for organizational work.

Data loss

Since these devices are owned by users, they are moved from the workplace to user's homes almost daily. In transit, these devices face the threat of being stolen or damaged. Such a loss translates to the loss of data that is stored in the devices. At times, these devices may contain sensitive data such as emails detailing an organization's trade secrets. Many organizations use Microsoft Outlook for emails and it is normally set to open and sync emails without necessarily requiring re-authentication. The only security barrier from these emails is the login functionality. Therefore, a loss of a device is always treated as a big loss since an organization will not be sure whether the thief will be interested in reading sensitive data within the hard disk. Physical damage leading to loss of data may cause unexpected loss of work data which might set back some work processes.

Mitigation

The best mitigation for data loss is a secure backup. Therefore, organizations should ensure that they remind their workers to back up their information on cloud platforms so that even if their devices are lost, the data will not be. To combat the security risk of organizational data falling into the wrong hands after a theft, organizations should give users software that encrypts hard disks. A good example is DesLock, which does full disk encryption and can be enabled for enterprise use where IT admins can ensure that all user devices are encrypted. This way, if a thief steals a user's device, the hard disk will be useless. Also, users should be discouraged from storing sensitive organizational data in their personal computers. They should only keep data that is essential for them to perform their duties. Lastly, organizations should set email client-software such as Outlook to request for authentication every time it is opened. This way, if a user's device is lost to thieves, they cannot open it and continue reading or receiving organizational emails on the device.

Insecure usage

Organizations do not have rights over the use of personal devices as they would if these were organizational devices. Therefore, they cannot regulate where these devices can be used or who can use them. These devices may, over the weekend, be used by an employee's friend. In the evening, they may be used by the employee's family. There are no rules to bar this from happening. When these people use the device, they might not be as security-minded as the employee. Thus, they may visit malicious sites that could compromise the devices. They may also be too curious and start eavesdropping on work emails and other sensitive data, thus introducing some security threats since they are not the authorized recipients of such data and information.

Mitigation

An organization may not be sure about the true intentions of their employee's friends and relatives who may have access to the computing devices after work. Therefore, a separation should be done between one's personal life and work life. The best way to ensure that an employee's personal life is separated from the workplace is requiring an employee to have two user profiles. One profile should specifically be designated for work purposes and is the one that should be able to access a user's work emails. This way, when a user leaves work, he or she logs in to their personal user account. This does not put the organization in inherent danger of third parties having extensive access to organizational data and emails.

Remote access by malicious parties

The use of personal devices means that users have to be given remote access to organizational systems. If not monitored, this remote access could be used by threat actors to gain access to the organization and steal data from the servers. This is possible if users are given access credentials that they can use any time they wish to remotely connect to the servers. If hackers get access to these credentials, they too can use them to access the servers. Also, if the connection between users and the servers is not secured, attackers may capture the packets being transmitted and later on read them to determine their contents.

Mitigation

The best mitigation for remote access threats is the use of an organizational application that can create an encrypted connection to the servers. This will give employees a convenient and secure mechanism to access the data that they want from the corporate servers. An addition to this would be a configuration to such an application to ensure that sensitive data from servers is only placed in the main memory and only when the application has been logged into by the user. When the application is closed, all of the data should be erased. Therefore, if a user's device is stolen, the sensitive data is never found on the hard disk by the thieves.

Malicious applications

BYOD might be applied to personal devices that may have existing malicious apps. For instance, attackers may already have installed spyware on a user's laptop. The purpose of the malware planted on the device might be to continually sniff data from the laptop and send it to the attackers. When such a device is made part of an organization's resources, it will inherently expose the organization to the malware it already has. Therefore, the organization's data will continue to be stolen by hackers without the knowledge of both the employee and the organization.

Mitigation

To mitigate this, organizations should check the machines that they allow employees to use for work functions. A malware check should be done to ensure that the personal device does not come with existing threats. Users should be encouraged to have an active and updated antivirus program on their personal devices. This prevents malware from being installed or run on the device that will be used for more sensitive purposes. Also, organizations can opt to give users client versions of enterprise antivirus programs. This way, the IT department will be able to tell if the threats exist in the personal devices remotely and safely remove them from the devices.

Insider threats

One of the most daunting threats in an organization is an insider threat. An insider threat is a threat actor that works or resides within the organization. This person has knowledge about the organization such as where sensitive data is kept, which users have rights to access it, and the existing weaknesses in the security infrastructure of the organization. Insider threats in organizations that have implemented the BYOD policy are quite dangerous. They can take advantage of the reduced monitoring of systems, access to servers by many employees, and the overburdening of the IT department by requests to attend different machines and systems. The insider threats can use all of these distractions to commit espionage of enormous proportions. Since the access to servers by employees is seen a quite normal, they may use this privilege to copy all the pieces of information that they can access on the servers. They may also use this privilege to plant malware in files stored on the servers. When other users access these files, their computers may get infected with malware. The damage they cause can range from stolen data to a compromise of all computers that employees use to access organizational files and data.

Mitigation

An insider threat is a powerful enemy and it is best to prevent this enemy from getting into an organization in the first place. Employees should be subjected to background checks to determine their work history and why they left their previous jobs and whether they present security risks to an organization. Also, the IT department should be most vigil when operating in an environment where BYOD is implemented. Instead of data being pooled by users on their machines, it should be temporarily accessed through a given application. Access to servers should also be role-based so that not just any user can access any file. Lastly, regarding the planting of malware in shared drives, the IT department should use permissions to give read or write permissions to users. Generally, most users should have read-only permissions, with write permissions being given to a select few. It is very challenging for the IT department to cover all of the activities of personal devices in a network and therefore organizations should ensure that they have enough staff and resources to meet the unique security challenges that come with BYOD policies.

Summary

Bring Your Own Device (BYOD) offers the business many benefits, but can be a burden for the IT and Security department. In the case of BYOD, it is important to find a balance between security and productivity. A good practice is to have a tier level approach to access the corporate resources and services, making sure that only the most secure BYOD device has access to all of the corporate resources and services that an employee requires. This way, the user has the choice of how much security they want to enforce on their own device.

Internet of Things

One of the new frontiers in cybersecurity attack surfaces is the IoT technology. It is quite a new technology that has probably been adopted at an accelerated rate, maybe too fast. IoT has seen the introduction of millions of new tiny computing devices on the internet. They are being used for diverse functionalities and in groups, and they are achieving marvelous results such as smart homes and smart cities. However, most of these have come laden with bugs and vulnerabilities that hackers have not hesitated to exploit. According to Symantec, an industry leader in cybersecurity products, there are some IoT devices that are being exploited barely two minutes after they go active. The reason for this kind of reception from attackers is that IoT devices are economically viable for attacks. These tiny devices can easily be ganged together and used for denial of service attacks. They are small, they are voluminous, and they are easier to control than zombie computers. In 2016, barely the second year of their adoption, there came to rise a new botnet that has been used in a number of DDoS attacks. This botnet has been named Mirai and it was made up of IoT devices instead of the usual computers. There are probably many other unknown botnets operating on IoT devices:

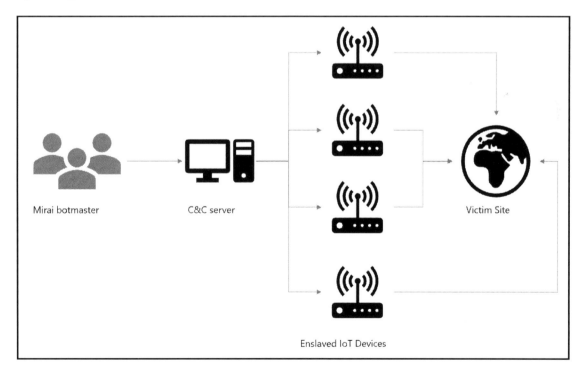

As a testament to their overwhelming power, IoT devices were found to be responsible for the most powerful DDoS attack ever. A hosting company called OVH was forced offline by an overwhelming number of IoT devices that bombarded it with 1 TBps illegitimate traffic. An almost comical attack was when a school was attacked by its own IoT-enabled lights, months after their installation in the school's premises. There are several threats facing IoT devices, most of which threaten to see these devices being recruited to botnets or having their functionalities altered by attackers. These threats are as listed in the following subsections.

Weak authentication/authorization

The biggest weakness in IoT devices, which falls back to the laziness of users, is the use of default passwords. Users have extended their preference for weak passwords from end host devices to IoT devices. In the case of IoT, users are hardly changing the default passwords that their IoT devices come with. Also, the users that change from the default passwords are not departing from the use of weak combinations of characters that they use for their passwords. It is, however, understandable why users are taking the issue of the credentials for these devices with laxity. A typical smart home will have smart lights, smart AC units, smart refrigerators, smart curtains, and smart entertainment systems among others. All of these will require the user to set up new, complex authentication credentials, a task that has proven to be too daunting for many. They therefore either opt to have the IoT devices remain with their default passwords or change the passwords to a weak but similar password. There are other challenges that are affecting the authorization of IoT device users into carrying out specific tasks. There is a lack of protection of credentials in the tiny memories of these IoT devices. There is also a challenge with password recovery on the tiny internet-enabled devices. Lastly, there is a lack of definition of different user roles and in most cases, anyone that can log into the device has the rights of an admin.

Mitigation

The threats for weak authentication are the prime culprits for the hacking of many IoT devices and their enlistment on botnets or the compromise of their functionalities. Manufacturers can help mitigate the challenge of weak passwords by setting up the devices with One Time Passwords which owners have to change after they activate their IoT devices. The passwords should be subjected to a complexity test and users should not be allowed to configure their devices with weak passwords. Manufacturers should also be made to ensure that they protect the authentication credentials. They should at least be encrypted so that a third party cannot directly read the authentication details from the memories of these devices. Also, manufacturers ought to separate the roles of users that log into the devices; there should be an admin account and a normal user account at the very least. Users should be encouraged to enable two-factor authentication wherever possible for their IoT devices. Lastly, IoT devices should be set so that they can request for re-authentication after some time so that if they are enlisted in botnets, hackers will lose control over them.

Insecure interfaces

Since they are internet enabled, the interfaces for configuring most IoT interfaces are web-based. A user has to visit a certain web address in order to interact with the devices wirelessly. While this remote control is highly convenient, it also places IoT devices at the risk of being compromised by attackers. The interfaces are reportedly also weak and do not have protection mechanisms against attacks. They have been found to be prone to both SQL injection and cross-site scripting attacks. They have also been observed to have poor session management. Some interfaces feature poor account logout configurations. Others are just supportive of weak username-password combinations from users.

Mitigation

The insecure interfaces have been interpreted as the cost of the rush by many manufacturers to meet the needs of the new IoT market that caused them to overlook security. To mitigate the flaws on the interfaces, there are a number of things that manufacturers ought to do to secure these devices from the threats that they are currently facing. They must begin by making sure that these interfaces are not prone to either SQL injection or XSS scripting attacks. These attacks are almost outdated since most websites have implemented code that can thwart attempts to hack them through these kind of techniques. The interfaces should feature some security in terms of encryption so that credentials are not transmitted in plain text from users to the web interfaces. If an attacker is capturing packets from the user's network, it will be easy to read the transmitted login credentials. The interfaces should also be made to be strict on the password requirements. Lastly, these interfaces should feature more robust password recovery mechanisms and also lock out login attempts after a number of failed sign-in attempts.

Lack of encryption

A problem facing most IoT devices is that most of them do not feature any type of encryption. Data stored in them and data in transit is not secured with any encryption method. Intruders are therefore having an easy time sniffing data in them or being transmitted to them and using it to compromise the operations of the device or, in the case of login credentials, using the data to gain control over the devices. The few IoT devices that have encryption are also not safe since some of them have poorly configured SSL/TLS protocols. This is what is making IoT devices easy to be commandeered by attackers.

Mitigation

The lack of encryption is a problem that should be solved by the manufacturers of these devices. Manufacturers should hire qualified personnel to ensure that data on the devices or data being exchanged between the device and a user is secured using SSL or TSL encryption protocols. Industry level encryption should be implemented to avoid weak encryption that can be easily cracked by hackers and the encrypted data deciphered. Manufacturers should also avoid using their own proprietary encryption protocols.

Insufficient configurability

A security threat facing IoT that can be traced back to the rush to flood markets with IoT devices is the lack of sufficient configurability of security settings in an IoT device. There are some devices where users cannot alter their inbuilt security controls. The web interfaces through which these devices can be configured offer limited security options. Therefore, even security-minded users cannot help much in securing their devices from attackers. Some manufacturers were not so much concerned about the security of their devices as that was not a priority in the manufacturing process, hence this weakness is being exploited by attackers.

Mitigation

To avoid such future problems, manufacturers should prioritize security in the design of their devices. Also, since most of the interfaces used to control IoT devices are web-based, manufacturers should take the responsibility of updating the interfaces to feature more security options. This should be done non-intrusively and carefully to avoid leaving users with unsecured devices in the process.

Summary

The **Internet of Things (IoT)** is a booming new market. The problem is that while these new microchips are getting installed everywhere, not many of the vendors focus on security today. This puts the end user at tremendous risk. A couple of things that are important to understand, verify, and implement are strong authentication, ensuring that the interfaces leveraged cannot be tampered with to perform a SQL-injection or cross-site scripting attack and ensuring a level of disk encryption.

Summary

Cyber threats have proliferated over the internet and have targeted both individual users and enterprises. Not only have threat actors caused enterprises to suffer financial loss due to cyber attacks, they have forced their businesses to dip due to a loss of reputation and the exposure of trade secrets to competitors. Individual users have lost private information and sensitive credentials to attackers. The threat areas in which both individual users and enterprises have been targeted and exploited have been discussed. Network security, which has been a core concern for enterprises, has been discussed and prevalent threats have been identified as denial of service, eavesdropping, and data breaches. These have been individually discussed, the threats they pose explained, and their mitigation measures have been given.

Regarding endpoint security, this chapter has looked into the issue of ransomware, spyware, Trojan horses, and viruses. In the discussion of these threats, there has been an emphasis on ransomware, which drew attention after a single ransomware program encrypted over 150,000 devices in more than 100 countries, causing sheer devastation in some victim institutions. Effective mitigation scenarios that can be taken against these endpoint threats have been discussed. We highlighted cloud technology since it is among the most promising technologies of the day and will see more adoption with time. The threats facing it, such as data breaches and Denial of Service attacks, as well as their mitigations, have also been examined.

Questions

- What are mitigation options to protect against ransomware?
- What is the name of the type of attack that can take down corporate networks?
- What are recommended mitigations against DDoS attacks?
- What is the most effective way to prevent a data breach?

Further reading

Below is a summary of recommended further readings.

- Kan, "DDoS attack on Dyn came from 100,000 infected devices", *Computerworld*, 2018. [Online]. Available: `https://www.computerworld.com/article/3135434/security/ddos-attack-on-dyn-came-from-100000-infected-devices.html`. [Accessed: 19- Mar- 2018].
- Smith, "US charges 3 Chinese security firm hackers with cyber espionage", *CSO Online*, 2018. [Online]. Available: `https://www.csoonline.com/article/3238828/security/us-charges-3-chinese-security-firm-hackers-with-corporate-cyber-espionage.html`. [Accessed: 19- Mar- 2018].
- Smith, "US charges 3 Chinese security firm hackers with cyber espionage", *CSO Online*, 2018. [Online]. Available: `https://www.csoonline.com/article/3238828/security/us-charges-3-chinese-security-firm-hackers-with-corporate-cyber-espionage.html`. [Accessed: 19- Mar- 2018].
- "The 25 Most Common Passwords of 2017 Include 'Star Wars'", *Fortune*, 2018. [Online]. Available: `http://fortune.com/2017/12/19/the-25-most-used-hackable-passwords-2017-star-wars-freedom/`. [Accessed: 19- Mar- 2018].
- Liptak, "The WannaCry ransomware attack has spread to 150 countries", *The Verge*, 2018. [Online]. Available: `https://www.theverge.com/2017/5/14/15637888/authorities-wannacry-ransomware-attack-spread-150-countries`. [Accessed: 19- Mar- 2018].
- Vonoepen, "Internet Security Threat Report 2017 - The threat of IoT | Symantec Connect", *Symantec.com*, 2018. [Online]. Available: `https://www.symantec.com/connect/events/internet-security-threat-report-2017-threat-iot`. [Accessed: 19- Mar- 2018].

11
Trends in Security Architecture Technology

Trends are always tricky to predict and quite honestly, typically the pablum that bloggers will put out to entertain the non-security media readers. But, as an Enterprise Security Architect, you have to be able to look at the direction that various different technology areas are going in. To do that, as with everything else in this book, it's best to fall back on our **Reference Security Architecture (RSA)**.

Cybersecurity has always followed new technology directions because, while new technologies are great, they are also filled with unintended consequences, and cybersecurity has always been about dealing with those unintended consequences. To look at what future trends in security technologies will bring, you need to understand where non-security technologies are going and then imagine what will have to occur in order to protect those new technologies. Most of the time, this will be some form of adjustment to existing technologies with the occasional brand-new security technology.

 History teaches us that progress is made, not through major jumps, but by incremental changes.

Remember that with any conversation, solution, or issue, there are always going to be three (or four) components; the people, process, technologies, (and governance) associated with the area you are looking at. The next chapter will talk about the future of security architects and security architecture and that, at the end of the day, falls in the people, process, and governance areas. With this chapter, we'll talk about the trends associated with security technologies. The conversation will be broken down into the different areas of the RSA and their associated trends.

One last thing to keep in mind before going into the various future trends is that there is a lot of hype that surrounds various technologies. You've seen it through the years. In the early 1990s, FDDI was hyped as the LAN technology of the future. In the late 1990s, everyone was talking about how biometrics was going to be the way to secure IT in the future. By 2005, Application Security was the key to making sure that vulnerabilities went away. **Digital Rights Management (DRM)** started to get popular in the 2008 timeframe. PKI was the security technology that was key to securing everything and became very popular around 2010. Around 2015, **Data Loss Prevention (DLP)** started to take off. Each one of these technologies (and there are plenty of other examples as well) had plenty of support because they were viewed as technologies that were going to solve all problems.

The problem is that these technologies never truly took into consideration the behaviors of people and why the issue was there in the first place. DRM and DLP both require changes in the behavior of people so that they actually have to do one additional task associated with documents that they are creating. PKI is used but not to the extent expected because it requires centralized control, which slows administrators down from doing what they want to do, biometrics feel physically intrusive to users, and so on and so forth. When you look at technologies, be wary of anything that requires a change in the behavior of users. It will mean that the technology will have a limited use.

We will cover the following topics in detail:

- Border protection
- Detection services
- Content control services
- Identity and Access Management
- Auditing services
- Configuration management
- Cryptographic services

Border protection

Border protection is all about defining borders for your organization's network as well as creating security zones. It's all about dealing with things at the network layer, so let's talk about the security technology trends associated with that layer.

Cloud security

The traditional view of where the network border of the organization has changed. No longer can you define the organization's border by an external router that dedicated leased lines are connecting to or the demarc associated with the internet. Now, organizations are trying to be more and more nimble as well as cost-effective, and that means shifting more and more of the information technology direction to cloud service providers. As a result, there will be more and more of a need to understand cloud security components, both within the cloud service provider as well as from your organization.

Cloud security will be driven by the security capabilities that the various IaaS service providers will be able to, or be willing to, provide to their customers. That means services such as Amazon Web Services, Google Cloud, and Microsoft Azure are going to grow their security offerings so that more and more of your organization's data centers can be located within their infrastructure.

AWS firewall capabilities are very limited compared to what you can find within your own dedicated firewalls, but that won't last. The ability to securely configure AWS buckets has been similar to the way servers originally were—the user's responsibility. If you remember back when Microsoft exploded on the scene with their servers, it was up to the user to configure the servers properly. But, as time went on, Microsoft's reputation became damaged by the poor security capabilities of their products and they started the entire Trustworthy Computing initiative. Now, their products are a LOT more secure. The same will occur with the various cloud vendors. Their cloud security capabilities will improve over time, which means that more and more people will feel comfortable with using cloud capabilities, but there will be a real need to truly understand how to securely design cloud environments.

Tokenization

With the edge of the organization's network border moving from blurred to non-existent (hey, we shifted to cloud a decade ago. Mobile devices have been around even longer. You tell me—where's the network edge to your organization?), the shift has been to focus on the data of the organization and protecting it. But how can you protect bits and bytes?

That technology is called **tokenization**. Tokenization was described earlier in this book but, basically, tokenization is the process of replacing actual usable data with a token that represents that data so that an organization can make use of a cloud-based application (for example, Salesforce) while ensuring that the data never leaves the actual organization's environment.

Because it's a token rather than the actual data that is being acted on, the ability to meet privacy legislation (such as GDPR) is much easier since you can account much more completely for what occurs with the personal information of customers and employees. The data never leaves your environment and you can clearly show who has accessed the data.

The downside of tokenization is that the cloud application has to be able to work with tokens rather than actual data. If the cloud application can't do that, then you are limited in its capabilities.

Disaster recovery

With more and more breaches occurring, there will be a growing demand for technologies that ensure a quick recovery to known good situations. This means that you will see backups and disaster recovery environments start to grow. Backups have always been important and a stable solution that has been used by administrators for decades, but disaster recovery environments have not been designed properly and are often viewed as secondary production sites.

What will probably happen with DR sites is that the criticality of applications will become more and more important and, as a result, you will see proper DR sites being designed. The thing to be aware of, though, is the cost. Having a data center, any data center, is expensive, and a DR site is just another data center but with a specialized purpose. With the move to cloud service providers, the cost of data centers drops dramatically and that means the cost of having a proper DR site will also drop. It's simple supply and demand—as the cost of a data center is reduced, the demand will go up. So, as the cost of having a DR site goes down, the use of stand-alone data centers will go up.

The use of a DR site as a secondary production environment will most likely continue as well. It would cost a lot to transition a poorly implemented DR site (being used as a secondary production center) to a new DR data center. As a result, expect to see a different approach to disaster recovery where a secondary production site can continue operations when isolated from the primary production site.

VPN

Have you seen the vendor that advertises on TV about a VPN technology that used military grade encryption? It's one of the most annoying commercials you can find if you are an actual security architect because the commercial is misleading the lay-person into thinking that there's a different type of encryption only available to the military. This tells you that VPN is really being over-hyped.

When you have a technology that is at this point in the hype cycle (thanks, Gartner, for that term!), you know that its use is ubiquitous and that there will be a new technology approaching that will start to replace it. VPN is discussed here in a chapter on trends, not because it will increase in use, but because it will most likely decrease in use in favor of a newer technology that is cheaper and easier to make use of. VPN was designed to allow an encrypted tunnel over a public network that allows your data to flow without allowing for data mingling or unauthorized access to your data. It was developed in order to reduce the cost of dedicated lines, but with the use of things such as SSL-based web protocols (for example, HTTPS, SFTP/FTPS, and so on), you have data flowing encrypted over public networks without the need for an encrypted tunnel.

Doing some research shows that there are a few alternatives starting to become available. You might just want to encrypt your own data without having to worry about a VPN tunnel. This provides the same type of protection and, with the expanded use of PKI service providers such as Entrust and Verisign, this becomes a possible option. Combined with the appropriate authentication/authorization mechanisms on either end of the communication path, you have a replacement for VPN.

Another option may come about if IPv6 ever starts to make headway. IPv6 has a requirement for encryption of data packets, and there are a few technologies that are focused on leveraging IPv6 because of its security capabilities.

In the long term, expect VPN to start to disappear in favor of a newer approach. It started with HTTPS and you can expect it to continue in other situations.

Detection services

Detection services are about detecting security breaches and unauthorized behaviour. Past technologies for this area were capabilities such as **Intrusion Prevention Systems** (**IPS**) and SIEMs, but as malicious behaviour becomes more and more sophisticated and the time to react becomes less and less, new approaches appear.

Artificial Intelligence

Artificial Intelligence, or AI, is what everyone seems to be hanging their hats on moving forward. It allows for more advanced logic in systems rather than the current A/B decision-making patterns. It allows for patterns of gray where there might be some decision-making that has to occur.

In cybersecurity, AI is meant to allow for an instant reaction to any perceived bad behavior. Currently, technologies such aslobally anti-virus and IPS use known malicious behavior patterns to prevent attacks from happening. These technologies are being replaced by whitelisting (more on this later), which recognizes known patterns of good behavior. But there will be situations where neither good nor bad behavior patterns are known. Or, and this is much more likely, there's a need to "self-heal" the environment, and decisions will need to be made based on the patterns of behavior.

AI will come into play in more and more ways from a cybersecurity point of view. But, and this harkens back to what was said at the beginning of this chapter, new technologies are put into place and then cybersecurity has to fix the unintended consequences. So, while AI may be a great technology in non-security ways, there will have to be corrective technologies to deal with the unintended consequences. And, in all likelihood, those corrective technologies will also be based on AI.

Incident response

Incident response isn't a technology. By its nature, it's a process. It deals without needing to respond when something inappropriate happens. The development of zero day attacks means that the incidence response has to happen even faster, but there's no way that a person can respond anything like as quickly as a piece of malicious software such as a virus or worm. As a result, there will be a need for automated responses.

Incident response will start to move towards some sort of self-healing network with the core of the response activity being tied to the SIEM. Currently, a SIEM will tell you when inappropriate activities are taking place, but then a person will have to make changes, which is slow. **Stix** a (structured language for cyber threat intelligence) and **Taxii** a (transport mechanism for sharing cyber threat intelligence) were protocols that were developed to allow for the communication of threat information so that secondary systems could anticipate a new attack vector.

The logical extension of Stix and Taxii is a common language among security technologies that allows for automated changes based on the information coming in. Imagine a firewall automatically changing its ruleset to prevent connections from a specific set of ports, or an anti-virus solution that automatically prevents communication on services because of an update to its signatures based on advanced warnings.

Expect security technologies to start to communicate to each other and allow for a faster incident response set of actions.

Content control services

Content control is about dealing with content that is coming into and leaving your organization. Spam, while nothing new, will always enter your organization. But what if spam was used in a different way?

Spam as a new phishing technique

Several months ago, the author of this book started receiving all sorts of new spam from organizations that were never asked for. Advertising from Old Navy and David's Tea were being received. The logical thing to do was to click on the unsubscribe link since I never asked to receive these advertisements to begin with.

But what if those weren't advertising but, were rather, methods of phishing or gaining access to one's computer? Traditional phishing techniques ask you to click on this link or ask whether you have an outstanding parking ticket, and so on. In other words, you receive an email that says that you have to click on a link to deal with a plausible situation. But there are other natural behaviors like trying to get rid of unwanted emails, and advertisements that you never wanted in the first place. A subtler way to phish would be to send an advertisement and then have the unsubscribe link create the issue.

Expect more subtle means of behavior to start occurring to replace the more obvious phishing techniques. As a result, the security architect will have to ensure that the spam filters and the anti-phishing techniques can deal with the subtler forms of attack.

Identity and Access Management

Identity and Access Management (IAM) is the primary focus when it comes to security. People automatically think passwords and access controls. What will the trends be with IAM?

Increasing use of two factor authentication

The use of two factor authentication is going to increase dramatically as the costs associated with two factor go down. Originally, the cost of two factor was quite high, not because of upfront technologies such as the servers, but because of the continuous cost of the key fobs. But, now, with the fact that the vast majority of people have smart phones and the ability to have apps on those phones, you are seeing the cost of two factor going down because the two-factor authentication fob is being replaced by the application that resides on the phone itself.

You see SMS messages all the time that confirm that a user is who they say they are when they register for some service on the internet. This is a form of two factor authentication simply because it's using the phone itself as the authentication mechanism. It's something that you actually have, which is what two factor is all about. There are three components associated with authentication: who you are, what you know, and what you have. The what you have has always been the domain of two factor authentication, but it used to be the key fob. Now, you can make use of your phone as the item that is what you have.

This will dramatically increase the use of two-factor authentication and will improve the authentication process appropriately.

Auditing services

Auditing services is all about auditing the activities that are going on and making sure that you are meeting compliance requirements. What trends will occur in this area?

Privacy/GDPR

With the advent of the European Union's GDPR for the protection of privacy, and with the massive breaches that have been occurring with multiple multi-national organizations, expect there to be an increasing demand for the protection of privacy and private information. This will increase the need for the appropriate protections on that specific set of data and the rise of additional legislation.

Your security budgets will start to increase as a result of these additional legislative requirements. We know that because of what has occurred in critical infrastructure areas and in association with the **Payment Card Industry** (**PCI**). As new compliance comes in, additional costs are needed to avoid fines.

While this isn't a specific technology, there will be a trend towards more legislation to require cybersecurity controls to be put into place. There has already been an increase in requirements for the Utility space and the Healthcare space, and there is a definite ROI associated with PCI. Don't be surprised if there are additional requirements associated with cybersecurity along the lines of:

- Publicly traded companies are required to communicate the steps they have taken to secure their environments. This could impact the prices that stocks are traded at and, as a result, will drive cybersecurity expenditures from a corporate dividend point of view.
- Manufacturers of devices with an operating system will be required to have independent assessments along the lines of CSA or UL certificates. There is already the ISA99 standard for assessing critical infrastructure components for known and unknown vulnerabilities. There could be an extension of this into other areas.
- International standards associated with cybersecurity could come into play. There are currently too many independent standards (for example, GDPR, PIPEDA in Canada, and so on), and it makes sense to have an international alignment of all standards.

Expect legislation to start to arrive over the next five years, especially in light of the national state attack on the US (specifically against their election systems).

Configuration management

Configuration management comes down to the actual setup of solutions. This doesn't mean the design of a solution but, rather, the configurations of the devices that make up a solution. Most solutions will have multiple components that are off the shelf, so making sure that they are at limited risk is important. From a security technology trend point of view, the following are things to keep an eye on.

Internet of Things

With the advent of the **Internet of Things (IoT)** a few years ago, more and more vendors started adding operating systems to non-traditional devices. But what we learned with traditional IT devices such as servers and desktops is that everything needs to be patched. So, for example, cameras that are IT enabled and positioned on the exterior of a building can potentially be used for accessing the interior networks, especially if they are wireless LAN-enabled.

This will drive forward a number of different changes to cybersecurity. First, there will need to be a vulnerability scanner that is able to scan non-traditional devices with reliability. Typical vulnerability scanners don't deal with IoT situations, so your organization is going to need to monitor IoT vulnerability scanning capabilities. Keep an eye on IoT vulnerability scanners as they become more and more capable.

A second area to keep an eye on will be managed service providers that focus on IoT security. As more and more devices become IT-enabled, there will be a growing demand for the management of these devices. This will include the management of the patching and security aspects of these devices.

The last thing to keep an eye on isn't so much a technology as much as a change to reference architectures. We are currently looking at traditional IT capabilities in our reference architectures, but IoT devices and areas aren't typically part of those reference architectures. This means that there aren't any strategies being created in these areas and that there aren't any IT management capabilities in place. Expect that the IT department and groups within the organization will end up having conversations about who is best able to manage these devices.

End point security

Traditionally, end point devices such as desktops, laptops, servers, and mobile devices are dealing with malicious applications that will be loaded onto the device's hard drive and then launched. But there is a trend towards malware that resides within RAM rather than on the hard drive. This means that end point security vendors are going to have to provide capabilities for protecting what occurs in RAM.

When you select your end point security solutions, make sure that you are looking at the roadmaps of those vendors in terms of where they are going to protect against fileless attacks.

New technologies — new breaches

As I mentioned earlier, security is used to deal with the unintended consequences of new technologies. It gets added to and, over time, the new technologies will build in security. For the next several years, imagine and monitor the risks that come with those technologies. The technologies that are being talked about right now are:

- **Artificial Intelligence (AI)**: With AI growing, there will be a dependency on programs to make the correct decisions. But, if people can be conned, then AI will be able to be conned. How will that be dealt with?
- **Digital centralization**: People have so many devices they have to deal with (not just traditional IT devices) that they are going to get tired of having to deal with it all. This will push people towards some sort of centralization effort, where one device will manage all devices (including all the various smart devices). Centralization means that one breach will make everything available, which is why **Single Sign On** (**SSO**) and provisioning came about. What impact will this have on security technologies
- **Data overload**: As we saw with the 2016 US election, data on everyone is available to anyone. While there is a move towards privacy legislation, this doesn't change the fact that all this information is available. Here's the question—if phishing attacks are made with little to no information about an individual, what types of attack can be made with some information?

- **Changes to user interfaces**: Originally, we had mainframes with green screen dumb terminals and keyboards with the use of dot matrix printers for outputs. Then came devices with traditional interfaces through keyboards and displays with a move away from printing and towards mobile information sharing through things like Dropbox or USB sticks. This has driven the rise in keystroke loggers and over-the-shoulder spying. But if the user interface changes (maybe to verbal rather than keyboard-driven inputs), how does that change how inputs to and outputs of IT devices are stolen?

Keep in mind the various new technologies that are in the pipeline and how you will have to deal with those.

Cryptographic services

Cryptographic services deal with encryption. PKI has been steady rising in usage and, where a decade ago it was okay to use unencrypted protocols such as HTTP and FTP, now there is an expectation to use SSL-enabled protocols such as HTTPS and SFTP. Encryption has become the expected technology that all security architects will focus on. There is one specific technology that the security architect should keep an eye on moving forward: Bitcoin.

Bitcoin and blockchain security

An area that has become very trendy is Bitcoin. But Bitcoin is a very specific application of blockchain technology, which is heavily dependent on encryption. More importantly, it's a whole new approach to identity and improving the integrity of information communication. Currently, it is being used for the exchange of money, but blockchain's capabilities are capable of being used in so many other areas.

Blockchain can be used for authentication purposes since it can legitimately be viewed as the what you have component for authentication purposes. You can actually see a time where it can be used to replace usernames and passwords.

With the lightweight nature of the blockchain wallet, it's a very good technology for use in Internet of Things components that may not have a large amount of memory for storage. IoT could then be able to use blockchain for authentication into a decentralized network.

Decentralization is the main reason for blockchain. Bitcoin is taking off because it allows the individual to avoid the use of financial institutes and deal user to user. This is a prime example of a user to user technology. Other examples might be media distribution where a user may want to make sure that a file makes it to a specific user without being intercepted. It could be used as a replacement for **Digital Rights Management (DRM)** or **Digital Loss Prevention (DLP)**.

There are so many possible applications for blockchain that this is one area that the security architect really should keep an eye on. Don't focus on Bitcoin—that's the hype that is in the mainstream media. Focus on the underlying blockchain technology.

Application security

More and more, you have to be aware of the cybersecurity aspects of applications, and not just for any custom-built application. In this space, there is one area that you will need to keep an eye on, and it may very well impact your requirement gathering for various projects, especially if you are associated with a critical infrastructure or with a government.

Applications serving their nation states

There have been more and more examples of nation states requiring applications written in their countries to include the ability for that nation state to access infrastructure within another nation state. Several years ago, Huawei was restricted in their ability to sell their telecommunication and networking gear in North America, both the US and Canada, because there were concerns about the equipment being used by China to access data flowing across a network for spying purposes.

More recently, Kaspersky (an anti-virus vendor based in Russia) was discovered to have a backdoor that allowed Russian cyber spies to access systems protected by Kaspersky anti-virus. The FBI has been pressuring Apple to build in a way to break into Apple devices so that they can monitor communications going through those devices, and it's been interesting that there hasn't been any public conversations around Android devices. This is not unusual and shouldn't be forgotten.

But the world is becoming more and more segmented, and old alliances are breaking down. This will impact your choice of vendors moving forward because you'll also have to keep in mind which country a technology came from and whether you want to run the risk of there being some sort of intentional vulnerability being built into that country's technology.

When you are collecting your requirements, and this goes for cloud service providers especially, you have to determine if your solution is okay using the assumption that all data will be made available to specific countries. The requirements chapter earlier in this book, goes into country-specific requirements. Give special focus to this area.

Summary

Always fall back on the three components of a solution (people, process, and technologies) when you are looking forward, whether from a strategic point of view or just to see what trends are coming and then plan for them. The easiest way to structure this planning exercise is to use your RSA and look at the individual areas to see what trends may be occurring. Doing that will help you moving forward.

This chapter has been all about security technologies. The next and the final chapter of this book will talk about the future of security architects and security architecture, and this will mean focusing on the people and process components of any solution.

Questions

1. What is the best tool to structure how you look at trends?
2. Is there one area that you think will bring the biggest change to cybersecurity?
3. How can you protect information classified as private but still make use of Cloud solutions?
4. There are areas in security architecture that aren't specific to technology products, but different approaches to solutions. What are they?

12
The Future of Security Architecture

Over the last 20 years, security architecture and the people that have performed security architecture have changed a lot. It used to be that security consultants provided security architecture services. Then, the term architect was created and security architects were born. When the concept of enterprise architecture was developed, there were disagreements with who should be an enterprise architect. Originally, the view was that an Enterprise Architect was someone that was an expert in several architecture towers. But that was slowly shifted to mean a master in a specific architecture field, and Enterprise Security Architects were born.

This book has talked about two different types of security architect: the solution security architect and the supporting security architect. We've also talked about the enterprise security architect as the role that focuses on strategy and program development in the security architecture space. That's three roles that currently exist. But will they continue to exist into the future, considering how IT is changing? Let's take a look at the entire role of security architects and security architecture from a strategic point of view.

We will cover the following topics in detail:

- Environmental variables
  - Political variables
  - Economic variables
  - Technical variables
  - Social variables
  - Competitive variables

- General future associated with security architects
    - Market consolidations
    - Breaches and reactions
    - Secure by design?
    - Managed Security Service Providers and outsourcers
    - The evolution of the security tower
    - Merging of cybersecurity and physical security

Environmental variables

Remember that, whenever we look at a situation, we have to consider the environmental variables. We went over this back in the Strategy chapter. Those variables, especially with regards to a role such as a security architect, which is industry-wide rather than company-specific, will definitely be impacted by those various variables.

For those who may not remember, here's a diagram showing how the various variables interact with the enterprise as well as with each other:

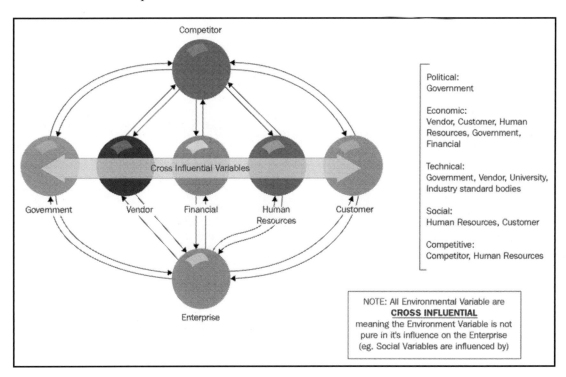

In the case of the security architect role, just replace the word enterprise with the phrase security architect. Also, keep in mind that the term security architect will have to deal with people and processes rather than technology, though the role focuses on technology. What do we get? Well, we will cover this in the following subsections, starting with political variables.

Political variables

This will go back to governments for anything that is industry wide. Political impacts will have to do with things such as legislation, both from a process and a people point of view. You won't see any legislation that's specific to security architects, but you can expect to see legislation around security. Expect over the next 10 years that you will see manufacturers required to meet certain security standards and that enterprises will be required to report on their security risks from a board point of view. This means that security measures will continue to have to be implemented and that means processes similar to PCI, HIPAA, and Sarbanes Oxley (but for security). Organizations will want to implement security controls that automate a lot of these capabilities, so expect to see an increase in expenditures.

Economic variables

This will go to the amount that organizations will spend on cybersecurity. Political variables will drive increases in expenditures, but companies will want to see some sort of **return on investment** (**ROI**). This will drive the conversation away from the typical insurance conversation (because that will be dealt away with because of the legislation) and require security to be talked about in terms of ROI and showing the lowest way to meet legislative requirements. People that talk in terms of ROI will succeed and those that talk in terms of "insurance" won't.

Technical variables

We talked about the technical trends in the previous chapter, so we won't say too much about them here. Needless to say, there will be changes that will occur, but the search for the silver bullet in security will disappear. Changes in technology will primarily be more incremental rather than towards something that is brand new (with a few noticeable exceptions like AI). Those people that have a good feel for what is currently in place and able to adapt will succeed. Those that get bored easily and that are looking for the brand new solution will be disappointed. Look for a shift to more quality control rather than having to deal with new technologies.

Social variables

We have had a dearth of security professionals in the industry for a few years, and companies have had to adapt because the other environmental variables aren't going away. While there will be people that continue to become experts in security, expect organizations to start to split the role into its different component parts. The support security architect is a role that doesn't need as much design experience as the solution security architect role does. This means that the support security architect role will evolve into more of an audit role with technical capabilities (you are seeing this more and more already). The solution architect role really isn't much different from that solution architect role, which isn't security-specific, so don't be surprised if you start to see solution architects performing the activities of implementing security technologies.

You will also start to see project-driven roles flowing out of the IT organization towards service providers. You currently see the PMO of IT organizations bringing in contractors to perform things like solution architecture work, but it will get to the point where projects will not be managed by the PMO but, rather, by service providers, and that means there will be boutique architecture firms as all those contractors start to consolidate into specific organizations. You can see this currently with the big consulting firms, but those organizations deal with all sorts of projects. Specialties will start and result in architecture firms, just like there are in the building industry.

A special note about enterprise architects: enterprise architects, whether they are Enterprise security architects or Enterprise Architects from some other architecture tower, are all about strategy. Here's a question for you — who trains and gets trained in strategy? Business schools, not computer/engineering schools. They have an entire field of specialty called MIS. They just haven't been very technical in nature and, as such, they will go into the IT departments but more into project or program management and less into architecture. Senior Enterprise Architects will start to shift into more senior roles such as CIOs, directors of IT, and the heads of PMO and the people that fill the architecture space will be more business-related and less technically driven.

Competitive variables

The last point from the social variables section talks about how the service provider industry will shift and states that you will see more and more boutique vendors focusing just on architecture. These boutique architecture firms will be more nimble and cost much less than the big consulting firms, and will push those firms to either partner with these boutique architecture firms or slowly move away from project delivery (focusing more on consulting activities). That's what will happen with regard to contract security architects.

Internally, though, there will be competition in providing security architecture capabilities within the organization. There will be CISO, PMO, and enterprise architecture organizations that will compete to deliver the services internally. The differences will be associated with the core competencies of each organization. Remember, security architects are a combination of security and architect.

The CISO group will believe that the security architect should be in that organization because of the focus on security. As a result, the supporting security architect role will evolve into the technical security analyst role will and no longer provide broader architecture capabilities.

The enterprise architecture group will believe that the security architect should be part of their organization because of the focus on design and implementation activities, which will align with the other architecture activities. This will drive the security architect role into a situation that will compete with the CISO for driving strategy. There is a risk that the enterprise architecture group will disappear because strategy will be taken over by the individual areas within IT.

The PMO group will believe that the security architect should be part of the PMO organization because of the focus on project delivery, and the security architect role should report to the project manager. As a result, the security architect role will evolve into the solution architect role.

The security architect role, regardless of where it currently resides, will start to break down into its constituent parts and leave us wondering in 10 years what happened to the internal security architect role.

This has given a view of the environmental variables and how they will impact the role of the security architect in the future. If you are a solution architect or an enterprise architect, you can expect your roles to slowly include more and more traditional security components.

General future associated with security architects

There are a number of specific things you can see happening with regards to the security architect and how security gets combined with architecture. Let's take a look.

Market consolidations

Whenever markets start to slow down in growth, there is a tendency for companies to start to consolidate, which shakes up the marketplace. We have been seeing this for a while with the big security technology companies and, as a result, I expect you'll start to see shifts in how security architects are deployed in the market. After all, organizations still look for technology to fix problems and, by the nature of that thinking process, there is a need for security architects.

Now, keep in mind that market consolidations are focused on the technology. This means that there will be a need for security architecture to adjust how it delivers specific vendor's capabilities. This will impact security architecture strategies and will require security architects and any architect with touch points into security to have to rethink how they get involved with security technologies. In fact, it's entirely possible that security technologies will be merged into non-security technologies.

Don't think this will happen? Consider the following three examples:

- Network equipment more and more often includes firewall capabilities.
- Workflow, formerly the domain of provisioning solutions, is being included in numerous other solutions.
- SIEMs are starting to be used for more things than just security events. They are starting to be used for all logging, regardless of whether they are logging security events, system events, or application level events.

A good parallel to look at would be the rise of quality control and quality assurance in the 1990s. During that time, software was starting to boom because, just a few years earlier, the personal computer had started to rise in demand. As the demand for more and more applications started coming out, there was a need to make sure the applications met the needs of their customers without bugs. And so came about quality assurance and quality control in software. Software was released but, slowly, QA started to be applied to the software as a control rather than a feature.

The same is happening with security. More and more products have security built-in or have been tested for security vulnerabilities. As a result, more and more products have built-in security capabilities and fewer vulnerabilities.

Breaches and reactions

As vulnerabilities are being discovered faster and faster and exploited even faster than this (giving rise to Zero Day Exploits), there is a growing demand for faster reactions to these vulnerabilities. There was a SANS Security Analytics Survey that was released in September of 2013 that indicated that:

- 72 of 345 respondents (21%) took 1 day to discover an attack
- 105 of 345 respondents (30%) took 1 week or less to discover an attack
- And 113 of 345 respondents (33%) didn't know the average detection time

Those averages are already coming down because the study was taken when the implementation of SIEMs was taking off, but any gap between a breach and discover is still too long, especially if there's a manual activity involved in the discovery.

If it takes that long to discover an attack, there's a lot of damage that can occur. The demand to react faster to attacks is highly dependent on how fast the attack is actually discovered. This leads to a number of changes to security architecture coming into your designs.

First, you will see a higher demand for all devices within a solution, regardless of what that solution is, to forward their security logs to the company SIEM. If the company doesn't have a SIEM, there will be a demand to see one put into place (though we are past that peak in the hype cycle). Prepare for your solutions to have to log appropriately.

Second, a faster reaction time will be dependent on actually understanding what we see. With the growth of analytics and of AI, you will see more automation associated with the triggering of incident response. From an architecture point of view, this will mean that you will need to include your solution components in the corporate incident response plan and ensure that the appropriate disaster recovery components are included. Again, there will be changes to the way architecture is created.

Third, and this goes more to technology trends rather than changes in architecture, you'll see a need to be able to hook up the various security solutions to a central self-healing mechanism that will be triggered by alerts from the SIEM, but none of this matters if solutions don't forward their logs to a SIEM.

Secure by design?

It used to be that networks and environments were designed in a very flat manner. You still have those types of environment designs, except they are created by very junior people. But, by and large, from an architecture design point of view, you will see an increase in security zones rather than a decrease. We are moving away from flat networks and, with the ability to have virtual firewalls within an environment, there's no reason why entire solutions should be isolated from each other.

Naturally, things will go overboard and there will be an overuse of firewalls (there are already some enterprises that have to consolidate firewalls). Consolidation in firewalls will occur, but it will be driven by a proper understanding of the security classification of the various pieces of information. There will be a fight between the enterprise architects and the CISO group, where the CISO group will want to have every solution making use of its own firewall whereas the enterprise architecture group will want to leverage and consolidate equipment.

As firewalls are upgraded, you will see a shift away from standalone **Intrusion Prevention Systems (IPSs)** to IPSs that are integrated into the firewalls. The use of standalone IPS's will slowly be reduced until there are only those IPS's that are needed for highly critical security zones.

But how does this impact the use of the cloud? Enterprises will make use of combinations of cloud environments, so how do you monitor the security aspects for each cloud environment? You could make use of each cloud's standalone security capabilities, but that's inefficient; or you could see the development of a security cloud environment where security devices from the various cloud environments are managed. A consolidation of cloud security events, if you will. If you are a security architect, look for solutions to appear that will talk about how to manage security solutions across multiple cloud environments.

There's already Identity Management as a Service (for example, CA has this service), SIEM as a Service (for example, ArcSight has this service), and IPS as a Service (for example, Qualys has this capability). This seems like an area where market consolidation could occur (see the preceding regarding market consolidation).

Managed Security Service Providers and outsourcers

Security has always been viewed as a cost to the bottom line. While the drive towards legislation will increase spending on security, it will still not be a profit center to any organization. Hence, you will see an increase in the use of Managed Security Services. This will be especially true since the drive into the cloud will create a consolidation of the various cloud security capabilities.

Managed Security Service Providers (**MSSPs**) will continue to grow but will move towards managing the various cloud capabilities. Among large service providers, you will see partnerships with the different cloud service providers to be able to manage these capabilities.

From an architecture point of view, you'll need to consider the security cloud as a separate security zone and manage it accordingly. The roles that you allow into that security zone will be limited to the personnel that are approved to manage the security for your organization.

Outsourcing has always been a cyclical situation. One CIO will determine that they can get budgetary savings by making use of an outsourcer and outsource as much of the IT capabilities as possible, including the security capabilities of the organization. Unfortunately, studies have found that the saving from using outsourcers is only, on average, something in the 4% range. But if the outsourcing isn't done properly or efficiencies are found, that 4% savings will actually be a higher cost.

This will typically cost the CIO their job and the next CIO will try to force the savings from the contract, but outsourcers, by nature, will always point to the contract and try to live by the word of the contract rather than the intent. This will result in components of the outsourcing agreement being brought back in–house. Usually, the first component brought back in-house is the security operations group.

There will be lots of work for security architects that understand the outsourcing industry because they will work on moving security operations away from the client to the outsourcer and from the outsourcer back into the client. This won't change but will start to look at how to move clients from one security cloud environment to another.

The evolution of the security tower

Security has evolved as the IT industry has grown. Originally, the IT industry was all about networking and the implementation of LANs, MANs, WANs, and so on. This created the security industry, and we have focused on network-level security.

Then came along the growth in infrastructure. You had improvements in servers, databases moving to SANs, and desktops giving way to more mobile end products. This drove the growth in end point security capabilities, and security became more and more concerned about malware.

Around the turn of the century, applications were booming and we had the Dot Com boom. SAP and other ERP products exploded in popularity and the security industry evolved yet again. They started to introduce the concepts of application security and securing these various applications.

By 2010, middleware was taking shape and applications were being integrated to each other in order to be more and more efficient. The use of XML exploded and the entire concept of **Services Oriented Architecture** (**SOA**) grew. TIBCO's middleware bus and other middleware capabilities were put into place and, with it, the need to include security controls in SOA. So, XML-based security standards grew and people that understood application security started to shift to middleware.

But the concept of shared resources created the concept of cloud architectures. The cloud allowed the enterprise to leverage economies of scale that weren't available to their own organization because you were now able to leverage the resources from multiple enterprises at once. Costs were driven down and the usage grew. Security had to figure out how to secure the cloud, and the cloud had to figure out how to provide security capabilities that were scalable as well. That's where we're at now.

Notice a pattern? If you know your OSI model, we started at the physical layer and moved our way up. We are now working at the data layer since it's all about managing the data and not the equipment. So, now, we're at the top of the OSI model and dealing with information architecture aspects of security. But what comes next?

Well, remember, there are three (or four) components to every solution: people, process, technology, (and governance). Technology has been covered by the various towers as we move up the OSI model. People are being dealt with by outsourcing and by MSSPs. The fourth component is governance. But governance is being dealt with by legislation, which we've talked about. So what's left?

Process!

One of the areas that you can expect to start to grow over the next few years will be **Business Process Automation (BPA)** and **Business Process Management (BPM)**. You are already seeing workflows shifting into multiple solution areas, and not just in provisioning for the processing of access requests. You'll see more and more automation of processes themselves with requests for purchases and requests for the movement of people, and the automation of all sorts of other processes occurring.

How does this impact security architecture? Well, it's the next step in the evolution of security. You can expect to see security ensuring that there are security steps in each process. You can't have new cubicles set up if there aren't appropriate physical access controls put into place to access these new cubicle areas. You can't have people being hired if they haven't gone through background checks. In short, you'll start to see the security architecture shift into the business realm, which, in itself, will trigger a different trend, which we will be covering next.

The merging of cybersecurity and physical security

It's always been a wonder that there are two separate security groups within an organization. One is tied to cybersecurity and the other is tied to physical security. With the growth of the Internet of Things, there is the bleeding of cybersecurity into the physical security space since physical security controls such as access control panels, wireless video cameras, and biometric access all make use of software and hardware. This is the realm of cybersecurity.

The problem is that each of the two groups views itself as more important than the other. It's very similar to the situation in Canada with the relationship between the provinces. Quebec views itself as one of two countries whereas the rest of the provinces view Quebec as one of ten provinces. Completely different views of each other.

If you go through your CISSP training, you can get the same sense. Physical security is one component of many domains in your training for the CISSP. Cybersecurity personnel are very technically oriented and tend to be much more comfortable in front of a computer than in front of a person, whereas physical security personnel are typically ex-cops and they are very real-world oriented, and much more comfortable dealing with people than machines. This leads to issues associated with combining cybersecurity and physical security.

Where do they reside? Do they reside together, or should cybersecurity be in IT and physical security in the facilities group? No one has really figured out how to deal with this dichotomy. And that doesn't even deal with how those two areas relate to the chief risk officer and the corporate risk department. But there is a sense of what is coming, and this is driven by the prediction around legislation.

If legislation is put into place where the corporate board will have to include cybersecurity in their corporate risk reports (which we talked about earlier), then you'll have a need for the chief risk officer to have a clear understanding of the security risks associated with the organization. If you combine this future trend with the view from the CISSP domains, you all of a sudden see that the chief risk officer will start to shift into the cybersecurity and physical security realms.

This makes double sense when, looking at the CISSP domains, you see two different domains that fit with risk: the security and risk management domain, and the asset security domain.

From an architecture perspective, you will start to see security being shifted more into a governance situation (with one of those components for every solution), and that means that the architecture will have to ensure that the appropriate security controls are in place to meet corporate governance. Simple corporate policies such as thou shalt have security won't be enough, and proper security policies and standards will be put into place. This is what will drive changes into architecture practices.

As an architect, regardless of architecture towers start to get used to following policies and getting the appropriate guidance in meeting policies and standards. It's ultimately where this is all going, even though it's taking decades to get there.

Summary

Security architecture has changed a lot over the years. We started off as part of networking and slowly evolved into a capability that had to be able to deal with any architecture tower. We had to be good at all architecture towers, but the master of none (except our own speciality). You could say that we have evolved into what the enterprise architect was supposed to be—an architect that has a good understanding of all architecture towers.

Unfortunately, what will end up happening is that we will slowly become absorbed into each of the architecture towers so that each tower architect is able to implement solutions that have security built-in rather than added on. From a security point of view, this is really good news because we've always said that security has to be the responsibility of all people in an organization, not just the security group.

The ironic part is that, in driving the organization to alignment with that philosophy, we may have gotten rid of our own jobs. So here's a philosophical question for you as we finish this book:

Isn't this the definition of success where we meet our goal of integrating security into everything? So, by evolving people roles to include security in everything they do, we have been successful and we've gotten rid of our jobs?

That, my friends, is the definition of irony is.

I hope this has helped.

Questions

1. Where do you see cybersecurity in your organization in 10 years time?
2. What new non-security technology do you see arriving in the next 5 years? How do you deal with security of that technology?
3. What do you see happening with the security within the cloud?
4. Do you see security architecture being absorbed into your architecture role? If so, how?
5. Your turn—what do you think will happen to security architecture in the future?

Assessment

Chapter 1, Security Architecture History and Overview

1. What is the key capability that a security architect possesses?

   A security architect is all about communication. Communication between stakeholders, communication with the business, and communication with the technical personnel.

2. What type of security architect deals with strategy?

   Enterprise Security Architect

3. What was the first architectural framework?

   The Zachmann Framework

4. What are the three primary components of a solution? Is there potentially a fourth and, if so, what is it?

   Every solution has technology, people, and process. The potential fourth is governance.

5. Does a nonsecurity project have a security component?

   Every architecture, regardless of tower, has security components. That does not mean security technologies, but rather a view from a security architecture point of view.

6. Which layer did security issues start showing up in first?

   The network layer.

7. What is the purpose of architecture?

   To communicate the solution that is intended to be implemented, covering the people, processes, and technology aspects.

Chapter 2, Security Governance

1. How long should a single principle be?

    The ideal principle is only one sentence long. When it gets too long, no one is able to remember or even use them.

2. What areas should principles cover?

    Principles should cover people, process, and technology (and governance, if that is one of the areas that your view architectures should cover).

3. When you put together either principles or policies and standards, how do you involve people outside your security or architecture group?

    Engage them directly. In other words, talk to them, consolidate what you hear, feed it back to them to make sure you heard correctly, and then finalize and communicate the principles.

4. What is the difference between a policy and a standard?

    Policies are the intent or goal of the organization and standards are how you measure where you are.

5. What policy domains does a security architect focus on?

    With regards to ISO 27001, the domains are communication and operations management, access control, and systems acquisition/development/and maintenance.

6. What areas does a security architect focus on when looking at architectures and designs?

    A security architect focuses on information classification, authentication/authorization, access controls, data in flight security, data at rest security, and audit logging.

Chapter 3, Reference Security Architecture

1. Apart from this book, what other sources are available for providing a reference security architecture framework?

   This is for you to find out for yourself.

2. How can you use network zoning, even though it's not really a security technology, for improving your security posture?

   Network zoning allows you to consolidate assets of similar security classification and criticality. Just remember not to overdo it—too many zones will increase complexity, which increases potential vulnerabilities.

3. On which side of a firewall should you be placing your scanning solution—the target side or the management side?

   The scanners should never scan through a firewall, so place the scanners on the target side of the firewall, but have them send their outputs to a central management console located on the management side.

4. Should you consider physical security technologies in your reference security architecture? If so, why? If not, why not?

   This is for you to find out for yourself, but remember that there can be some correlation between physical security activities and cybersecurity activities.

5. Why do most projects fail? And where are most vulnerabilities introduced?

   Most projects fail because they have not collected requirements properly and, as a result, don't meet client requirements. Most vulnerabilities will be introduced during design.

Chapter 4, Cybersecurity Architecture Strategy

1. When you are creating your strategy, what are the four core components that you need to include?

   The four components are the current state of the environment, the future state of the environment, the resources you can use to get to the future state, and the path or roadmap you use to get to the future state.

2. There are five environmental variables that you need to consider when you create your strategy. What are they and are they within your control?

   The five environmental variables are political, economical, technical, social, and competitive environmental variables, and they are all outside of your control.

3. From a time management point of view, where should you live and where do most people actually live? What's wrong with that?

   You should live in Quadrant 2, which is the "important but not urgent" quadrant because it will allow you to prevent those urgent tasks from reoccurring. Unfortunately, most people live in Quadrant 1, which is the "important and urgent" quadrant and are constantly putting out fires.

4. Why are metrics important? If you were going to measure your strategy, what (in your mind) would you be focused on?

   Is that a strategic measurement or a tactical one? If you don't measure how you are doing, how would you know if you are doing well? The measurements that you choose are specific to you.

5. If your financial department tells you that they don't have enough money for all your initiatives, how can you get around that?

   Try to leverage all projects that are being planned so that you can leverage the funds in those projects.

Chapter 5, Program–and Strategy–Level Work Artifacts

1. What is the best way to approach creating a **Key Decision Document (KDD)**?

   The KDD is meant to describe the process that you went through to make a decision and what that decision is. You can explain the different options you had and why you ended up with the decision you made.

2. What are the different types of risks?

   There are multiple different types of risks, such as, security risk, business risk, project risk, and architectural risk.

3. Why would you want to have a fixed score decision tree for RIAs?

   So that personal biases don't come into play and so that the process can be used by anyone and still get a consistent result.

4. What is the purpose of a whitepaper?

   The whitepaper is used to communicate thoughts and ideas by the Enterprise Architect.

Chapter 6, Security Architecture in Waterfall Projects

1. What is the most important phase of any project delivery methodology?

   In the following order, requirements gathering, requirements gathering, and requirements gathering. Get it yet?

2. What is the main risk in using the Agile methodology?

   That people will use Agile as a reason to not do things properly, just quickly.

3. What is the downside of using the waterfall methodology?

   It takes longer and is very structured. This can lead to growth in bureaucracy.

4. What is the difference between a solution security architect and a supporting security architect?

   A solution security architect pulls solutions together while a supporting security architect supports the Solution Architect from other architecture towers.

5. What stakeholder group is very commonly not interviewed for their requirements, and if you have gotten to the **Production Turn Over (PTO)** phase without talking to them, will it lead to issues?

   Operations is an extremely important stakeholder group and seldom gets talked to.

Chapter 7, Security Architecture Project Delivery Artifacts

1. If you have new requirements come up after a project has moved past that phase, what should you do?

   Put them aside for a different phase in the project.

2. What is the purpose of the SDA workbook?

   The Security Design Assessment workbook is where you put your workings.

3. What is the difference between functional and nonfunctional requirements?

   Nonfunctional requirements can be measured (that is, are quantitative in nature), whereas functional requirements are more qualitative in nature.

4. Once you create your requirements, how are they used?

   Every phase in a project delivery should go back and confirm that the requirements are being met.

Chapter 8, Architecture Design Document

1. How should you document security architecture components in the target architecture?

   Security architecture components should be part of every architecture layer and tower and not be put aside in it's own section. Remember, Security Architecture is more of a quality assurance view on the different solution components.

2. When would you document the current state architecture?

   When you are making changes to the current environment, you need to make sure you properly understand what is in place.

3. What two other architecture artifacts are essential when putting together your target architecture?

   The Key Decision Document (**KDD**) and the Requirements Document.

4. Why is documenting the out-of-scope aspects of the architecture important?

   It's important to describe where the limits are for where the solution should go.

5. Is an SDLC a security architecture activity or a security practice?

   This is a security practice (though you can talk about the security architecture of an application within the SDLC).

Chapter 9, Security Architecture and Operations

1. Why is it important to talk with the operations group for input into security architecture strategy?

   They are the people who will have the best view on how security technologies and the current state security architecture are working since they are hands on with it.

2. What tool can you use so that you don't forget about a solution that is in production?

> The asset inventory is important for tracking what solutions are in production. The **Reference Security Architect (RSA)** is also a very important tool to organize your solutions.

3. What are some of the considerations you have to think about when it comes to the staff of the operations groups?

> The number of staff members, experience, expertise, staff turnover, and staff organization.

4. Do you just have to think about the security operations group or all operations groups? Why?

> All Operations groups have to be thought about because they are all touching on security in some manner.

Chapter 10, Practical Security Architecture Designs

1. What are the mitigation options to protect against ransomware?

> The best way to recover from a ransomware attack is by having a backup of the encrypted data. In addition to that, you want to make sure that your **Endpoint Protection Platform (EPP)** is updated.

2. What is the name of the type of attack that can take down corporate networks?

> Denial of Service.

3. What are recommended mitigations against DDoS attacks?

> Ensure your organization has an alternative site that is kept in a ready state.

4. What is the most effective way to prevent a data breach?

> Driving user awareness on accidental data leakage and social engineering is critical. Make use of intrusion prevention systems as well as Firewall on the network layer to sniff out malicious requests.

Chapter 11, Trends in Security Architecture Technology

1. What is the best tool to structure how you look at trends?

   Make use of your Reference Security Architecture to structure your view of trends.

2. Is there one area that you think will be the biggest change to cybersecurity?

   This is based on your own opinion.

3. How can you protect the information classified as private but still make use of Cloud solutions?

   One good tool is to use tokenization, which substitutes data for a representative token that can be sent to the cloud. Unfortunately, not all SaaS cloud solutions can make use of tokens.

4. There are areas in security architecture that aren't specific to technology products but provide different approaches to solutions. What are they?

   Focusing on people and process aspects of solutions will allow you to look at different ways to create solutions that aren't technology driven.

Chapter 12, The Future of Security Architecture

Each of these questions don't have a definite answer, but are instead provided just for you to contemplate. Remember, this is the future you are looking at, so it's always possible that we will all be wrong:

1. Where do you see cybersecurity sitting in your organization in 10 years' time?
2. What new nonsecurity technology do you see arriving in the next 5 years? How do you deal with the security of that technology?
3. What do you see happening with the security within the cloud?
4. Do you see security architecture being folded into your architecture role? If so, how?
5. What do you think will happen to security architecture in the future?

Other Books You May Enjoy

If you enjoyed this book, you may be interested in these other books by Packt:

Mastering Linux Security and Hardening
Donald Tevault

ISBN: 978-1-78862-030-7

- Use various techniques to prevent intruders from accessing sensitive data
- Prevent intruders from planting malware, and detect whether malware has been planted
- Prevent insiders from accessing data that they aren't authorized to access
- Do quick checks to see whether a computer is running network services that it doesn't need to run
- Learn security techniques that are common to all Linux distros, and some that are distro-specific

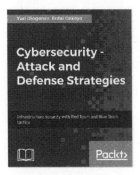

Cybersecurity - Attack and Defense Strategies
Yuri Diogenes, Erdal Ozkaya

ISBN: 978-1-78847-529-7

- Learn the importance of having a solid foundation for your security posture
- Understand the attack strategy using cybersecurity kill chain
- Learn how to enhance your defense strategy by improving your security policies, hardening your network, implementing active sensors, and leveraging threat intelligence
- Learn how to perform an incident investigation
- Get an in-depth understanding of the recovery process
- Understand continuous security monitoring and how to implement a vulnerability management strategy
- Learn how to perform log analysis to identify suspicious activities

Leave a review - let other readers know what you think

Please share your thoughts on this book with others by leaving a review on the site that you bought it from. If you purchased the book from Amazon, please leave us an honest review on this book's Amazon page. This is vital so that other potential readers can see and use your unbiased opinion to make purchasing decisions, we can understand what our customers think about our products, and our authors can see your feedback on the title that they have worked with Packt to create. It will only take a few minutes of your time, but is valuable to other potential customers, our authors, and Packt. Thank you!

Index